The Cambridge Companion to Edith Wharton offers a series of fresh examinations of Edith Wharton's fiction, designed to meet the needs of students or general readers encountering this major American writer for the first time but also to interest scholars looking for new insights into her creative achievement. The essays cover a broad span of Wharton's most important novels, including *The House of Mirth, The Age of Innocence, The Custom of the Country, The Fruit of the Tree, Summer, The Valley of Decision,* and some of her shorter fiction. The essayists – established commentators on Wharton as well as several exciting newcomers – utilize both traditional and innovative critical techniques, applying variously the perspectives of literary history, feminist theory, psychology or biography, sociology or anthropology, and social history. Particularly noteworthy is the fact that as a whole the essays represent a new turn in the criticism of this highly individual writer – a searching into the social and historical context out of which her writing grew and which it comments upon, a discovery of her sociological vision.

The Introduction, a valuable review of the history of Wharton criticism, demonstrates that her writing has provoked varying responses from its first publication and shows how current interests have emerged from earlier ones. A detailed chronology of her life and publications and a useful bibliography of important books for further reading are also provided.

THE CAMBRIDGE
COMPANION TO
EDITH WHARTON

Cambridge Companions to Literature

Continued on page following Index

THE CAMBRIDGE
COMPANION TO
EDITH WHARTON

EDITED BY
MILLICENT BELL

CAMBRIDGE
UNIVERSITY PRESS

PUBLISHED BY THE PRESS SYNDICATE OF THE UNIVERSITY OF CAMBRIDGE
The Pitt Building, Trumpington Street, Cambridge CB2 1RP, United Kingdom

CAMBRIDGE UNIVERSITY PRESS
The Edinburgh Building, Cambridge CB2 2RU, United Kingdom
40 West 20th Street, New York, NY 10011-4211, USA
10 Stamford Road, Oakleigh, Melbourne 3166, Australia

First published 1995
Reprinted 1998

Printed in the United States of America

Typeset in Sabon

A catalogue record for this book is available from the British Library

Library of Congress Cataloguing-in-Publication Data is available

ISBN 0-521-45358-5 hardback
ISBN 0-521-48513-4 paperback

CONTENTS

CONTENTS

CONTRIBUTORS

ELIZABETH AMMONS is Professor of English and American Studies at Tufts University. She is the author of *Conflicting Stories: American Women Writers at the Turn into the Twentieth Century* (1991) and *Edith Wharton's Argument with America* (1980), and the editor of *Critical Essays on Harriet Beecher Stowe* (1980), *Short Fiction by Black Women, 1900–1920* (1991), and *Tricksterism in Turn-of-the-Century Multicultural U.S. Literature,* with Annette White-Parks (1994).

MILLICENT BELL is Professor of English, Emerita, Boston University. She is the author of *Hawthorne's View of the Artist* (1962), *Edith Wharton and Henry James* (1965), *Marquand: An American Life* (1979), and *Meaning in Henry James* (1992).

NANCY BENTLEY is Assistant Professor of English at the University of Pennsylvania. She is the author of *Ethnography of Manners: Hawthorne, James, and Wharton* (1994), and has published articles on issues of race in American fiction as well as essays on James and Hawthorne.

GLORIA C. ERLICH is an independent scholar who has written essays on Hawthorne, Thomas Mann, and biographical theory, as well as on Wharton, and is the author of *Family Themes and Hawthorne's Fiction: The Tenacious Web* (1984) and *The Sexual Education of Edith Wharton* (1992).

MAUREEN HOWARD is a professor in The School of the Arts, Columbia University. Her latest novel, *Natural History,* was published by W. W. Norton (1992) and is now a Harper Perennial. An autobiography, *Facts of Life,* won the National Book Critic's Circle award and is published by Viking/ Penguin.

PAMELA KNIGHTS lectures on English and American Literature at the University of Durham, England. She has published essays on Faulkner and other American writers and provided the introduction for the Everyman's Library edition of *The House of Mirth.*

ELAINE SHOWALTER is Professor of English at Princeton University. Among her books are *Women's Liberation and Literature* (1971), *A Literature of Their Own* (1977), *The New Feminist Criticism* (1985), *The Female Malady: Women, Madness, and Culture* (1985), *Speaking of Gender* (1989), *Sexual Anarchy: Gender and Creativity in the Fin de Siècle* (1990), *Sister's Choice: Tradition and Change in American Women's Writing* (1991).

RHONDA SKILLERN, a writing instructor for the Success Program at the University of Texas, has published two study guides for American Literature correspondence courses. She is completing her dissertation, entitled "From the Land of Unlikeness: Ritual and Resistance in Edith Wharton's Novels." A version of the essay presented in this volume was presented at the International Conference on Edith Wharton, held in Paris in 1991.

JAMES W. TUTTLETON is Professor of English at New York University. He is the author of *The Novel of Manners in America* (1972), compiler of "Edith Wharton: A Review of Research," in *Fifteen Women Writers in America* (1983), and coeditor with Kristin O. Lauer and Margaret P. Murray of *Edith Wharton: The Contemporary Reviews* (1992).

WILLIAM L. VANCE is Professor of English at Boston University. He is the author of articles and review essays on Hawthorne, Whitman, Dreiser, and Faulkner, and on American painting, and author of *America's Rome* (1989).

VERNON LEE, born Violet Paget (1856–1935), was the author of over forty volumes of poetry, fiction, plays, works of cultural and aesthetic criticism, and numerous uncollected magazine and newspaper essays. Her *Studies of the Eighteenth Century in Italy* (1880) attracted wide attention; Browning wrote in *Asolando* (1889): " 'No, the book / Which noticed how the wall growths wave,' said she, 'Was not by Ruskin.' I said, 'Vernon Lee.' " Her personal brilliance was acknowledged by a wide circle of intellectual acquaintances, including Henry James, Maurice Baring, Bernard Shaw, Roger Fry, and Edith Wharton, who met her in Italy in 1894.

1862	Born New York City, third child of George C. Jones and Lucretia Rhinelander Jones.
1866–72	Fall in family income, owing to economic depression, prompts move to Europe. The Joneses spend most of 1867 in Rome, travel in Spain and settle in Paris in 1868, move to Germany in 1870 and to Florence at the end of 1870.
1872	Family returns to the United States, living in New York City and spending summers in Newport, Rhode Island.
1876–81	Juvenile writings: a manuscript novella, *Fast and Loose;* a volume of poetry, *Verses* (1878), published privately by her mother; a poem, signed "Eadgyth," printed in the *New York World* (1879); and one or more poems published in the *Atlantic Monthly* (1880) at the recommendation of Henry Wadsworth Longfellow.
1880–2	With parents in southern France, where George Frederic Jones dies in 1882. She inherits $20,000 trust fund. Engaged to Newport socialite Henry Stevens but engagement broken.
1883	Meets Walter Van Rensselaer Berry and Edward Robbins Wharton in Bar Harbor, Maine.
1885–8	Marries Wharton, and couple move into cottage on her mother's Newport estate and spend February through June in Europe each year. In 1888, they cruise the Aegean for four months. Develops friendship with cultivated member of her social circle, Egerton Winthrop. Inherits $120,000 from a Jones cousin.
1889	Whartons rent house on Madison Avenue, New York City. Four poems accepted for publication by *Scribner's Magazine, Harper's Monthly, Century Illustrated Monthly Magazine.*

1891–2	Buys house on Fourth Avenue (later Park Avenue) in New York City. First published short story, "Mrs. Manstey's View," in *Scribner's*.
1893–4	Buys Newport house, "Land's End." Visited by French novelist Paul Bourget. Publishes three more stories in *Scribner's*. Travels in Italy and meets English writer Vernon Lee.
1895–7	Experiences prolonged periods of depression and writes only sporadically. Begins work on *The Decoration of Houses* (1897), collaborating with architect Ogden Codman and counseled by Walter Berry, and book is published by Scribner's which will continue to publish her without interruption until 1912.
1898	Undergoes Dr. S. Weir Mitchell's rest cure for female neuroses as an outpatient at the Philadelphia Orthopedic Hospital.
1899	Whartons stay for four months in Washington, D.C., where Berry, Washington lawyer, is her supportive friend and literary adviser. *The Greater Inclination* (1899), collection of stories. Summering in Europe, the Whartons tour northern Italy with the Bourgets.
1900	*The Touchstone* (1900), a novella. Travels again in Europe with the Bourgets and begins work on *The Valley of Decision*.
1901	Buys property in Lenox, Massachusetts, and begins planning house modeled after Christopher Wren's Belton House in Lincolnshire. *Crucial Instances* (1901), second story collection. Mother dies, leaving trust fund which will bring her $90,000.
1902	*The Valley of Decision* (1902). Henry James praises but urges her to "do New York." Moves into The Mount.
1903	*Sanctuary* (1903). Divides year between Italy (where she inspects Italian villas for a series for the *Century* and sees Vernon Lee), The Mount, and England (where she visits Henry James).
1904–5	Buys first motor car: tours in south of France and visits Bourgets at Hyères; in England, tours Sussex with James. Entertains at The Mount a succession of guests, including James. *The Descent of Man* (1904), third story collection. *Italian Villas and Their Gardens* (1904). *Italian Backgrounds* (1905). *The House of Mirth* (1905). Literary income for 1905 over $20,000.

1906	In Paris, makes new friends in elite social circles; in England, becomes part of circle at Queen's Acre, home of James's friend Howard Sturgis, where she meets Percy Lubbock and Gaillard Lapsley. Play version of *The House of Mirth* opens in New York. Literary income for year nearly $32,000.
1907–8	Rents apartment in rue de Varenne, where her Paris social life accelerates, and, with her husband, takes James and Lapsley on motor tours through France. Meets another friend of James's, William Morton Fullerton, and in March 1908 their love affair begins while Teddy goes to Hot Springs, Arkansas, to relieve his depression and gout. Sees much of James at his own house at Rye and at Queen's Acre and tours with him in England. Makes two new younger English friends, Robert Norton and John Hugh Smith. *The Fruit of the Tree* (1907). *A Motor Flight through France* (1908). *The Hermit and the Wild Woman* (1908), fourth story collection. Earnings for 1908: $15,000.
1909–10	Edward Wharton's medical and emotional problems increase; in November 1909 she discovers that he has embezzled $50,000 of her trust funds. In January 1910 he enters Swiss sanatorium, while she remains in new Paris apartment, 53, rue de Varenne. Following September she returns with Wharton to New York, after which he leaves for world cruise. Affair with Fullerton has come to an end. *Artemis to Actaeon* (1909), a book of poems. *Tales of Men and Ghosts* (1910), fifth collection of short stories.
1911–12	In 1911, promotes, unsuccessfully, the nomination of Henry James for Nobel Prize, and, the following year, arranges that $8,000 of her own royalties be transferred to his account. Separation talks with Edward begin. The Mount (where she entertained James in July) is put up for sale in September 1911 and sold the next June. Tours Italy that October, visiting Bernard Berenson, and, in the spring, returns to Tuscany with Berry. *Ethan Frome* (1911). *The Reef* (1912), published by Appleton.
1913	Sues Edward for divorce on grounds of adultery; divorce granted April 16. Travels with Berry in Sicily, with Berenson in Germany, and makes new friend, Geoffrey Scott. Attends premier of *Sacre de Printemps* in Paris. *The Custom of the Country* (1913).

1914–16   Tours in Algeria and Tunisia with Percy Lubbock, returning to Paris three days before outbreak of World War I. Establishes workshop for seamstresses. Directs, with Elisina Tyler, American Hostels for Refugees. Visits Argonne, Verdun, and Vosges fronts. Establishes homes and training schools for Flemish refugee children. Continues war work and is made Chevalier of the Legion of Honor. *Fighting France, from Dunkirk to Belfort* (1915), her frontline reports. *Xingu and Other Stories* (1916), sixth story collection. Death of Henry James, February 28, 1916.

1917–19   September 1917, tours Morocco with Walter Berry. In 1918, buys Pavillon Colombe at St. Brice-sous-Fôret. *Summer* (1917) and *The Marne* (1918) published by Appleton, henceforth publishers of all her fiction except *A Son at the Front*, published by Scribner's in 1923. *French Ways and Their Meaning* (1919). *Pictorial Review* pays $18,000 for serial rights to next novel.

1920–4   This turns out to be *The Age of Innocence* (1920), which wins Pulitzer Prize and yields royalties of $70,000 by 1922. *The Glimpses of the Moon* (1922) sells 100,000 copies in first six months, is made into a film, and earns $60,000. *In Morocco* (1920). *A Son at the Front* (1923). *Old New York* (1924), four novellas. Receives National Institute of Arts and Letters Gold Medal.

1925–6   *The Mother's Recompense* (1925). *The Writing of Fiction* (1925). Ten-week Mediterranean cruise on chartered yacht. *Here and Beyond* (1926), seventh story collection. *Twelve Poems* (1926). Elected to National Institute of Arts and Letters.

1927–9   *Pictorial Review* pays $40,000 for serial rights to *The Children* (1928). *Twilight Sleep* (1927) earns $95,000 from book and film receipts. *The Age of Innocence* earns $25,500 as successful play. *Hudson River Bracketed* (1929). Berry, after two strokes, dies October 2, 1927. Edward Wharton dies in New York, February 7, 1928. In 1929, she suffers severe case of pneumonia.

1930–4   Elected to American Academy of Arts and Letters. *Certain People* (1930), eighth story collection. *The Gods Arrive* (1932) sold to *Delineator* for $50,000. *Human Nature* (1933), eighth story collection. In 1933 begins *The Bucca-*

neers (never finished). *A Backward Glance* (1934), her autobiography. Catherine Gross, companion since 1884, dies October 1933.

1935–7   Beloved sister-in-law, Mary Cadwalader Jones, dies, 1935. Play versions of *The Old Maid* and *Ethan Frome* successes in New York in 1935 and 1936 and net her $130,000. *The World Over* (1936), ninth story collection. Sends final story, "All Souls," to her agent. Suffers stroke June 1, 1937, and dies at St. Brice August 11. Buried, by her instructions, beside Walter Berry in Versailles cemetery.

THE CAMBRIDGE
COMPANION TO
EDITH WHARTON

MILLICENT BELL

Introduction: A Critical History

Edith Wharton, who was never obscure or forgotten, has been rediscovered a number of times. In 1938, the year after she died, Edmund Wilson published a famous essay, "Justice to Edith Wharton," because he felt that the notices at her death had underestimated her achievement. Between *The House of Mirth* (1905) and *The Age of Innocence* (1920) she had attained, he thought, an intensity – the consequence of secret personal anguish – which made her "important during a period . . . when there were few American writers worth reading."[1] He deplored the lowering of her reputation by the effect of her later, inferior works, written when some of this anguish had passed. Unquestionably, Wharton's powers had waxed and waned, as Wilson said. But the life curve of her reputation, whether measured by critical blame or esteem or by popular success or failure had not been governed by the issue of literary achievement alone; it was her subject matter and presumed personal attitudes that chiefly provoked response.[2]

Before the triumph on all fronts of *The Age of Innocence,* she pleased some readers, but by others she was considered too refined or too intellectual or too snobbish or not cheerful enough or too much like Henry James. At the same time, the avant-garde champions of the new naturalism found her inadequately realistic, setting her well below Dreiser or Norris. In the 1920s, the period of her greatest commercial success, her books still seemed to indicate, the serious critics thought, that she had turned her back on the truths of common life, and if she wrote about the rich it was in a way inferior to F. Scott Fitzgerald's. Writing about the rich was less appealing in the depression 1930s, when she seemed to have found, as Henry Seidel Canby said, only the "soiled egret feathers and false decorations"[3] of a degenerate upper class to write about.

The House of Mirth, the first complete triumph of her art, had been met with some enthusiasm, despite its subject, and speaking against prevailing prejudice one reviewer wrote that it was "far and away the best novel of society written by an American . . . deeply moralized because it is deeply humanized," and because it made no concession to "the optimistic mood which is supposed to dominate American readers" (111–12). But another expressed a common opinion in remarking that the magazine readers who were pleased by the serial installments of the novel had found there only the equivalent of the society gossip column (207). That the writer had chosen to show the sordid rather than the glamorous side of upper-class life did not please; another reviewer said, "If this is American society, the American House of Mirth, it is utterly unsuitable for conversion into literature" (116). And Wharton's attitude toward her characters, even toward her heroine, Lily Bart, was at the same time felt to be too frigid, too distant, showing, as the English writer Alice Meynell said, an "extremity of reserve" which hid her feelings too well (125).

Yet when *The Fruit of the Tree* (1907) came along, it was unfavorably compared with its predecessor – which had meanwhile become a popular success despite its detractors. The critical jury found the presentation of a "mercy killing" repulsive and one commentator pictured Wharton writing it in a state of mind "as detached as a scientific student viewing bacilli under a microscope" (154). Soon after, her *Ethan Frome* (1911) – which would eventually become the favorite both of critics and of the general reader – seemed even more repellently grim to many. Though the short novel's technical mastery impressed some of these first readers, they called her vision "relentless" (186), and she was reproached with an inability to see life "with the deep sympathy, smiling tenderness, and affectionate tolerance of the greatest novelists" (181). She had not succeeded in depicting "normal people and situations" (183), and the ending was "something at which we cover the eyes" (186). When she returned to the scene of upper-class life in *The Reef* (1912), the jury of journalistic censors continued the indictment of cruelty. One reviewer defined Wharton's method in this novel and its two predecessors as "taking a human being and subjecting him or her to a cumulative process of torture . . . a primitive method of entertainment" like that offered by the writhings of Christian martyrs in the Roman colosseum (193).

The Custom of the Country (1913) struck a nerve in the American consciousness. The subject of the rich American matron, with her tough tenacity in the service of absolute frivolity and selfishness, her ambition to "climb" socially, her divorces and remarriages, was too well known to newspaper readers to be denied. But reviewers still shrank from Wharton's strong portrait. Undine Spragg was a "monster" – the word was used repeatedly (202, 203, 208) – so monstrous that she seemed inhuman. Gentle Lily Bart, victim rather than victor in the savage social game, was recalled wistfully as a type one would rather read about.

Such a book as *The Custom of the Country* could not expect to please those who enjoyed contemporary best sellers like Eleanor H. Porter's *Polyanna,* Henry Sydnor Harrison's *V. V.'s Eyes,* and Gene Stratton Porter's *Laddie,* examples of a genre critics were dubbing "molasses fiction."[4] Wharton was well aware of this and saved a clipping of an advertisement of *Laddie* which called it a "true blue story." She underlined in red the admonishing information that *Laddie* had sold 3 million copies, being a book that "goes to the heart of a vast reading public because it is true to life, a picture of genuine American people, people who love their homes, who figure neither in newspaper nor divorce court; who are the source of the vitality of the nation."[5] Her next production was intended to deal with the "common" person, certainly, but it was hardly in the vein of *Polyanna* – a name which would become a word for foolish cheer. In *Summer* (1917), written in the midst of the war, she had chosen to write again, as in *Ethan Frome,* of obscure and straitened American lives. Though the *Boston Evening Transcript* felt that the New England scene had been maligned (252), outside of Boston others found her to have created a masterpiece. In truth, like *Ethan Frome,* it had almost no real precedent in its boldness in treating sexual passion and in its sense of regionality, except for *The Scarlet Letter.* But the writer was thought by a lingering minority to be colder than her New England snow. "It is one of those stories of the inexorable that seem perfectly to lend themselves to Mrs. Wharton's icy restraint. . . . What one dislikes in *Summer* is the undoubted purpose of the author to dish the heroine for the sake of the sensation of dishing her," one of the leading literary reporters said (249–50).

Yet subjects aside, her literary competence did not always win her plaudits. From the first, even when her themes were deemed tolerable, she was still reproached for being an accomplished writer; the very elegance of her style was somehow felt to be a limitation that expressed a temperament too inhospitable to the emotions animating great art. She was said to have "that rare thing, distinction in literary style, . . . but it is like the fine gowns of her heroines, a fashion of the times for interpreting decadent symptoms in human nature" (110). She writes "too consciously well," said a rival novelist, Robert Herrick, in 1915, setting himself deliberately against the laudatory summary of her accomplishments to that date by Wharton's friend Percy Lubbock.[6] Her American male critics would sometimes express the ingrained native distrust of "cleverness" as somehow undemocratic and something no real man cared for, something respected chiefly by women. Surveying the work she had done by 1914, John C. Underwood acknowledged her "brilliancy" but observed that brilliancy was "a patrician quality, of the superficial, by the superficial, for the superficial. It is intrinsically alien to the genius of the Anglo-Saxon world, in particular to that of its male half; and the great mass of the world in general has some reason for looking at it with suspicion."[7] One can see why Wharton came to feel that America was still a culture of cave dwellers.

Her literary sophistication was often confused with a supposed resemblance of her art to that of the most sophisticated of American writers, Henry James. When her first collection of stories, *The Greater Inclination* (1899), was published, reviewers, as one of them admitted, formed "a critical chain gang"[8] in agreeing that she was James's imitator. And the refrain that she copied his choice of motives and even his style continued in reviews of her next books, with the exception of her first long work, a chronicle novel about eighteenth-century Italy, *The Valley of Decision* (1902) – too obviously an experiment utterly unrelated to James's model. In the case of some of her stories of this period there was some superficial truth to these charges, a theme or situation paralleled in James. But her treatment was already quite different from his; she was less interested in the deeper reverberations of character than in situation, and her crisp style, already showing her bent for satire, predicted the direction, quite divergent from his, that she would soon take in *The House of Mirth*.

The assertion that she was James's literary heiress annoyed Wharton at the start of her career as well as later.[9] James's more rarefied late writings did not appeal to Wharton at all, though, paradoxically, even while she was reading them the older novelist himself was becoming one of her most cherished friends. Returning a batch of the reviews of her third collection of stories, *The Descent of Man and Other Stories* (1904), she wailed to her Scribner's editor, W. C. Brownell, "The continued cry that I am an echo of Mr. James (whose books of the last ten years I can't read, much as I delight in the man) makes me feel rather hopeless."[10] A particular embarrassment created by the charge of her dependence upon James was the fact, probably, that it did her no credit with an anti-Jamesian literary establishment – and she was used as a paddle with which to spank him. "No one except perhaps Mr. James can present a revolting scene with more delicacy,"[11] a reviewer of her novelette, *The Touchstone* (1900), wryly declared. Another deplored the fact that she had "enveloped all she touched in a thick Jacobean atmosphere, in which nothing human, not even an emotion, could stir."[12]

The House of Mirth may have reflected the effect upon her of James's advice that she embrace the subject she knew best and tether herself in native ground.[13] But it had no Jamesian qualities. This was true despite a certain correspondence between Selden, its principal male character, and some of James's heroes. It was more of a naturalist novel than any of James's, its heroine down-spiraling through the layers of a realistically observed social world, a structure remote from his tightly centralized designs, his preoccupation with mental events. For a while, in her next writings, the comparison despite differences could still be made. Unlike *The House of Mirth,* the international *Madame de Treymes* (1907) was a step backward, and the reviewer for *Putnam's Monthly* had some right to complain, "After granting the unfairness of comparisons which Lily Bart's successor would inevitably be compelled to undergo, it was positively exasperating for *Mme de Treymes* to hark back to Henry James."[14] The story had analogies with the Master's *Madame de Mauves* and *The American.* But even these resemblances were less significant than the differences; her interest in Franco-American cultural comparisons was more objective than his, more a question of the precise observation of real manners.

In the case of *The Fruit of the Tree,* with its complex incorporation of social issues, one might possibly say that some elements of the plot were Jamesian, but there was now no question at all that Wharton could write without owing anything substantial to the older writer's example and was serving interests totally unlike his. James, himself, reacted to the casualness of the book's design – so different from his own – and told a friend, "It is of a strangely infirm composition and construction."[15] Her masterpiece in consistent point of view and tight structure, *Ethan Frome,* he would call a "gem,"[16] but, still, nothing could have been more unlike his studies of complicated human subjects. *The Reef,* on the other hand, like *Madame de Treymes,* did take up again more subtle characters and a Jamesian international theme, and James told its author that he had adored "the unspeakably *fouillée* nature of the situation between the two principals" and its "Racinian" unity.[17] The terms of James's praise suggest that *The Reef* may have been Wharton's most serious effort to adapt his method to her own purposes.

But, if so, it was pretty much her last attempt in this direction. When *The Custom of the Country* appeared, it was clear that she had taken up again the line begun with *The House of Mirth,* reversing the earlier novel's spiral, episodic downward design and substituting the picaresque ascent of a heroine who would never have interested James, taking liberties of authorial intrusion into the narrative that must have gone against his grain, illuminating her scene with her own "almost scientifically satiric . . . light," as James himself saw.[18] He made this book the occasion of his only published comment on Wharton, a complimentary review in the London *Times Literary Supplement,* although he told her privately that she had slighted the kind of interest that he himself would have found in her heroine's penetration into the labyrinth of the old French aristocracy.

In any case, she really never wavered afterward in her attachment to the mode most natural to her. In 1913 she was groping for a new novel, wavering between two subjects, she told her publisher, but certain only that both "would be planned somewhat on the lines of 'The House of Mirth' and 'The Custom': that is, they would deal with a group or groups of people, and with a series of events rather than a central situation"[19] – a clear declaration of anti-Jamesian intent. World War I interrupted her work, and during the war years she produced only a single important work, *Summer*. Among the larger projects laid aside may have been "Literature," a chronicle of the literary life she never completed.

The other may have been *The Age of Innocence* (1920). Here, one might say, was a novel dealing with those familiar Jamesian antonyms, innocence and experience, America and Europe. But Wharton is not really interested in the abstract moral comparisons that had preoccupied James; her American "innocence" of Old New York is quite ironically regarded, her "Europeanized" woman of experience is more vulnerable, ultimately; it is New York society itself, the organism of the tribe, that is her chief actor. Above all, the novel's objective narrative eschews immersion into that internal world which preoccupied James.

And it is her observant gaze upon outward things that Wharton turned, henceforth, not only on the ordered life of the past but on the present in which she found herself growing older, the America she now regarded from the distance of her settled expatriation in France. Her late novels have suffered in critical esteem from the fact that they were written for serialization in "women's magazines," but they are deft, ironic studies of personal passion set in the spectacle of a disintegrating social world. She was mining her own vein to the end. At the last, she wrote, in two joined novels, a somewhat rambling chronicle of the modern artist's career. *Hudson River Bracketed* (1929) and *The God's Arrive* (1932), despite obvious weaknesses, still showed some of her storytelling strength and her social vision.

Despite the consistent cavils of critics, Wharton's career is a model of market success attained fairly early and never altogether surrendered. She really had no need to envy the author of *Laddie*. *The House of Mirth*, after all, had been at the top of the best-seller list for four months, and 140,000 copies were sold during the first year after publication.[20] And critics themselves surrendered to this popular vote of approval – the *New Republic* reviewer of her *Xingu and Other Stories* (1916), for example, who said that her clever satire "came very near to affording complete satisfaction" even though her characters were not "the kind of people with whom you share cracker-jack in a day-coach" (237). The literary world was ready for *The Age of Innocence,* which won the Pulitzer Prize for being, in the incongruous language of the award, "the American novel published during the year which best presented the wholesome atmosphere of American life and the highest standard of American manners." That the reading public now had acquired a tolerance for social satire is indicated by the fact that Sinclair Lewis's *Main Street* led off the best-seller list in which *The Age of Innocence* ranked fourth. (*Main Street* had been the choice of the Pulitzer jury, but the Columbia trustees, who had final authority over the award, had balked at Lewis's more mordant mockery of contemporary life.) And the book was a money-maker. The *Pictorial Review* had already paid $18,000 for the right to run it in the magazine, and her new publishers, Appleton, put down a $15,000 advance on book royalties even before the sales began. These were not paltry sums in 1919, and by 1922 her income on the book's sales and film rights mounted to $70,000.[21]

Going back to the New York society world of her own youth in the 1870s, she had, it was recognized, painted her scene with Meissonier-like brilliance of detail (283). The generals of the book-reviewing army – William Lyon Phelps, Carl Van Doren, Henry Seidel Canby (283–9) – all agreed that *The Age of Innocence* was an ironic masterpiece enclosing a tender story of love and sacrifice. It was held to have topped all of her previous books; Phelps said, "Edith Wharton is a writer to bring glory on the name America, and this is her best book" (285). There were a few dissents. In England, the rival novelist Katherine Mansfield found Wharton's art too orderly and of the surface and asked for "a little wildness, a dark place or two in the soul" (292). In America, only the leftist critic Vernon L. Parrington, though he praised her "immaculate art," insisted that she had wasted it on trivial material and said that there was "more hope for literature in the crudities of the young naturalists. . . . She is too well bred to be a snob, but she escapes it only by sheer intelligence. . . . She belongs in spite of herself to the caste which she satirizes. . . . If she had lived less easily, if she had been forced to skimp and save and plan, she would have been a greater and richer artist" (295).

Wharton could have answered that in *The House of Mirth,* at least, her interest had been precisely in the situation of persons who find themselves, despite their upper-class origins, on the slippery slope of economic insecurity. And now, her next novel, *The Glimpses of the Moon,* was hailed by Katherine Fullerton Gerould as "Mrs. Wharton's new *House of Mirth*" (307). Wharton seemed to have continued the story of Lawrence Selden and

Lily Bart – who had been too poor to marry each other – in the story of a similar pair, who, living by one dodge or another with the help of affluent friends, decide to make it as a married couple. But without quite realizing it, Wharton had made Nick and Susy repulsive in their adaptation to this end – and then, in depicting their renovating conversion, the happy, moral ending she had denied Lawrence and Lily, she had simply been sentimental. None of the critics, with the exception of Mrs. Gerould, a personal friend, failed to see the novel's weaknesses, and it was called an "improbable jambalaya," nearly "totally devoid of interest" (315) and "a puppet show" (318). And such things could be said without resort to the old charges. For once, she was accused of technical ineptitude. Gibert Seldes wrote, "I am convinced that this failure is due not to Mrs. Wharton's preoccupation with any given social set nor to the domestic ideals which she gives to her hero nor to the celebrated coldness of her treatment of love; it can be explained only by the structural fault in the work itself" (316). In England, Rebecca West wrote that she could understand "the mood of despair that makes people declare that all is up with the novel when one reads Mrs. Wharton's *The Glimpses of the Moon*" (313).

Glimpses of the Moon sold over one hundred thousand copies in six months,[22] a more resounding applause than any Wharton had previously received from readers. But the gatekeepers of criticism were never again to see her in the light in which she had stood in 1920. Her war novel, *A Son at the Front* (1923), probably had more qualities to praise – and it was praised by a few – but most deplored her attempt to write about the feelings of the elderly, wealthy relatives of a young combatant. Again, commentators reminded themselves that her qualifications were of the wrong kind, her "chill temperament [making her] the last person in the world to write a war novel" (331) and that she could be expected to see the war myopically, "snobbishly blind to every point of view but that of her class" (331). Anyhow, by 1923 the war was a stale topic. A younger generation of male participants had already treated the subject quite differently: Cummings, Dos Passos, Boyd, among others. Yet when Hemingway published *A Farewell to Arms* still later, in 1929, everyone suddenly realized that the war novel had arrived that would define that experience for all time.

Her quartet of novelettes, boxed handsomely together by her new publisher, Appleton, under the title *Old New York* (1924), must have been designed to win back the joined critical and popular support that had met *The Age of Innocence,* and the responses were at least respectful. It began to be felt, however, that her talent might be running thin. This was the regretful observation now offered by Wilson, who had liked *A Son at the Front.*

Recalling her earlier work about the city of her birth, he expressed the belief that she was "probably the only absolutely first rate literary artist, occupying himself predominantly with New York, that New York has ever produced" (365). Again she had reached back to view with studied grace and only a mildly mocking humor the society she had known as a child and even the earlier New York of her parents.

Wharton's reputation never returned to its 1920 high point in her lifetime. She had a while to go, industriously turning out, in the next few years, novels that were greeted respectfully; her preeminence was not really denied. Her "consummate art" (399) in *The Mother's Recompense* (1925) was still acknowledged, although at least one reviewer called it "competent, skillful work, adequately chiseled and polished like a painting by a competent, but rather tired, artist" (402). Her touch seemed to be growing lighter and more uncertain, and Wilson said, in his review of *Twilight Sleep* (1927), "We may regret that she should have lived so long abroad that her pictures of life in America have a tendency to seem either shadowy or synthetic" (435). Now and then the dismissal was more harsh; one reviewer said, after reading *The Children* (1928), "Mrs. Wharton has already told us everything she knows, and now she has got to be judged on her merits. She is becoming an old-fashioned writer, with two plots, and everything handsome about her" (457–8). *Hudson River Bracketed* seemed only "a good old-fashioned novel of huge proportions" to V. S. Pritchett, who found its picture of the literary life unalive and the plot contrivances arbitrary (474). *The Gods Arrive* was "workmanlike" and yet, one critic objected, only journalistic; Wharton's attempt to represent the literary bohemia she hardly knew sounded "distressingly like Sunday-supplement comment" (498).

Some of the criticisms reviewers had offered her novels as they appeared remained staples of summary judgment for some time after her death, and justice, in the form of a serious, full-scale study of her work came late to Edith Wharton. Perhaps the slowness of the critics to attempt to give her a place, to evaluate her as a candidate for the canon of American literature, is an index of the resistance of the canon to the intrusion of a major female novelist, for even so astute a critic as Alfred Kazin contrasted Wharton with Dreiser in an essay titled, "The Lady and the Tiger" (1941), complaining that even in her earlier, better books she had generally been interested only in the destruction of the finer spirits among the socially privileged and had missed "the more important subject, the emerging new class of industrialists," which the masculine Dreiser had grasped.[23] It was a view not far from Robert M. Lovett's earlier conclusion that she showed herself "profoundly ignorant of the relations of class with class, which is the vital issue of social morality today." In 1925, in the earliest attempt to treat Wharton's work at length, Lovett had summed her up dismissively as "among the voices whispering the last enchantments of the Victorian age."[24]

But while some continued to think that Wharton had concerned herself with the wrong class of society and showed ignorance of the social forces governing all lives, it also became possible, as the years passed, to see how well she had understood the process that drove Lily Bart into penury and despair – a process no less significant than the destiny that had directed Dreiser's Carrie Meeber. In 1947, Diana Trilling went so far as to identify *The House of Mirth* as, in fact, a "class" novel, "one of the most telling indictments of a social system based on the chance distribution of wealth, and therefore of social privilege, that has ever been written." Nevertheless, Mrs. Trilling dismissed *Ethan Frome* almost in the same terms as its earliest critics had; she called it "a cruel book."[25] Other major rereaders, including Lionel Trilling, would find the famous novella not merely cruel but factitious; once reproached for her preoccupation with the wealthy, now she was criticized for having strayed from familiar scenes.[26] *Ethan Frome*, the eminent F. O. Matthiessen had written, "is the work of a woman whose life has been spent elsewhere [than in New England]."[27]

Finally, in 1953, Blake Nevius's *Edith Wharton: A Study of Her Fiction*, put together the whole of Wharton's career in a comprehensive, carefully balanced fashion, detecting the continuities that made her books, taken as a whole, an *oeuvre*. Nevius argued that Wharton had not only successfully exhibited an important historical subject, the "feudal remainder" that had dominated American society and the invasion into its ranks of newcomers. Threading through almost all of her fiction he saw preoccupation with a tragic theme of classical simplicity: "the spectacle of a large and generous nature . . . trapped by circumstances ironically of its [own] devising into consanguinity with a meaner nature."[28] It was a theme that united a study of vanished patrician manners such as *The Age of Innocence* with *Ethan Frome,* a description of the humblest rural lives in present-day America. The suggestion for this analysis was, probably, the biographical insight that Wilson had offered as a key to understanding the writer. Probably it had been her own unhappy marriage that inspired her vision of the "trapped sensibility," even if the protagonists of the books just mentioned were male. For it had been *she,* after all, who had had to escape from the snares of the society in which she had been bred, a society that defined her as a woman in ways from which she had to break free by making herself a writer. The entrapment from which she had had to escape had been precisely defined also in *The House of Mirth* and *Summer,* which illustrated the condition of female imprisonment both in the milieu of wealth and in the most limited of social circumstances.

And so, her life began to be looked at more closely. It was true that a notion of her personal character had always affected responses to her work. From the fact that she was rich and aloof, the reader of the early Sunday-supplement articles had been encouraged to imagine an art inhibited by class condescension and prudery. Her own autobiography, *A Backward Glance* (1934), did not help enough to change this picture, and Percy Lub-bock's *Portrait of Edith Wharton* (1947) tended to increase the impression that she was supercilious, stiff, without heart – and this connected with the view of her books that, as we have seen, convicted her of limited response to common experience, discovering in her elegance of style a reflection of the well-dressed woman of fashion.

Yet even *A Backward Glance* had told much that might suggest the woman beneath her armor of public appearance. Wharton had been born, as she herself related, to parents who were members of the exclusive heredi-tary aristocracy of Old New York. This class was puritanical and stodgy. A "well-bred" girl was not only abysmally ignorant about real culture; she was also kept in the dark about sex. Young Edith, with an active, searching mind that hardly knew where to find its sustenance, and totally unprepared for sexual relations, made the expected marriage to a Bostonian sportsman without any ideas. The marriage was a catastrophe in every way. She was forty when, in 1912, she divorced Teddy Wharton and settled in Europe, having already published eighteen books. There had never been such a thing as a professional writer among the Joneses and the Rhinelanders from whom she came, but she was a person of will who had *made* herself, in a very American way, out of her own idea of selfhood. She knew that she could not survive in the world that had bred her, and she had already shown that she could create her own space and choose her own company in her house, The Mount, which she built in a secluded spot in rural Massa-chusetts. Europe represented a better refuge from the world that had almost extinguished her, a larger, more congenial cultural environment. In France, she established herself in a circle of cultivated men and women who found intelligence and artistic creativity acceptable feminine attributes.

The liberation had not been easy, and the autobiography acknowledges gratefully the help of certain friendships – that with the great James and with lesser intellectuals from her own New York like Egerton Winthrop and Walter Berry, who read her first stories and helped her write her first book, a manual for the decoration of upper-class homes. Berry was more than a mentor; it is plain that she loved him for almost all her life. She calls him "the one friend in the life of each of us who seems not a separate person, however dear and beloved, but an expansion, an interpretation, of one's self, the very meaning of one's soul,"[29] and he died in her arms. In Europe she found others who encouraged her to be a writer, like the novelist Paul Bourget. She became, at last, a productive professional.

This, however, was not the whole story. The desperation underlying her outward composure during the years while she struggled to free herself from her sterile marriage was hidden from general view but obvious to her intimates. In time it became obvious to readers of her previously unpublished private letters, especially of the letters to her and about her written by James, the keenest of these observing intimates.[30] James's remarkable letters show a brilliant woman driven by frenetic restlessness arising from her hidden frustration. What James also knew more about than most was a long-delayed outburst of the inner Wharton, her catapult into a secret love affair with the American journalist Morton Fullerton. Not as profound as her feeling for Berry – which may never have reached full expression in the sexual sense – Wharton's brief experience with Fullerton apparently freed her from the frigidity of her marriage. Excerpts from a private diary, published in 1958, hinted at this episode,[31] but a complete view of it became possible only after all of her sealed papers were made available to her biographer, R. W. B. Lewis, and disclosed to the reading public in 1975, nearly forty years after her death. Lewis's biography also brought into print a document – previously known only to some other scholars – that had long rested in the open files of Wharton's papers at Yale. This was a story fragment depicting a scene between an older man and a young woman, perhaps his daughter, engaged in varieties of sexual activity rarely described outside of deliberate pornography. Though it was of no great literary merit, the "Beatrice Palmato" fragment made it finally impossible to describe Wharton as someone ignorant of the nature of sexuality or immune to its force. Too many had misinterpreted her as prudish, as had André Gide, who recorded waiting for her to leave the room before discussing "sexual perversions" in his own writing.[32]

In other ways, also, the image of an invulnerably ladylike Wharton came to be modified. Letters exchanged with her publishers and editors from the start of her career to the climax of her popularity revealed that she had transformed herself into an author with no old-fashioned inhibitions about moneymaking. As practically as though she possessed no private income inherited from generations who had never had to work gainfully, she adapted herself with determined toughness to the modern book market. She learned to look after her interests as well as any agent might have done for her, pressing her publishers for advertising and promotional effort, insisting on royalties commensurate with her market value, and shifting without any sentimental regrets to new publishers who maximized her earnings. At whatever cost, she made herself in more senses than one into a "new woman" who seized her own identity.[33]

As this personal image became more distinct, it was not surprising that a sense of identification with Edith Wharton was felt by women of a later time and condition. Somewhat inexactly, she began to be seen as one of feminism's foremothers – who, though talented and rich, suffered the persisting ordeal of all women struggling for personal and professional self-definition in a male-dominated world. That she was a "lady novelist" had been a somewhat invidious characterization made throughout her career. Perhaps a few early readers perceived how valuable her insight into women had been – a forgotten popular reviewer, Aline Gorren, for example, who commended her first stories for "the genius with which she brings to the surface the underground movements of women's minds" (33). Recognition of her insight into female feeling was apt to be but another form of condescension, however, as when another reviewer praised *Sanctuary* (1903) for the "beautiful, tender sentimentality peculiar to women whether they are writers, mothers or missionaries" (71). When her art was approved by male critics, she was held to have somehow "transcended the limits of her sex," as E. K. Brown, put it.[34] Even Henry James, responding to *The Custom of the Country,* had resorted to a conventional distinction between male and female mentality when he declared that her talent was a rare instance "of the dry, or call it perhaps even the hard, intellectual touch in the soft, or call it perhaps even the humid temperamental air; in other words of the masculine conclusion tending so to crown the feminine observation."[35]

In the last third of the twentieth century, readers began to see it differently, and a series of studies appeared which concentrated on Wharton's objectified analysis of femalehood and on the relevance of her personal experience to the study of her art, which, if it was "feminine," was feminine in a new sense altogether. Though she was no conscious feminist, it was felt that she had expressed her own struggles in fiction that showed her clear understanding of what it had meant to her to be a woman. By the end of the 1980s, feminism had produced a flood of books and articles on Wharton. The new interest promoted biographical studies which boldly speculated about the element of trauma in the writer's private history, seeing her life in terms of a feminist psychopathology. In 1977, Cynthia Griffin Wolff, in *A Feast of Words: The Triumph of Edith Wharton,* applied the theories of Erik Erikson in a diagnosis of Wharton as someone whose early loss of her father and "oral deprivation" had arrested her development but motivated her to find an outlet in language. It was the first attempt to propose a narrative of Wharton's life laying primary emphasis on the thesis that she had been emotionally starved as a child. Fifteen years later, in her psychobiography *The Sexual Education of Edith Wharton* (1992), Gloria C. Erlich drew upon the theories of Freud, D. W. Winnicott, and others. She saw Wharton's life as a never-ended effort to gain maternal love from alternate mothers who reenacted the division she had felt between her own mother (the bad mother) and her nurse (the good mother). Both Wolff and Erlich detected the replay of childhood's primal drama in Wharton's stories and novels. The "Beatrice Palmato" fragment played a role in these interpretations and even promoted the unverifiable guess that Wharton had been sexually abused by her father.

But other feminist critics saw Wharton's writings as reflections of a woman artist's lifelong struggle against social proscriptions and saw how she described the process of "commodification" – to use the Marxist word – in the formation of female character.[36] Elizabeth Ammons, in *Edith Wharton's Argument with America* (1980), approached the writer sociologically as someone who expressed the fact that the American patriarchy had robbed women of control of their own lives. Carol Wershoven, in *The Female Intruder in the Novels of Edith Wharton* (1982), showed how the woman who is in some way outside her society was an embodiment of the author's rebellion. Wendy Gimbel's *Edith Wharton: Orphancy and Survival* (1984) took its interpretive impulse from a view of Wharton's personal alienation and search for selfhood and habitation. Judith Fryer's *Felicitous Space: The Imaginative Structures of Edith Wharton and Willa Cather* (1986) explored the relation of Wharton's imagination to her concepts of space, both in her views of house decoration and in her fiction. Katherine Joslin's *Women Writers: Edith Wharton* (1991) detected in all of Wharton's writing about women, including her autobiography, the struggle experienced by so many women for "relational selfhood" (i.e., personal definition within rather than outside of the social context) and analyzed Wharton's literary tone and style as an assumption of male disguise.

In the mid-1990s, Wharton is again almost a popular author. Her books sell well in paperback and are made into big-budget movies (both *Ethan Frome* and *The Age of Innocence* have recently been made into successful commercial films, and a paperback edition of *The Age of Innocence* with a cover picture showing Michelle Pfeiffer in the role of Ellen Olenska went to the top of the best-seller list in the fall of 1993). Wharton is also more important than ever before to the critical-academic world. But shifts in the fashions of criticism have begun to modify the feminist emphasis of the preceding two decades. The time seems to have come around to reconsider her writing in whole and in part, restudying problems of intrinsic content and literary form, and to evaluate her artistic success or failure. Biographical interpretation of her fiction may have done its work. She, herself, it should be remembered, did not deny the direct pertinence of her life to her readers merely out of fearfulness or modesty. She saw herself, like George Eliot, as an intellectual, interested in her culture in a broad sense – in questions of nationality and sociology and history as these affected all mankind, male and female. Much of the feminist platform of her own time did not arouse her sympathy, but she had been, from her own young womanhood, stimulated by nineteenth-century evolutionary theory and by the new field of anthropology, and she was undoubtedly affected by the naturalists, like Dreiser, who have been wrongly contrasted with her. Her sense of history was profound. She saw herself not merely as, like James, an "historian of fine consciousness" but as an historian of class shifts and of changes in manners.

So, psychology, no longer focusing exclusively on feminist issues, returns to the study of Wharton's work, merging with a general interest in the cultural formations of the self which help to explain her own history as well as the histories of her characters. She is again seen as a writer who worked in ungendered generic traditions. Current redefinitions of Realism and of Naturalism include her in a new historical context, and her works now are being studied as part of the complex cultural and political dynamics of the early twentieth century. As contemporary critics look at Wharton, questions of class and even of race, of sociological and anthropological ways of viewing, are as important as questions of gender.

Certain of Wharton's works, always favorites of the general reader, remain still of central interest, but particular novels or shorter fictions now take the lead instead of others. *The House of Mirth,* for example, has recently provoked more study than almost any of her books, outdistancing even *The Age of Innocence,* once her most famous. But there are signs that *The Age of Innocence* is becoming interesting again in a new way – not so much for the frustrated romance of its hero and heroine as for its social vision. *The Custom of the Country,* whose ascendant heroine has generally failed to attract the attention of feminists, now seems fascinating for the brilliance of its representation of class mobility. And works formerly passed over seem to invite a fresh approach. One may still feel, as Wilson or Louis Auchincloss did, that Old New York was her most authentic subject, but her stories, short and long, about New England now seem to represent one of her major statements, and it is now *Summer,* once thought to be the lesser companion to *Ethan Frome,* that some think the more exciting, original, deeply resonant member of the pair of novellas, and one of her greatest books. Critics are turning to the works done outside those fifteen years between *The House of Mirth* and *The Age of Innocence* – to, for example, her first, unjustly forgotten novel, *The Valley of Decision,* and to her early novellas and short stories, or to the late writing so invidiously remembered as having been done for "women's magazines."

The essays in this collection represent some of this newest thinking about Edith Wharton. Pamela Knights demonstrates how completely Wharton, in *The Age of Innocence,* lived up to her own view that character "flows imperceptibly into adjacent people and things" and that consciousness is created by social typologies and conventional paradigms of behavior. Knights invites us to "read the hieroglyphs" of Wharton's descriptions, to see how the drama of conformity is enforced by the dynamics of change and regulation. Nancy Bentley's essay on "Wharton and the Science of Manners" is an appropriate companion study to Knights's in its demonstration that Wharton's imagination was given a language of conceptions and descriptions by the contemporary rise of scientific anthropology, and although Bentley's discussion ranges over Wharton's fiction it is not surprising that a primary illustration is, again, *The Age of Innocence.* The shift to see Wharton sociologically is also illustrated in Elizabeth Ammons's essay on the role of race in Wharton's fiction. Although the issue of race definition and race conflict plays only a minor role on the surface of the writer's narratives, Ammons argues that the essential American conflict over race is enacted in Wharton's representations of privileged "whiteness," that "blackness" is its "hidden signifier." And Elaine Showalter discovers in *The Custom of the Country* a brilliant anticipation of modern business personalities and their material self-expression; she shows how Undine Spragg's survival is complexly achieved by determinants of class as well as of gender.

Critical study of Wharton seems, at last, to have become more rich, to match the challenge of a major writer whose work derived from complex inspirational sources. For Gloria Erlich, these are still chiefly personal, and she argues that Wharton's imaginative themes derive from the earliest tensions of childhood, a divided motherhood creating a contest to be found in tales like the mysterious ghost stories, "Bewitched" and "Afterward," and the early novellas of moral dilemma, *Sanctuary* and *The Touchstone.* Another use of modern psychological theory, drawing upon French feminism and the psychoanalytic theory of Jacques Lacan, and blending these with the insights of modern anthropology, is to be found in Rhonda Skillern's analysis of *Summer*. Several of the essays in this collection try to come to terms with the nature of Wharton's artistry, her place in literary tradition, and, above all, her use of literary genres – questions long neglected in the rush to extract her thematic messages. Was she a traditional "novelist of manners"? Bentley suggests that she substituted a "science of manners," in the sense of the phrase employed by anthropologists, for the novel's old way of ranging social types and forms of behavior in a comic exhibition. Maureen Howard shows how Wharton modifies and blends comedy of manners, melodrama, and naturalism in *The House of Mirth*. James Tuttleton discovers *The Fruit of the Tree*'s membership in a popular realist genre of factory novels aimed at reform of the abuses of the industrial system but also sees how its structural difficulty arises out of an attempt to write, at the same time, a novel about marriage, yoking the issues both of class and gender by a linking theme, "the perils of abstract idealism."

Finally, the collection presents two essays on Wharton's earliest long work, *The Valley of Decision*. It has seldom been discussed by modern critics and is still little read, often dismissed as an overloaded pastiche of guidebook scenes and potted history. But William Vance shows how this impressive historical romance helped Wharton to create a personal "mask." The collection closes with a newly rediscovered critical essay on *The Valley of Decision* written by Wharton's contemporary, the English writer Vernon Lee (Violet Paget), whose own writings on Italy greatly influenced Wharton's novel. The essay was contributed to an Italian periodical in 1903 and is here republished and translated into English for the first time. It is an essay whose brilliant insight into the major work of Wharton's early period should promote further study of this novel today.*

NOTES

1   Edmund Wilson, "Justice to Edith Wharton," *New Republic* 95 (June 29, 1938), 209–13. Reprinted in Wilson, *The Wound and the Bow* (Boston: Houghton Mifflin, 1941).
2   The impression that Wharton's work was generally received favorably throughout her career is one that she herself promoted in her autobiography *A Backward Glance* (New York: Appleton-Century, 1934), but contemporary reviews give a mixed picture. A generous representation of these is to be found in the recent

*Christine Richards drew my attention to the existence of Lee's essay, published in Italian in *La Cultura* 21, no. 20 (1903), 305–7. The translation has been provided by Marcella Barzetti.

collection *Edith Wharton: The Contemporary Reviews,* ed. James W. Tuttleton, Kristin O. Lauer, and Margaret P. Murray (Cambridge: Cambridge University Press, 1992). When reviews of Wharton's books are cited from this collection, they will be referred to parenthetically in the text.

3   Henry Seidel Canby, "Edith Wharton," *Saturday Review of Literature* 16 (August 21, 1937), 7.

4   Frank Luther Mott, *Golden Multitudes: The Story of Best Sellers in the United States* (New York: Macmillan, 1947), p. 220.

5   Millicent Bell, *Edith Wharton and Henry James* (New York: Braziller, 1965), p. 328. The clipping is in the Wharton Collection, Beinecke Library, Yale University.

6   Robert Herrick, "Mrs. Wharton's World," *New Republic* (February 13, 1915), 40–2; Percy Lubbock, "The Novels of Edith Wharton," *Quarterly Review* 222 (January 1915), 182–201.

7   John C. Underwood, *Literature and Insurgency: Ten Studies in Racial Evolution* (New York: Mitchell Kennerley, 1914).

8   *New York Musical Courier* (May 1899). Cited along with other minor newspaper notices in Bell, *Edith Wharton and Henry James,* p. 217.

9   Wharton's biographer, R. W. B. Lewis, states that the assertion of her resemblance to James by early reviewers "was not yet vexatious to Edith Wharton, particularly since it was made in her favor." *Edith Wharton: A Biography* (New York: Harper & Row, 1975), p. 89. This may not be correct. The remarks of one reviewer of *The Greater Inclination,* John D. Barry, of the *Boston Literary World,* probably did vex her, for she remembered them all her life. In her autobiography she recalls with distaste Barry's declaration that she was ignorant of the rudiments of the storytelling art in failing to open her tales with a short phrase or with dialogue, though she does not disclose his declaration that in this error and others she had reproduced some of James's "worst faults of style." This ground of her annoyance with the reviewer evidently became known to him, for he observed in print several weeks later: "She is said . . . not to relish the frequent references made by her readers to her indebtedness to Henry James, so her next book will probably not be marked by slavish adherence to the method of a very questionable literary model." She saved clippings of both of Barry's columns until her death. Bell, *Edith Wharton and Henry James,* pp. 218–20.

10   Edith Wharton to W. C. Brownell, June 25, 1904, *The Letters of Edith Wharton,* ed. R. W. B. Lewis and Nancy Lewis (New York: Scribner, 1988), p. 91. All subsequent references to Wharton's letters are from this edition (except where letters are only available elsewhere) and are cited parenthetically in the text.

11   *The Independent* 55 (December 10, 1903), 2933–5.

12   Percival Pollard, *Their Day in Court* (New York: Neale, 1909).

13   Henry James to Mary Cadwalader Jones, August 20, 1902, *Henry James Letters* ed. Leon Edel (Cambridge, Mass.: Harvard University Press, 1984), vol. 4, p. 247. All subsequent references to James's letters are from this edition, except where letters are only available elsewhere.

14   *Putnam's Monthly* 3 (1907–8), 593.

15   Henry James to Mary Cadwalader Jones, December 8, 1907, quoted in Bell, *Edith Wharton and Henry James,* p. 259.

16   Henry James to Edith Wharton, October 25, 1911, *Henry James Letters,* vol. 4, p. 588.

17   Henry James to Edith Wharton, December 9, 1912, *Henry James Letters,* vol. 4, p. 644.

18   *Henry James: Literary Criticism,* ed. Leon Edel (New York: Library of America, 1984), p. 155.

19   Edith Wharton to Charles Scribner, May 19, 1913, quoted in Bell, *Edith Wharton and Henry James,* pp. 290–1.

20   Bell, *Edith Wharton and Henry James,* p. 320; Lewis, *Edith Wharton: A Biography,* p. 151.

21   Lewis, *Edith Wharton: A Biography,* pp. 429–30.

22   Lewis, *Edith Wharton: A Biography,* p. 444.

23   Alfred Kazin, "The Lady and the Tiger: Edith Wharton and Theodore Dreiser," *Virginia Quarterly Review* 17 (Winter 1941), 101–19.

24   Robert Morss Lovett, *Edith Wharton* (New York: McBride, 1925).

25 Diana Trilling, "*The House of Mirth* Revisited," *Harper's Bazaar* 81 (December 1944), 126–7, 180–6.
26 Lionel Trilling, "The Morality of Inertia," *Great Moral Dilemmas in Literature, Past and Present*, ed. Robert M. MacIver (New York: Institute for Religious and Social Studies, 1956), pp. 37–46.
27 F. O. Matthiessen, "New England Stories," *American Writers on American Literature* (New York: Liveright, 1931).
28 Blake Nevius, *Edith Wharton: A Study of Her Fiction* (Berkeley and Los Angeles: University of California, 1953).
29 Edith Wharton, *Novellas and Other Writings* (New York: Library of America, 1990), p. 870.
30 Most of these letters were published for the first time in *Edith Wharton and Henry James* in 1965. A selection of James's letters to Wharton and to others about her can be found in Edel's *Henry James Letters*. Wharton's letters to James are now available in Lewis and Lewis, *Letters of Edith Wharton*. The correspondence between James and Wharton has also been recently published in *Henry James and Edith Wharton, Letters: 1900–1915*, ed. Lyall Powers (New York: Scribner, 1990).
31 Wayne Andrews, "The World of Edith Wharton: Fragment of a Biography in Progress," introduction to *The Best Short Stories of Edith Wharton* (New York: Scribner, 1958).
32 André Gide, *Journals*, vol. 2: *1914–1927*, trans. Justin O'Brien (New York: Knopf, 1951).
33 Described in detail in Millicent Bell, "Lady into Author: Edith Wharton and the House of Scribner," *American Quarterly* 9 (Fall 1957), 295–315.
34 E. K. Brown, *Edith Wharton: Etudes critiques* (Paris: Droz, 1935).
35 Edel, *Henry James: Literary Criticism*, p. 155.
36 An influential argument to this effect was made by Judith Fetterley in "The Temptation to Be a Beautiful Object: Double Standard and Double Bind in *The House of Mirth*," *Studies in American Fiction* 5 (1977), 199–211.

I

PAMELA KNIGHTS

Forms of Disembodiment: The Social Subject in *The Age of Innocence*

"Everything may be labelled – but everybody is not."[1]

In 1921, excited by news of a plan to stage *The Age of Innocence,* Edith Wharton responded immediately with proprietarial advice about getting the 1870s right – the moustaches ("not tooth brush ones, but curved & slightly twisted at the ends"), the clothes and the buttonhole flowers (violets by day, gardenias by night), the manners and the language (no slang, no American-isms – "English was then the language spoken by American ladies & gentle-men").[2] Since she had insisted that she did not want the novel taken as a "costume piece" (*Letters,* 433), this punctiliousness might seem surprising. But in *The Age of Innocence,* social details matter: "As Mrs. Archer re-marked, the Roman punch made all the difference: not in itself but by its manifold implications" (1276). Reconstructing knowledge of half a century earlier, Wharton writes as if she has forgotten nothing. Social forms, her letters explain, are imprinted young and are impossible to erase. Her story, she tells one friend, was about "two people trying to live up to some-thing . . . still 'felt in the blood'" (*Letters,* 433); anxious about the drama-tization, she exclaims, "I could do every stick of furniture & every rag of clothing myself, for every detail of that far-off scene was indelibly stamped on my infant brain" (*Letters,* 439).

For some readers, the interest of the novel is psychological: some ask what the act of returning to that childhood scene meant to Edith Wharton in 1919. Others, abetted by Newland Archer, speculate about the nature of "real" experience (passion, perhaps, or art?) as something apart from the "tyrannical trifles" (1188) which bind one hour to the next and tie the self firmly into the everyday social world. But the text makes it hard to sustain readings that dismiss cultural furnishings as "background" (whether pictur-esque or oppressive) or that see characters as discrete beings, with an inde-pendent "selfhood" separate and intact from any social inscriptions. Whar-ton was critical of modern fiction that took its bearings entirely within the flux of the subconscious; for her, the novel had found its form when it became aware "that the bounds of a personality were not reproducible by a sharp black line, but that each of us flows imperceptibly into adjacent people and things."[3] *The Age of Innocence* lives up to her paradigm. Readers soon discover that any observation about an individual character – about his or her consciousness, emotions, body, history, or language – also entangles us in the collective experience of the group, expressed in the welter of trifles, the matrix of social knowledge, within and out of which Wharton's subjects are composed.

Where and how far that entanglement extends is one of the novel's questions. Its hero, Archer, raises the inquiry, but by the time we hear that he "had long given up trying to disengage her [May's] real self from the shape into which tradition and training had moulded her" (1276), we realize his limits. Though acknowledging social formation, he still assumes that somewhere a "real" self survives. The suggestion of the unfolding narrative is, more radically, that without the shape, the social mold, there may be no self at all.

Wharton was always interested in what happens to the self when separated, by will or circumstance, from the world that has formed it. Archer is her specimen rather than her spokesman. In examining him, *The Age of Innocence* goes beyond his brand of analysis to parallel, in its own terms, contemporary debates about the social basis of consciousness. In turn-of-the-century writings by, for example, William James, Charles Horton Cooley, or (slightly later) George Herbert Mead, we find early explorations of the idea that, to use Ian Burkitt's helpful summary, "personality develops within discourse," that is . . . "self" and "mind" are formed within the "communicative activity of the group."[4] For Mead, the self developed through language, above all, in the very processes of thinking, grounded in an inner dialogue with the social group. Wharton, in *French Ways and Their Meaning* (1919), essays that she assembled for publication as she was working on *The Age of Innocence,* suggested that looking at a race's preponderant words is one of the best ways of getting at its nature. *The Age of Innocence* contains a glossary to old New York. The quoted terms ("nice," what was "not the thing," and the rest) take us a long way into what Society feels in its blood, and in reading it becomes hard to think outside their limits – or to know whose words they are. Frequently we meet objective narrative commentary, often at the start of a chapter, which suddenly relocates itself in Archer's focalizing vision: "These things passed through Newland Archer's mind" (1063); "Newland Archer had been aware of these things ever since he could remember" (1097). As we continue, then, public and private, personality and surroundings, begin to fuse, as New York's consciousness and Archer's emerge in the text together.

Archer is a thoroughly middle-of-the-road subject. *The Age of Innocence* begins with him solidly the gentleman, brushed and white-waistcoated, his coordinates clear. Everything about him proclaims his firm insertion within the symbolic order, from his secret satisfaction in his mastery in the home to his work as legal caretaker of the large estates and "conservative" investments (1115) of New York gentility. Putting Archer in the office of a Mr. Letterblair, with a roll of dead names on the letterheads and a senior partner who "was, professionally speaking, his own grandson" (1089), the text could not have inscribed him in a more patrilineal institution – worlds away from the "real" life of letters that tempts him in imagination.

Despite his intellectual pretensions to be a person of "advanced culture" (1051), Archer's reading, too, confirms him in the assumptions of his class and gender. He consumes science and literature in his upper-floor quarters, while his mother and sister squeeze themselves into the narrower space below. Later he uses history as a shield against his wife (1249). He chooses Michelet, a historian, so Ludmilla Jordanova tells us, "obsessed with sexual difference."[5] He pursues his beloved through the pages of Rossetti. Even his anthropology is far from radical. Archer's London bookseller sends him Herbert Spencer and, we suppose, other dominant thinkers of the decade (Sir Edwin Tylor, Sir John Lubbock, or John F. McLennan, for instance) who could supply him with the templates for marriage by capture, the service of the prospective son-in-law, the parental feints of reluctance, and so on, through which he characterizes his own experiences. According to the historian Elizabeth Fee,[6] these writers were conservatives to a man, lawyers and amateurs like Archer himself. (One of them, McLennan, shared Archer's taste for pre-Raphaelite verse and, under the pseudonym of "Iconoclast," even wrote a volume himself.)

Viewing the sheltered reserve around Washington Square through their terminology of "inscrutable totem terrors" (1018), "sacred taboos," and savage practices, Archer shapes the 1870s for us into the customs and ceremonies of a vanishing tribe. There is no denying the extent to which his model pervades the text. But against the more sophisticated ethnological eye of the novel as a whole, Archer's anthropology has a distinctly old-fashioned air. By the 1900s, the evolutionary discourse of "survivals" was being replaced by an interest (which the narrative shares) in "functions," the interpretation of social features in terms of their contemporary meanings. From the vantage point of 1920, then, we see farther than Archer does. (We shall find that while Archer gazes smugly on archaisms, the text shows us an active system.) *The Age of Innocence* asks us to explore questions of social process; the "books on Primitive Man" (1051), in contrast, assure Archer of the hazardousness of women and the primacy of the patriarchal modern family. As McLennan was certain, "With the advance of society . . . the superiority of the male sex must have everywhere tended to establish that system."[7]

So, far from being the enlightened ethnologist, Archer himself is structured by the discourse of Family. At every step, his life embodies the family design, and the novel takes form around it. In the narrative of engagement, marriage, and fatherhood, Archer's identity is always positional: he is a son, brother, part of an affianced couple, caught in the "bridegroom's convulsive gesture" (1162), unable to break free even when he realizes his own condition ("'What I am? A son-in-law,'" 1186), trapped, finally, by May's victorious news of his forthcoming paternity. His role is compounded by his casting as the official voice, the spokesman for Firm and Family, who has to represent the word of all the tribal fathers in the containment of the woman who threatens them, until he even hears himself talking of "our ideas" in a voice that sounded like Mr. Letterblair's (1103).

As the novel proceeds, Archer begins to try to talk his way out of these words (the "categories like that" [1245] that make his world. In his anguished (and much-quoted) discussions with Ellen Olenska, he always comes up against Ellen's paradoxical certainties that they cannot exist beyond their social roles; for her, there can be no new entity ("no *us* in that sense!," 1246), except in a disembodied, romantic union, possible only if they never meet. Otherwise Archer will always be "the husband of Ellen Olenska's cousin" and she "the cousin of Newland Archer's wife" (1246), involved in shabby liaisons.

Ellen's parodic genealogy holds Archer (and us) firmly within the tidy structures of New York. If Archer remains a social agent stuck inside his culture, we must read his story in the broader context of class survival. *The Age of Innocence* looks back to the New York of Wharton's parents, a place Wharton located on the edges of history or myth, like Schliemann's Troy or the vanished Atlantis.[8] In the Metropolitan Museum, we see the newly recovered fragments of Ilium first through Ellen's sympathetic eyes, as small domestic objects, poignantly broken and labeled "Use unknown" (1262); then, in the final chapter, as scientifically catalogued treasures. Either view offers a possible approach (*The Age of Innocence* has been seen as both a sentimental and a dispassionate record), but the narrative also enables more active readings. Its pace and chronology (the leisurely scenic presentation of two years in the 1870s, the precipitate switch in the last pages to two days in the early 1900s, all read with hindsight from the immediate postwar years) allow us to see the items both labeled and successfully in use, and encountering the pressures of change.

When the novel opens, the old New York families seem secure but are already under threat. Although the Academy still keeps the "new people" out, a new Opera House (with boxes for anyone who can afford them) is already being talked of, and from 1920, the concealed narrative standpoint, we know its building is imminent and that we are watching the rituals of an imperiled class. *The Age of Innocence* maps its field with the air of a textbook in systematic social observation. As Elsie Clews Parsons, a near contemporary, advised students in 1906, it was important, as a base for more advanced social analysis, to consolidate one's data: "The bounds and nature of the inhabited territory, the size of the group, its modes of subsistence, its economic and political classes, and its general social organisation, tribal, monarchical, democratic, etc. . . . In particular, the prevailing means in general of enforcing custom should be noted."[9] (And all this in one's first report.) We can try out her scheme against Archer's New York: details of territory (the streets, houses, rooms, furnishings, clothes, ornaments), subsistence (the menus? or the pastimes? – the Chivers's house parties, the van der Luyden's perfect lawns, or the Archer women's ferns in Wardian cases), hierarchies (a guest list ticked off with Mrs. Archer's sharp gold pen, precedence at table, a silent butler), or the invitations, visits, dinners, opera going, dances, and weddings that keep it all in place. All these take us into the language and being of the 1870s leisure class and together make up the cultural capital through which it maintains and reproduces itself, and, as critics demonstrate, any might do as an opening into the world of the novel.

For an example here, we might as well remain with the Roman punch and the dinner table (as ethnology knows, always a cultural minefield). There is a lot of dining in *The Age of Innocence*. In the 1870s, when the Newland Archers inaugurate themselves as a married couple, the punch, unambiguously, signified exclusiveness and accompanied "either canvas-backs or terrapin, two soups, a hot and cold sweet, full *décolletage* with short sleeves, and guests of a proportionate importance" (1276). By 1922, Emily Post was warning, "To eat extra entrées, Roman punch, or hot dessert is to be in the dining-room of a parvenu."[10] New York, as the novel's first paragraph tells us, is drawn to the new people, even as it dreads them: meanings are in contest and will shift as society changes.

To help us read the hieroglyphs, to know just who is an acceptable guest and why, *The Age of Innocence* supplies experts, who come confidently equipped with opera glasses and innuendo, axioms, long memories, and forests of family trees, to instruct us in social placing. We learn to read gesture and to listen to the unspoken. In polite voices, even gaps between syllables ("'Anyhow, he – eventually – married her'") teach "volumes"

(1044). At dinner in a room which speaks loudly of social purity, Mrs. Archer and Mr. Jackson securely query others' origins. Family portraits guarantee their own. Dark frames on dark walls oppose the crude glossiness that marks the upstart. (Here, real ladies put their Paris dresses away for at least two seasons to rebuke the vulgarity of fashion.) The grandfathers still rule the table: Grandfather Newland's voice giving advice about how to keep the dynasty pure ("Don't let that fellow Beaufort be introduced to the girls," 1043), and Grandfather Archer's picture, in front of his white-columned country seat, giving an ever-present reminder of social stability and family property in the face of the socially suspect. Mr. Jackson's "sniff" at the mushroom sauce is "scarcely perceptible" but is enough to suggest that he "would probably finish his meal on Ellen Olenska" (1045). Women and mushrooms are hard to label, might well be poisonous, grow in dubious places, and it may be unwise to admit them to the table.[11] In the next chapter New York refuses a dinner invitation to meet her and, at the end of the novel, stages the final party to expel her permanently from society.

The dinner-table topics are central to the novel. *The Age of Innocence* is transfixed, as the speakers are, by outsiders and by the problems of classification. In a world where mobility is dangerous, to define is to begin to control. The Archer voice declares itself the social norm; its social distinctions, Mrs. Archer claims, have "nothing to do with rank or class" (1054); it lies somewhere between the "plain people" and the aristocracy, and its wealth and its morality are the standard. Mrs. Archer makes clear that her family fortune came from good clean stock. With this world view, everyone else embodies deviant forms. Extreme wealth and sexual excess are displaced elsewhere – Mrs. Struthers's saloon in the West, the Tuileries or Count Olenksi's acres of roses, historic pearls and Sobieski emeralds in Europe. Extreme poverty appears only obliquely in a passing simile: the specter of killing time haunted Mrs. Welland "as the spectre of the unemployed haunts the philanthropist" (1190). Here rises up the ghost of what lies beyond the farthest boundaries of the Family's territory: the persistent depressions of the 1870s and the thousands of homeless on the streets of New York. From within the heart of the citadel, Archer, we learn, feels caught between "the bosses and the emigrant" (1115), who, he believes, possess the country. His worries are those of his class, afraid of new forms of money, civic expansion, ethnic and social fluidity. To maintain the "middle way" requires constant vigilance. Afraid of politics, "decent people" (1115), the elite, intent on keeping their place and their privileges, need other means of social control. The discourse of social categories provides it:

the pervasive nineteenth-century rhetoric of "types" that, through indexing faces, features, temperamental and intellectual qualities, identified the "right" people and could eject the socially dubious – or, in this novel, anyone outside the slippery pyramid of leisure-class New York. (Archer is a quick reader. He sees in an instant that Monsieur Rivière is a misfit in a crowd of "American hotel" faces, 1212.)

In a society that sees itself as beleaguered, desire follows cultural conformity. In Edward Westermarck's summary (of 1894), "Men find beauty in the full development of the visible characteristics belonging to the human organism in general; of those peculiar to the sex; of those peculiar to the race"; and, we might also add, of those peculiar to the class.[12] For New York in *The Age of Innocence,* replication seems everything. In domestic space, we frequently hear of characters growing into copies of their parents; May Archer, we are told, dies content, leaving a daughter of whom she is as sure as of her own self. In the larger public scenes, we see heritage made visible. The opera repeats itself season after season; the wedding places Archer in a rite going back to the dawn of history; and even an archery match produces a diamond arrow to be passed on to the eldest daughter.

The spectacle is self-confirming, but it also aims outward.[13] At Archer's wedding, the family row over whether the presents should be "shown" is not childish, as he imagines, but highlights the problem of how to exhibit the class to a wider audience. Mrs. Welland would as soon "turn the reporters loose" (1159) in her house; her fears are picked up in the reference to "the mob of dressmakers and newspaper reporters . . . outside fighting to get near the joints of the canvas" (1160). The family finds "painful" the idea of the "monstrous exposure" of Granny Mingott's person, compounded with the menace that " 'they might take a photograph of her [May] *and put it in the papers!*' " (1160). But though Mrs. Archer claims that the "aristocracy" is a journalistic invention (1054), wealthy society needs the press to represent its exclusivity to the outer world. We hear on the novel's first page that the newspapers have already learned the appropriate discourse. The Assembly at the opera is seen by "an exceptionally brilliant audience" (1017); the "most brilliant wedding of the year" (1164) will presumably attract a glowing paragraph. Mr. van der Luyden can read about his own important guests in the list of ship arrivals in the *Times*. But society does not want to meet cheap copies of itself in every carriage in the street. A photograph of May is for a bridegroom's desk, not for the fashion pages of *Hearth-fires*, next to New England love stories and advertisements for temperance drinks. By the turn of the century, if we remember the van Osbrugh wedding in *The House of Mirth,* the press are already through the canvas and at large in the house, and the leisure class has been reproduced in cinematograph throughout the land. By the 1920s, showing the presents was well established, and etiquette books were warning of more mundane burglaries: "When valuable presents are on view, one or more detectives should be engaged, and if the wedding is a large one the police should be informed, for pocket-picking often takes place on such occasions in the church porch," enjoined Lady Troubridge.[14]

Occasions like this reinforce images of exclusiveness, of a class reproducing itself without contamination. The novel's formal structure underlines the pattern, as scenes reenact themselves in a closed number of variants and the family names reappear in everlasting permutations, filling the text with the paper dolls and stenciled patterns that haunt Newland Archer (and the reader) with sameness (1082). Nevertheless, the rituals allow us the measure of change. At Grace Church, Julius Beaufort sits inside the white ribbon that marks the preserve of the family, and on summer afternoons his lawns host the archery contest and his wealth upgrades the prize. The leisure class is caught in a dilemma of wanting sameness but needing difference. Outsiders may mean disintegration or renewed strength. The accommodations operate in a very narrow realm. If artists will not decorate the salon, they are kept at a distance. Radical groups remain at the edges of the novel, and, Ellen's voice aside, the tone of high comedy in which Mrs. Welland reads out Professor Emerson Sillerton's invitation is used by the text of most of its agents of political or intellectual difference. We never join the Wednesday Afternoon Club, where, presumably, as Julia Ward Howe remembered, ideas, literature, and talk of reform "made it possible to be sensible even at Newport and during the summer"),[15] and we never enter the dissident house of "long-haired men and short-haired women" where the Sillertons once gave "a party for a black man" on the day of a *thé dansant* (1189–90).

But even limited transitions must be carefully managed, to maintain the boundaries against the outside as class identity alters. When it suits the group, society can relabel, forget origins, and assimilate. Despite Mrs. Struthers's beginnings in the dirt of western expansion and industrial manufacture (the "pit," for Mr. Jackson, 1044), society digests her before the end of the novel: "Once people had tasted of Mrs. Struthers' easy Sunday hospitality, they were not likely to sit at home remembering her champagne was transmuted Shoe-Polish" (1222). Good looks, a spell in Europe, the support of a duke, a famous pianist, dull Sunday evenings, and an outbreak of chicken pox smooth the process. (It was thus that New York "managed its transitions," 1222.) In the same way, when the novel opens, it has accepted Julius Beaufort. Deploying all the tactics Thorstein Veblen would itemize in his *Theory of the Leisure Class* (1899), Beaufort has thrown a screen over his shady past, married an impoverished beauty from "one of America's most honoured families" (1030), set her up for display in his brownstone palace ("dressed like an idol, hung with pearls," 1031), designed her smile and her drawing room, and kept all his work behind the scenes, to turn himself into the portrait of a gentleman: "and two years after young Mrs. Beaufort's marriage it was admitted that she had the most distinguished house in New York" (1031). Society preserves its health and its definitions by attributing the inclusion of Beaufort to "miracle" (1031), a sudden and inexplicable transformation in nature. But miracle masks corporate self-interest. The glitter of the Beauforts' ballroom, the "hot canvas-back ducks and vintage wines" (1031) at their dinners, and the careful exhibition of Mrs. Beaufort's perfect profile to the admiring stalls at the opera (1109) all contribute conspicuous evidence of New York's prosperity: "The Beaufort house was one that New Yorkers were proud to show to foreigners" (1032).

Old Mrs. Mingott sums up the process: "we need new blood and new money" (1039). Having heard this near the start of the novel, from a speaker described as "carnivorous," we soon begin to sense, more generally, that a social body with its own collective, even physical, identity is at large in the text. Some of the effect is built up by the rhetoric which speaks of "tribe" and "clan" but more substantially by a myriad of small references to an entity which can recoil with a collective shudder at the unthinkable, draw a breath of relief when it retreats, assume one voice on what "was generally agreed," and assemble in a "silent organisation" (1285) to act on it. Its interests, reactions, and mechanisms of survival go beyond those of any single member of the group but are variously focused for us in vivid individual figures.

Old Catherine's vast body is society's weightiest incarnation and holds its liveliest blood, energized by the Spicer past, life at the Tuileries, the pioneering house, and the goddesses on her ceiling. Change comes from this quarter, as Catherine recognizes more diverse ways of surviving than do most of the clan. This self-preserving dynamic of "Family" has one of its most cautious embodiments in Mr. Welland, whose careful attention to his bronchial tubes and, by extension, to the perfect plumbing of his daughter's married home, is only an extreme manifestation of the economies of self-conservation. Other family Elders consolidate the image of social purity and power successfully preserved. Mr. van der Luyden's patriarchal hand may be "bloodless" but, "weighed down by the Patroon's great signet-ring," it knows its authority (1087). His houses suggest a society kept on ice; his wife is the perfect replica of her aristocratic ancestress and of her own younger self, striking Archer as something "rather gruesomely preserved . . . as bodies caught in glaciers keep for years a rosy life-in-death" (1056). If Mrs. van der Luyden is deep-frozen, Mrs. Manson Mingott is petrified, her body submerged in accreted flesh "like a flood of lava on a doomed city," within which "traces" of her face "survived as if awaiting excavation" (1036). At the center of the family nervous system, mystery protects them: they keep their influence, as Ellen knows, by making themselves so rare.

On a first reading, we may miss the signs of active life in all these images and see New York through Archer's eyes as tame and unsurprising at best, a paralyzing Gorgon at its deadliest. But (as Archer finds out) the social body is a highly alert and powerful working system, with "countless silently observing eyes and patiently listening ears" (1282), alive to what will advantage it and prompt to respond to danger. No experience is private. The family gaze marks Archer's entire narrative. From the first, it sees the signals – the conversation pursued too long, Archer's thrill at the touch of Ellen's fan. The weight of an "admonitory glance" (1067), the look "from the pure eminence of black velvet and the family diamonds" (1068), warn and correct; and delicate asides gain a double edge: "As Mrs. Archer remarked: when the van der Luydens chose, they knew how to give a lesson" (1068). Others take up the task: Mrs. Welland's "reproachful eyebrows" (1069) that pin Archer to a long engagement or, when he seems on the point of flight, the glint of more dangerous weapons – Old Catherine's "round eyes suddenly sharp as penknives" (1255), or Mr. Jackson's "tranquil gaze" hardening into a trap, which "held Archer's face as if in a spring of steel" (1225).

For this highly tuned organism, women are an obvious site of danger. As Elsie Clews Parsons knew, "The more thoroughly a woman is classified the more easily is she controlled."[16] The "Egyptian style" of Mrs. Struthers (1044) or the golden beauty of Fanny Ring (like the intellectual ambition of Elsie Clews) make the signs unreliable and send shudders through the family. (When Mrs. Archer was a girl, "only the people one knew had carriages," 1097.) Anyone outside the usual range of types is hard for those at the center even to see: just as May thinks Monsieur Rivière common, so Ellen knows that in America she is not thought handsome. An extreme case of downward mobility shows us the strength of the system. Medora Manson never stays long in any one social category, and her body seems to have lost its form accordingly. She is "long, lean and loosely put together . . . , clad in raiment intricately looped and fringed, with plaids and stripes and bands of plain colour disposed in a design to which the clue seemed missing" (1140). What is the "clue"? a tinct of the Rushworth imprudence? or of friends and marriages in foreign places? or, as some critics think, of transgressive energy – her introductions of outsiders to New York and her forays into various utopian cults? (When we meet her, she is poised on the edge of plunging into the Valley of Love with the ominously named Dr. Carver.) Though it is tempting to admire Medora under a New Woman label, she has other, contradictory shapes ("Marchioness" and Count Olenski's envoy, for example), as tradition bound as any in the text. To New York she remains unreadable; her narrative takes her farther and farther away from acceptable spaces, as she resettles "each time in a less expensive house" (1062), until she loses her fortune in the Beaufort crash, finishing in Paris with Ellen.

If Medora is the "disastrous exception" (1022), the novel is full of women who have been more consistently formed by New York: among them, Janey as Old Maid, complete with suppressed springs of romance in slackening virgin body, or Mrs. Welland as Dutiful Wife, clad in an "automatic" "armour of cheerfulness" (1190, 1238). The text, like society itself, outlines its categories through the extended binary set of May and Ellen, inserting them in the structural slots they occupy in Archer's desires.

In New York's eyes, May is the "Nice Girl," the Angel and Diana of public statuary.[17] Seen from the male club box, everything about her signals purity – an "innocence" which licenses her appeal and guarantees the survival of the family. As Mrs. van der Luyden reminds Archer, at their dinner May is thought the handsomest girl in the room (1068). Archer recognizes marriage as an "association of material and social interests" (1050), and family councils legitimate his own: "There was no better match in New York than May Welland" (1044). The contract is hedged round with sanctions, " 'Twelve dozen of everything – hand-embroidered' " (1069), to ensure that "Form" prevails. Safely married, May exults that no horrors "ever *can* happen now" (1163). To her new husband, she looks like "a type rather than a person," a model for "a Civic Virtue or a Greek goddess," with "preserving fluid" for blood (1164). Family blood and property are safe for another generation: May is not a foolish Rushworth, an insane Albany Chivers, a widow, one of Archer's "clever people" (1112), a "foreigner" of doubtful origins, or an unnamed hazard from the "Siren Isle" (1044).

"Innocence" is a powerful force in the narrative. Enacting "blameless domesticity" (1044) and social stability, May writes Archer back into class and family. Her telegrams to and talks with Ellen close down the novel's two main sections, blocking Archer's attempted flights outward. (Even the Miss du Lacs' leaky water tank conspires to ensure that the correct couple honeymoons in the Patroon's house.) May can detect a household menace in Ellen and utter her challenge in an exchange about a smoking lamp: " 'They smell less if one blows them out,' she explained, with her bright housekeeping air" (1228). After this, her timely pregnancy almost seems self-generated, an affirmation of the community's claims as well as her own.

Seen through Archer's eyes, innocence is altogether simpler. Once again, although he believes himself detached from his cultural preferences, he embodies them in basic forms. At the opera, his version is comically disposed of in Madame Nilsson's caricature of the blonde ingenue in the garden of love, but his "thrill of possessorship" makes it plain that at this point Archer wholly approves of May's blushing ignorance, as he dreams of a honeymoon initiation via the "masterpieces of literature which it would be his manly privilege to reveal to his bride" (1020). As he begins to question these gendered patterns of power and passivity, the text produces what many readers find its most disturbing reflections: May is an "image made of snow," designed to flatter the "lordly pleasure" of the husband who smashes it (1051); a horribly adapted Kentucky cave fish (1081); a curtain dropped before an emptiness (1182). Archer decodes male gratification (at least to a degree) but never escapes it. Few critics, certainly, rush to congratulate him on his feminism. His similes (the flip side of his opera-box fantasies?) hardly go farther than dissatisfaction with the sexual temperature of a New York marriage. Before the honeymoon has ended, he has reverted to "all his old inherited ideas about marriage" (1170) and, though May is excited by seeing Parisian *cocottes* in the *cafés chantants,* he censors the words of the songs.

Archer locks May in the virginal script he criticizes. So do some readers; for at least one critic, May "fades out" in the latter part of the novel. For others, she has her own story as an unappreciated victim (of husband, patriarchy, or convention), or as the lovers' malign and implacable enemy.[18] If her blushes are a "red flag," signaling the knowledge for which a lady is permitted no language, then May speaks volumes: "Good gracious, look at her blushing again all over her blushes" (1184). The blushes, like the blue dazzle in May's eyes, witness to the interior self, the imagination, blood, and feeling that Archer prefers to overlook. Before their marriage, he credits her with a single "effort of speaking" (1134) but otherwise construes her only in the rhetoric approved by his society. He makes her eyes transparent, blind, and bandaged, and stops trying to read meaning in her silences. She remains a vacuum and a blank for him, the white page of convention, asexual, infantile, boyish, solid, cold, and suffocatingly present. (" 'The room is stifling: I want a little air,' " 1250).

Ellen, in contrast, seems cast as the Woman of Experience, presented in typical postures from melodrama.[19] In Archer's scheme, set against May's emptiness, Ellen represents unattainable plenitude. From the start, he fills her with "suggestion" (1021) – of enigma, passion, womanliness, Europe, mysterious joys, appalling suffering, conversations, art, music, literature, expressed in the exoticism of her room, the authority in her beauty, and the expression in her eyes. He imagines her as a shrine and a relic, a traveler in Samarkand and a vision in Rossetti, and sees her in terms of images of candle beams, butterflies, flickering fires, summer lightning, pre-Raphaelite haziness, the effulgence of Titian, and the golden light of Paris, "too dense and yet too stimulating for his lungs" (1300).

With yellow roses heading Ellen's column, as lilies of the valley do May's, the lists could lengthen indefinitely. Archer's terms are conventional ones: though he romanticizes Ellen and society fears her, she remains the unsettling Other. New York, like Archer, is clear about May but cannot decide about Ellen: born a Mingott, she has been fashioned in other circumstances that make her radically unstable. Fleeing her husband, she leaves a trail in different places and companies – Lausanne, West Twenty-third Street, "diplomatic society" (1185), the female house of the Blenkers. Entering the Mingott box in the first chapter, she is introduced in a paragraph framed by astonished exclamations from the arbiters of "form" and "family," while the men wait in "visible suspense" (1023) for a judgment. Like Mrs. Archer, society prefers young women to be "simple" (1136). Ellen has only to walk alone across a drawing room to offend its definitions. A lady should be an "idol," all surface, inert, an ornament meant to rest the gentlemen's eyes after their talk. Ellen's "animated" talk and relaxed posture are alarming signs of self-will and vitality (1065), and, faced with her documents, the lawyer, Mr. Letterblair looks "like the Family Physician annoyed with a patient whose symptoms refuse to be classified" (1089). If the symptoms are what he suspects, "unpleasantness" threatens the health of the family. Accordingly, much of the narrative is spent in trying to put Ellen in her place, whether by reabsorbing her into the clan, finding her a little house, sending her back to her husband, brooding endlessly about her intentions, or consecrating her in a small dim chapel in the memory.

Readers find Ellen even less simple than New York does. She is an endlessly variable text, impossible to read with any certainty. Though she has experienced other forms of existence, the novel leaves them mysterious. Her husband's letter is a "grimacing . . . spectre" that we are never allowed to see (1102); her secrets remain in a locked drawer at Mr. Letterblair's. Her European life (with Count Olenski or with Monsieur Rivière) is, in both

New York and the narrative, literally unspeakable. Though readers can try to shape it out of the gaps of her story, to represent it would need a different kind of novel altogether: a turn-of-the-century feminist one, for example, or a genre outside of realism. Ellen's past, after all, lies in the fantastic realm of *Dracula:* "a kind of sulphurous apotheosis" of marriage to a "white sneering" count with "many square miles of shooting in Transylvania" (1063, 1027).

Unreadability is part of the standard construction of the enigmatic woman, but beyond this stereotypical vision we may be seeing a more interesting figure, who writes her scripts herself. Ellen knows how to manipulate signs or to confound them. She is astute about men's use of women as badges of respectability: she saves her aunt from being exploited by Dr. Carver, refuses to lend herself to head her husband's table, and, when Regina Beaufort has no more value than an out-of-date banknote, restores her credit by driving the Mingott carriage to her door. As a girl, she looked like a gypsy child, in crimson; as a debutante, she wore black. Her room is an oriental mystery, and the litany of her fabrics and her furs (which begins to look to the 1990s like a list of endangered species, including green monkey, sealskin, eagle feathers in her fan, a heron wing in her cap) codes the erotic for everyone who sees her. (Ellen is as "romantic"-seeming for Miss Blenker, Medora, and Janey as she is for Archer.) Presenting herself as the image of sexuality (in a "sheath-like" robe of "red velvet bordered about the chin and down the front with glossy black fur" (1099), she seems unequivocally the type of the sensual. In a draft, she even advocates what is in effect a trial marriage, but she leaves Archer because she has "eaten of the Pomegranate seed and can never live without it."[20] But if we can find *Ur*-images of sexuality in the manuscripts, the text as published never confirms them. Behind Ellen's veils and screens might equally be self-containment and chasteness, just as unthinkable to the family. The clan holds that a woman can be defined only in relation to men; even Medora preaches the ideology of marriage as sacrifice, and old Catherine believes a married countess better than a single Mingott: whatever the source of Ellen's energies, unclassifiable or "'classed' . . . irretrievably" (1124), she remains an embarrassment.

If unregulated women trouble New York, so does unregulated capital. Perhaps because the novel makes its points so succinctly, some readers have felt that *The Age of Innocence* is less interested in the dynamics of money than is some of Wharton's earlier fiction. But from start to finish, the text has money on its mind: its sources, legitimacy, and limits. Whereas it distributes different aspects of femininity between a set of different characters, it largely concentrates finance into one: that of Julius Beaufort. Like Ellen, he is a perpetual riddle in the narrative: any answers only produce the same question: "Who was Beaufort?" (1030). We meet him as a New Yorker by custom, but at every appearance in the text he sets up currents of disquiet. Like Simon Rosedale in *The House of Mirth,* he is an outsider, possibly Jewish (he "passed for an Englishman" [1030],[21] whose rumored excesses set whispers murmuring "not only in Fifth Avenue but in Wall Street" (1181). Whether in monetary or sexual versions, Beaufort is viewed in terms of spending, with all its suggestion of fluidity, bleeding, giving out too much, being used up: "Some people said he had speculated unfortunately in railways, others that he was being bled by one of the most insatiable members of her profession; and to every report of threatened insolvency Beaufort replied by a fresh extravagance" (1181).

Lavish outgoings, speculation, risky investments, tainted capital, all run counter to the image of the self as constituted in leisure-class New York. Good form restrains other men. (Lefferts's mistresses do not drive bright-yellow carriages at the fashionable hour.) Cautious, conservative, resistant to indiscreet expenditure, New York reigns in passions and capital; the self remains solvent, its moral and its business consciences sound, and its identity clear. While Beaufort simulates integrity, he is acceptable. Once he overreaches, his smash threatens the whole of New York: " 'Everybody we know will be hit one way or another'" (1230). As both sexual and financial disasters rise to a crisis, shock waves pass through society. Mr. Letterblair, the family's legal conscience, is left "white and incapacitated" (1230), and in the body blow to "Family," Mrs. Mingott suffers a stroke. Less "mysterious" (1231, 1236) to readers than to her relations, Beaufort's fall registers the worst that can happen – an intolerable rupture at the center of New York that lays it open shamefully to the world: "That afternoon the announcement of the Beaufort failure was in all the papers. . . . The whole of New York was darkened by the tale of Beaufort's dishonour" (1236).

This is the place to return to Archer. A novel's central character, as Wharton suggested in *The Writing of Fiction,* often seems the emptiest. Archer is no exception. The other figures represent social power, in concentrated and vivid forms. Archer, for most of the novel, is a subject in the process of disintegration: "Absent – that was what he was: so absent from everything most densely real and near to those about him that it sometimes startled him to find they still imagined he was there" (1224). Given his formation in the society we have been looking at, it is hardly surprising that the two figures who most disturb him are the two who most trouble his class. Both Ellen Olenska and Julius Beaufort set up vibrations that threaten his very structure. At Ellen's name, his heart stops; he wonders "if, whenever he heard those two syllables, all his carefully built-up world would tumble about him like a house of cards" (1165); in Beaufort's presence, he feels "an odd sense of disembodiment" (1123) and angry perplexity. In this state, Archer fights to maintain his ground and, contradictorily, to escape from the words and role that trap him.

But if social role seems constriction, declassification is loss of being. At his wedding, as he waits at the chancel step in the part of the eager bridegroom, signs come adrift from their meanings:

> The music, the scent of lilies on the altar, the vision of the cloud of tulle and orange-blossoms floating nearer and nearer, the sight of Mrs. Archer's face suddenly convulsed with happy sobs, the low benedictory murmur of the Rector's voice, the ordered evolutions of the eight pink bridesmaids and the eight black ushers: all these sights, sounds and sensations, so familiar in them-selves, so unutterably strange and meaningless in his new relation to them, were confusedly mingled in his brain.   (1162)

The structure of the paragraph is familiar: the catalogue of effects, followed by its location in Archer's consciousness; but this time, the scene consists of disconnected sense data, with no unifying narratorial exposition, and when we join Archer it is to find the known defamiliarized. It is as if, at the moment of his public commitment to the body of New York, he reverses the entrance into the symbolic order and comes apart again. Critics have enjoyed Wharton's slip in the first printing which opened the wedding with the words of the burial service.[22] (Archer, too, might have learned from his anthropology that "the bridegroom's soul is apt to fly away at the wed-ding.")[23] But the funereal hints go farther than simply placing a tombstone on marriage to May; instead they seem to take Archer altogether out of the social world. Details, even of ordinary language (Archer's heart "stopped beating," the sight of the "apparition," the "fantastic figure" of Medora Manson, 1161), take on more spectral resonance. Archer wonders whether he is hallucinating. Possibly he is – but the text itself seems, too, to be flickering with glimpses of a different kind of discourse, as social surfaces become "unutterably strange." It is in passages like this, when Archer seems to be pushing toward a different kind of self (one, impossibly, beyond the social), that the mimetic mode of realism, where detail metonymically holds in it the larger scene, seems to feel beneath it other pressures, as the novel of manners shifts into the fantastic. In the terrain of fantasy, Allon White argues, "Corporal disintegration is the reverse of the constitution of the body during the mirror phase and it occurs only at those times when the unified and transcendent ego is threatened with dissolution."[24]

We do not have to be familiar with French psychoanalytic theory to see this process at work in *The Age of Innocence*. In Archer's world, identity is formed within social consciousness, and when Archer is confronted with a challenge to his categories he begins to come apart, losing his sense of himself, his language, position, bodily space. Some readers would agree with Archer that to be locked in the family is to be buried alive, but the text also suggests, conversely, that *loss* of social being is a form of death. In *A Son at the Front,* the war novel Edith Wharton laid aside to write *The Age of Innocence,* her painter, Campton, cannot see when the frame goes from round his world; Archer, too, does not know how to look at things. When Ellen asks if he takes the family view, he can only wander across the room and stare with "void eyes" (1104); he loses his voice in the family – "they never quote you when they talk about its being her duty to go home" (1255) – and his most ordinary words sound like "a strange language" (1198). Imagery of graveyards, tombs, and vaults surrounds him, as his body dies, cut off from the circulation of the collective. Dropped from any source of meaning, he is open to possession: "demons" and "inner devils" move in to haunt him (1288).

The text calibrates this in violent figures of racking bodily disturbance which run against the composed detail through which the social world is narrated. It notes Archer's loss of control as he blushes, laughs hysterically, winces, slams down his fist, leaps from his chair, flings open a window, frightens people with his gaze. Inside his head, the confusion he feels at the altar is a symptom repeated time and again, as Archer's brain whirls and the blood beats in his temples. (Mrs. Mingott's stroke hovers in the text in these moments, long before it channels itself through her.) Displacing Archer from the New York drawing room, the text produces hints of different spaces altogether. Emptied of its certainties, Archer's mind becomes an "empty and echoing place" (1181), an interior where doors slam (1180) – or an even wilder landscape, where blood rushes to the temples "as if he had been caught by a bent-back branch in a thicket" (1214), or he pitches from a precipice (1153), or an evening sweeps by, "running and running like a senseless river that did not know how to stop" (1286). Here, Archer loses his foothold entirely: he feels as if he had "slipped through the meshes of time and space" (1197) or "as if he floated somewhere between chandelier and ceiling" (1282). This topography of the unreal exists for readers only through the narration, but Archer begins to act as if it could become material, in fantasies of flight ("His own fancy inclined to Japan" [1258], of "plunging" (a favorite term) out of the here and now, or of reversing time and returning to childhood.

Many of the episodes readers find most resonant are ones which concentrate these motifs, where the landscape is at once internal and external (or as Wharton expressed it rather more poetically, "an event in the history of a soul").[25] There is space here for only one example: the encounter between Archer and Ellen in the Patroon's house. The episode is a wonderful instance of the fusion in the text of smooth surface and deep disarray, and of a space which is both public and private, enacting at the same time a fantasy and a critique of individual freedom. (Monsieur Rivière may speak of "quant à soi," but it remains a myth.) The house itself occupies multiple levels of space – psychological, social, and historical – and (with Ellen in a red cloak, looking like "the Ellen Mingott of old days," 1119) becomes a fairy-tale gingerbread cottage for two lost children: a fantasy of privacy and escape. This is the original Dutch governor's cottage and, as Chandler emphasizes, represents the guarantee of leisure-class power itself – in its original stamp, built in 1612 – virtually on the edge of historical time in the colonial settlement of the United States.[26] Much of its fascination is this suggestion that Archer and Ellen can go back, escape from their history and begin again. (The famous last paragraph of *The Great Gatsby* reaches out to that same historical moment, the sighting of the unspoiled continent.) Wharton duplicates the desire in the biographies of the characters – to Archer, Ellen looks as she did when they were children – and beyond this lies the dream of escape from any social category at all. Impossible though we know this is, here, for a moment, where the house looks "as if magically created" for them, there is the illusion that the "miracle" will happen (1122): that they will meet in a fairy-tale world transcending time and history.

But, as we have seen, because society has taught the individual how and what to feel, once Archer loses touch with his social role he has lost himself. Here the text presents him as completely paralyzed. He desires intensely but cannot act: he moves away from the hearth to look out at the snow. It is an attempt to bring life back to rule; "black tree-boles against the snow" (1122) have style and form and suggest prison bars, as Newland tries to close up his awkward senses. The inner pressure blurs the distinction between outer and inner worlds. Archer's perception is radically disarranged: first he sees Ellen and the fire, as he will see her lifelong, imposed on everything, like an image imprinted on a white sheet. And then, in the same mode, just as he feels he is about to break all the rules, he sees the banker Beaufort. As Chandler reminds us, this ironic arrival keeps the mythic world entangled with the commercial one of Beaufort's version of the "perfect little house" (1123).[27]

But social comedy also veers at the same instant into darker fantasy. We know that Beaufort is the strongest image for Archer of lust and impropriety but also a figure fascinating for its difference. From unknown origins, Beaufort offers the possibility of multiple, alternative selves, created through money, women, languages, foreign places, and new careers. He even speaks Ellen's dialect, inaccessible to Archer. As Archer suggests, Ellen likes Beaufort "because he's so unlike us" (1207). The narrative precipitates him at pressured moments, as his "unexpected figure" (1039) shadows Archer's encounters with Ellen. Even a thought of Ellen can produce him: Archer "saw the lady of whom he was thinking seated in a box with the Beauforts" (1108). In the Patroon's house, in the context of stirred emotion and disturbed vision, Beaufort seems to arise from Archer himself, a strange externalization of his guilt, projected onto the snow in the shape of his dark rival.

The moment stays with Archer, powerful and haunting: "he could never hear the name without the sharp vision of Beaufort's heavy figure, opulently furred and shod, advancing through the snow at Skuytercliff" (1223). In Wharton's ghost stories and elsewhere, she was interested in the double, the Other who is the dark side of the self.[28] In "Afterward," the ghost is specifically an economic and moral one, who rises up to haunt the man whose wealth is founded on his labor. Instead of a book entitled *The Economic Basis of Culture,* the rich man meets his material unconscious in the shape of a gray figure, face shaded by a hat. This is how the text consistently represents Beaufort: muffled, faceless or threatening, "darkly projected against a blaze of light" (1096). One answer, then, to the persistent question of who Beaufort "really" is might be that he is a version of Archer – a self who enacts all that Archer cannot.

Contesting the same slot, socially and psychologically, Archer feels "invisibility . . . non-existence" (1123) in the banker's presence. He winces when Ellen joins their names, but the coupling happens again and again, as meeting by meeting, bouquet by bouquet, the men pursue Ellen side by side. Thoughts of Beaufort provoke some of Archer's most profound moments of disturbance; "insinuations about Beaufort made him reckless" (1226). All of his questions to Ellen deny the identity but confirm it also, coming to a head when he asks directly whether Beaufort is to replace him. His conscious ambition is to make Ellen see Beaufort as he "really was, with all he represented – and abhor it" (1077); his darker one, to become him. It is impossible for Archer to take Ellen without taking on the role of Beaufort. (At dinner, the talk about Beaufort's extinction warns him of his own.)

The deeply held assumptions about the behavior of a gentleman, the morality that is felt in the blood, mean that Wharton cannot write Archer an ending with Ellen. When she experimented with offering her lovers some life together, she could not complete the story. In the published text, Archer cannot think beyond the limits of his society: conversation with Ellen leaves him "dumb" and "dazed" with "frozen tears" (1245–7). (A gentleman, even when facing the unthinkable, he lowers his voice, so that his wife's coachman will not hear.) Nor can he become the figure of Beaufort. To ensure a future, the figures who threaten structural collapse, to self and to society, must be expelled from New York and from the narrative. To write otherwise would be to pronounce an end to the values of a class. An un-categorized woman (not married, divorced, single, or mistress) has no place in the culture: Ellen is sent to Paris. Beaufort's excesses must be rebuked while society heals itself. New York redescribes Mrs. Mingott's stroke as an attack of indigestion and wipes out the scandal. Beaufort is "heard of in Constantinople, then in Russia; and a dozen years later . . . in Buenos Ayres" (1295). Neither exile is seen again directly in the final chapter. Within this closed space, the options for the self are firmly controlled: in banishing desire and excess, it resists fragmentation and so never tests the possibilities for different forms of being: Archer is reintegrated into a stable, if frozen, identity. Holding to known forms, the text, too, lets go of other modes of representation and comes home to the bounds of realism. Another kind of novel (fantastic, modernist, or contemporary feminist) might see fragments as a liberation from traditional forms, from constructs of class, gender, and "character."[29] Here, social, psychological and narrative order cohere.

If the novel ended with May's announcement, we would be left seeing the leisure class as an effective self-regulating system. In a nineteenth-century novel, a coda in the present tense might confirm the choices and suggest that now, at last, all was in place. Instead, *The Age of Innocence* throws every-thing into the air. First, there is the surprise of the final chapter, which sweeps the 1870s into the distant past and seems to overturn all its values. The immediate impact is of dramatic social transformation, of emotions released, in exuberant images of mobility, in behavior, appearance, phy-sique, and relationships. With telephones and Atlantic crossings, the bound-aries seem to be gone. The modern generation has swept away "the sign-posts" and "the danger signal" (1300), to create a world where "all the social atoms spun around on the same plane" (1296). But then there comes a secondary jolt, when we realize that, from the reader's position with the gulf of World War I between, even this vision of the contemporary is itself now an irretrievable past. (The war, Wharton's letters tell us, insists on a historical imagination: neither novelist nor reader can simply ignore the fact that the novel is set in the prewar years.) Perhaps, then, within the narrative, the continuities matter more than the changes? How much change, indeed, is there? Does the last chapter project the demise of the leisure class or its survival? Where, if at all, are the gains – and the losses?

The complex crosslights make any of these questions difficult, even impossible, to answer. The narrative performs a careful balancing act – "After all, there was good in the old ways. . . . There was good in the new order too" (1291–2) – and it takes this farther in a sequence of figures who, among them, embody what previously would have seemed impossible reconciliations. Though by their very existence they seem to turn Archer's old New York into the ruins of Troy, equally they might be seen as successful adaptations of that world, replete with the new blood and new money Mrs. Mingott recommended, maintaining its cultural heritage in the face of the twentieth century.

The text does not directly restore those it has expelled, but to a certain extent it legitimates their energies. Where their counterparts in a nineteenth-century novel might have been decisively extinguished, Beaufort and Ellen live on in new social spaces and maintain their influence. Though kept at a distance (he is dead by the end of the novel), Beaufort, we hear, is allowed both another fortune and another marriage (this time producing a child), and Ellen's life in Paris, as recent feminist criticism suggests, points toward new roles for women, even if it is not the novel's task to take them up. In her apartment, empowered by an allowance from Mrs. Mingott, living separately from her husband, she is not a gothic heroine imprisoned in a tower, Isabel Archer in a dark house, or another nineteenth-century rebel, doomed and dead.[30] (She is more like Ida Lewis, the heroic lighthouse keeper we heard of living in her Lime Rock tower [1185] or, as critics remark, Edith Wharton herself, a wealthy, independent expatriate in Paris.) Archer preserves Ellen as a picture in his head, but the text allows the reader to imagine more dynamic possibilities.

But this final chapter gives more space to characters new to the text. Just as *The House of Mirth* produced Netty Struther, who offers a solution (at least in fantasy) to many of the contradictions of the rest of the novel, so *The Age of Innocence* generates answers in figures who carry, in nonexplosive versions, forms of energy blocked in the main narrative.

The most commented on is, inevitably, Fanny Beaufort, who emerges to confound Lefferts's ironic prophecies by supplying one of "Beaufort's bastards" (1284) to be married to Archer's first-born son. In Fanny's multiple parentage (she has been raised by an unlikely team of Beaufort, Fanny Ring,

Ellen Olenska, and Mrs. Jack Welland), the narrative brings back its exiles and incorporates them into the social structure. In an "almost cousinly relationship" with Archer's children (1295), Fanny provides a "foreign" marriage from within the safety of the endogamous group; happy to look like an Isabey miniature in emeralds and pearls but at home with Debussy and with Paris theaters, she safely combines the modern with the ancestral, and it is into her hands that the family heritage is placed when Janey makes her bridal gift of Mrs. Archer's jewels.

Will the jewels be safe with Fanny? Though Archer registers a trace of doubt – "Fanny Beaufort, whatever one might think of her" (1293) – the reader would imagine so. In presenting a society that thrives on the vigorous "bastard" blood, *The Age of Innocence* is not showing us social overthrow, or even much readjustment. Mary Archer may be more tolerant than her mother and interested in philanthropy, but she grows up to a Grace Church wedding, not, say, to work in a settlement house. Edith Wharton was not Upton Sinclair: responding to his novel *Oil,* she agreed that corrupt capitalists would make anyone desire "some radical change in the organization of society," but she loathed his socialist solutions and his overtly political writing (*Letters,* 501). Her narrative, in contrast, preserves an image of "civilized living," supported on money and tradition, while regulating its unacceptable versions.

In negotiating this delicate middle way, both art and politics come back into service, cleansed of "unpleasant" (or subversive) associations. Dallas Archer inherits his "vague leanings towards 'art'" (1290) from his father but translates them into a profession. Where Archer's taste led him merely to the right desk and the right engagement ring, Dallas's is potentially more far-reaching; architects have tremendous power to reshape or reproduce social forms. Dallas remains in exclusive regions, but his work, nevertheless, registers change: in the first description of his current project, we learn that he is directly creating spaces in which the newly rich can operate. The "millionaire grocers of the suburbs" insist on "Colonial" houses (1290); Dallas's clients will be housed with better taste. Dallas can be sent to Europe to look at Italian gardens, perhaps with Wharton's recently published *Italian Villas and Their Gardens* in his pocket, and can be relied upon to house a young millionaire in a lakeside palace that matches Mr. van der Luyden's: "People had always been told that the house at Skuytercliff was an Italian villa" (1118). But if class boundaries can be stretched to Chicago, what is left? Dallas belongs "body and soul to the new generation" (1298); he has no more nuance than Beaufort and a breezy lack of regard for psychological interiors. Does he represent the end of his class, the erasure of all its values? or is he a fresh beginning – working within its sphere, with a cultural memory of how things used to be?

Whatever Dallas is, his social function is to channel new energies into older forms. As Beaufort remained safe while contained within the norms of New York, so his successors need controlling through older principles. Cultural practice does this one way, but the 1900s needed more immediate forms of supervision. In the 1870s, Archer's anxieties about the boss, the emigrant, and the financier never take shape in action. He remains the gentleman, vapid and inert, shrugging off Winsett's advice to "roll up your sleeves and get right down into the muck" (1115). (In a house with perfect plumbing, one never has to.) In the 1900s, the novel (like this essay, in its final pages), at last produces its hidden hero, and its most important dinner guest, who bangs a clenched fist on the table, gnashes his eyeglasses, and attempts to stir the leisure class into action.

There can be few readers who would predict Theodore Roosevelt as Archer's compensation for Ellen Olenska. If she becomes "the composite vision of all that he had missed" (1291), Roosevelt emerges as his reward for staying in place. On the level of character, we might suspect that Archer would have preferred, like Monsieur Rivière, to have known Maupassant, but in terms of the direction of the narrative, Roosevelt is far more interesting. Most obviously, he retrieves the image of the gentleman; here, in his most character-building form, is the manly, active opposite of Archer's wavering emptiness, bringing into the text exemplary patrician origins, best-selling books, scholarliness, literary enthusiasm, physical prowess, and legendary charisma – as a hero, even a last-minute one, he has perfect credentials. Indeed, his face would even pass into the ethnic pattern books as the ideal of the American type: "Active, progressive, industrious, full of business and thought" (1910).[31] And as president (and patriarch), he would maintain the advocacy of the upper-class family, worrying about "Race Suicide" and urging the leisured elite to breed.

Through this muscular paragon, the novel offers a different model of a social agent, reinstating a vigorous public voice turned on more disorderly enemies than a single woman. We hear it directly in the text, making its appeal for an effort of herculean housekeeping: "You're the kind of man the country wants, Archer. If the stable's ever to be cleaned out, men like you have got to take a hand in the cleaning" (1290). Within the general glow of knowing the president, Archer's memory frames a moment in 1899 or 1900, during Roosevelt's brief career as governor of New York. Although the timing may have been dictated by verisimilitude (a base in Albany makes dinner invitations more convenient than one in the White House), the speech is impeccably placed to recall the novel's broader concerns. Roosevelt not only echoes Ned Winsett but sets the example: as governor, he took on the bosses and set about regulating the evils of capital. As president, he repeatedly spoke in the terms of Archer's New York, deploring excessive growth and blatant irregularity but alive to the benefits of new commercial wealth. Though he is wrong about Archer's efficacy in the state Assembly, he guides him into a new identity as "a good citizen" (1291) (a rhetoric which was beginning to expand the concept of "Family") and a writer for a reforming weekly. Later, Roosevelt might well have found one of his new men in Dallas: it was an architect, Herbert Croly, whose book *The Promise of American Life* (1909) provided a philosophical base for Roosevelt's own reforming program.[32]

In his immediate incarnation in the narrative, Roosevelt is a deus ex machina, produced to save gentility in peril; in hindsight, he looks more like the last specimen of his kind. He was, we know, Edith Wharton's own model of a statesman, a close friend and also a family member through marriage to one of her network of cousins. After his death in January 1919, she drew on anthropology to write a commemorative poem, in which, as her biographer tells us, using a legend from *The Golden Bough,* she ferried him to meet friends in the land of the dead.[33] For Wharton, this hero certainly left traces in the blood; she reported, in an image alarming to the 1990s, that each of her encounters with him "glows in me like a tiny morsel of radium."[34]

The Age of Innocence was composed and first read in the aftermath of Roosevelt's death and in the immediate wake of World War I. We frame the ending remembering the multiple losses that occurred in the gap between the end of the novel and the moment of reading: not only the loss of Roosevelt but the destruction of the prewar world and all that Wharton valued in it. Even Dallas bears a strong resemblance to the cheerful young men killed in the war whom Wharton, at the same time, was painfully memorializing in *A Son at the Front.* This knowledge makes the rest of the novel, in turn, radically unstable. In *A Son at the Front,* Wharton worried about the heritage for art. (Her "son" has two fathers, a banker and a painter.) To look back to the past is a highly ambiguous act: reviewing sketches he had made of his son, the painter feels that he is digging up the dead. A memorial may merely recycle old forms, or it may produce new ones. In these years, Wharton wondered whether she could go on writing:

"the world I had grown up and been formed by had been destroyed in 1914, and I felt myself incapable of transmuting the raw material of the after-war world into a work of art."[35]

If a subject has been fabricated through one kind of discourse, when society changes that subject is disembodied, loses its voice. Interested in staging *The Age of Innocence*, Wharton seems concerned with settling interpretation, re-creating a solid image of the past. But in narration, the novel resists stability, pursuing old traces, fragments of a dead world, reassembling them even while they vanish like the "visions of the night" (1126). For its hero, to know at last that he had been read aright releases him, taking "an iron band from his heart" (1299), retroactively making his life coherent. The novel remains more difficult: a moral tract, rewarded by the Pulitzer trustees; a memorial to Realism and to an extinct social order; a piece of covert modernism, radically taking apart old forms; "the spoils of the ages" (1289), waiting for the opening night of a multi-million-dollar movie at the end of the century. All these (and more) cross and recross a reading: "Is New York such a labyrinth?" Ellen wonders. "I thought it so straight up and down –" (1076).

NOTES

1 *The Age of Innocence* in *Edith Wharton: Novels,* ed. R. W. B. Lewis, Library of America Edition (Cambridge: Cambridge University Press, 1985), 1076. All references are to this edition and are given in the text.

2 Edith Wharton to Mary Cadwalader Jones, February 17, 1921, *The Letters of Edith Wharton,* ed. R. W. B. Lewis and Nancy Lewis (London: Simon & Schuster, 1988), 439. Hereafter cited in the text.

3 Edith Wharton, *The Writing of Fiction* (1925; New York: Octagon, 1966), 7.

4 Ian Burkitt, *Social Selves: Theories of the Social Formation of Personality* (London: Sage, 1971), 29.

5 Ludmilla Jordanova, *Sexual Visions: Images of Gender in Science and Medicine between the Eighteenth and Twentieth Centuries* (Hemel Hempstead, U.K.: Harvester, 1989), 67.

6 Elizabeth Fee, "The Sexual Politics of Victorian Social Anthropology," in *Clio's Consciousness Raised: New Perspectives on the History of Women,* ed. Mary S. Hartman and Lois Banner (New York: Octagon, 1976), 86–102.

7 John F. McLennan, *Primitive Marriage: An Inquiry into the Origin of the Form of Capture in Marriage Ceremonies,* ed. Peter Rivière (1865; Chicago: University of Chicago Press, 1970), 91.

8 Edith Wharton, *A Backward Glance* (New York: Appleton-Century, 1934), 55.

9 Elsie Clews Parsons, *The Family: An Ethnographical and Historical Outline with Descriptive Notes, Planned as a Text-book for the Use of College Lecturers and of Directors of Home-Reading Clubs* (New York: Putnam, 1906), 7–8. Whar-

ton's anthropology may also be discussed in more modern terms. See, for instance, Mary Ellis Gibson, "Edith Wharton and the Ethnography of Old New York," *Studies in American Fiction* 13.1 (1985), 65–8, and Judith Fryer, *Felicitous Space: The Imaginative Structures of Edith Wharton and Willa Cather* (Chapel Hill: University of North Carolina Press, 1986), 116–42.

10 Cited by Margaret Visser, *The Rituals of Dinner: The Origins, Evolution, Eccentricities, and Meaning of Table Manners* (New York: Grove Weidenfeld, 1991), 76.

11 For more on Mr. Jackson's taste buds, in the context of manners, money, and types, see Richard Godden, *Fictions of Capital: The American Novel from James to Mailer* (Cambridge: Cambridge University Press, 1990). 12–16.

12 Edward Westermarck, *The History of Human Marriage*, 2nd ed. (London: Macmillan, 1894), 264–5. This monumental work was much reprinted.

13 For general arguments on these lines, see Amy Kaplan, *The Social Construction of American Realism* (Chicago: University of Chicago Press, 1988), and Godden, *Fictions of Capital*.

14 Lady Troubridge, *The Book of Etiquette*, vol. 1 (U.K.: Associated Bookbuyers, 1926), 46. Archer's wedding followed "English" models.

15 Julia Ward Howe, *Reminiscences, 1819–1899* (1899; New York: Greenwood, 1969), 406.

16 Elsie Clews Parsons, *Social Rule: A Study of the Will to Power* (New York: Putnam, 1916), 55.

17 Martha Banta's formulation, placing May and Ellen in a brilliant and encyclopedic survey of American types: *Imaging American Women: Ideas and Ideals in Cultural History* (New York: Columbia University Press, 1987), 448–9.

18 For examples of "strong" readings of May, see Susan Goodman, *Edith Wharton's Women: Friends and Rivals* (Hanover, N.H.: University Press of New England, 1990), 96–104, and Mary Suzanne Schriber, "Convention in the Fiction of Edith Wharton," *Studies in American Fiction* 11.2 (1983), 195–7.

19 Banta, *Imaging American Women*, 448–9.

20 Candace Waid, *Edith Wharton's Letters from the Underworld: Fictions of Women and Writing* (Chapel Hill: University of North Carolina Press, 1991), 12.

21 Marilyn R. Chandler's suggestion in *Dwelling in the Text: Houses in American Fiction* (Berkeley and Los Angeles: University of California Press, 1991), 159.

22 R. W. B. Lewis, *Edith Wharton: A Biography* (London: Constable, 1975), 430.

23 Elsie Clews Parsons, *The Old-fashioned Woman: Primitive Fancies about the Sex* (New York: Putnam, 1913), 263. Parsons is reviewing the extensive discourse of "The Jeopardized Male."

24 Allon H. White, "L'éclatement du sujet: The theoretical work of Julia Kristeva," cited in Rosemary Jackson, *Fantasy: The Literature of Subversion* (London: Methuen, 1981), 90.

25 Wharton, *Writing of Fiction*, 84.

26 Chandler, *Dwelling in the Text*, 171.

27 Ibid., 172.

28 See Kathy A. Fedorko, "Edith Wharton's Haunted Fiction: 'The Lady's Maid's

Bell' and *The House of Mirth*," in *Haunting the House of Fiction: Feminist Perspectives on Ghost Stories by American Women,* ed. Lynette Carpenter and Wendy K. Kolmar (Knoxville: University of Tennessee Press, 1991), 80–107.

29 See Jackson, *Fantasy,* 61–91.

30 See, for example, readings by Katherine Joslin, *Edith Wharton* (Basingstoke, U.K.: Macmillan, 1991), 89–107; Sandra M. Gilbert and Susan Gubar, *No Man's Land: The Place of the Woman Writer in the Twentieth Century,* vol. 2: *Sexchanges* (New Haven: Yale University Press, 1989), 123–68; Fedorko, "Edith Wharton's Haunted Fiction," 81–2.

31 V. G. Rocine, *Heads, Faces, Types, Races* (1910), cited (with an accompanying illustration) in Banta, *Imaging American Women,* 121.

32 Gwendolyn Wright, *Moralism and the Model Home: Domestic Architecture and Cultural Conflict in Chicago, 1873–1913* (Chicago: University of Chicago Press, 1980), 275–7; also cited by Fryer, *Felicitous Space,* 31.

33 Lewis, *Edith Wharton: A Biography,* 391–2.

34 *A Backward Glance,* 317.

35 Ibid., 369–70.

2

NANCY BENTLEY

"Hunting for the Real": Wharton and the Science of Manners

Edith Wharton was present at the famous 1913 debut of Stravinsky's *Le Sacre du Printemps* when the Parisian ballet patrons erupted in protest at the work's cacophonous sounds and sacrificial themes. She therefore witnessed two ongoing dramas of early modernism: the absorption of primitivism into the high arts, and the outrage it could provoke among the arts establishment. It is not surprising that the cosmopolitan Wharton, by this time a famous expatriate, was on hand for one of the signal events of European art history. But her reputation as a cultural conservative distrustful of avant-garde experimentation offers little to account for her deep admiration of the ballet: her notebook records that she found it "extraordinary."[1] The gap between reputation and reality here is provocative, for it hints at the complexity of Wharton's relation to her cultural context – and to the changing concept of culture itself, the subject at the heart of her fiction.

Of particular interest is the historical turn to primitivism reflected in both Stravinsky's score and Nijinsky's choreography, for this contemporary trend can also provide an illumination of Wharton's own art. Her intellectual interest in the subject of tribal or "primitive" culture is well known; R. W. B. Lewis writes that she was "passionately addicted" to anthropology from an early age, and it is easy to speculate that her ethnographic knowledge provided much of the pleasure she took in the ballet's harsh ritualism.[2] Like many contemporary artists Wharton had a taste for the exotic. At first glance, though, it may appear that ethnographic themes appear in Wharton's fiction merely as a marker of taste, only one among the hundreds that she records in her novels. Newland Archer in *The Age of Innocence,* for instance, is drawn to "books on Primitive Man that people of advanced culture were beginning to read," and, like his Eastlake furniture, anthropology is a sign of a new intellectual fashion.[3] Unlike Stravinsky, Wharton does not draw upon the ethnographic to radically refashion a traditional aesthetic form. Instead, she appears to subordinate the current vogue for the exotic to the conventions of a long-established genre, the novel of manners. One can imagine, indeed, that for Wharton it was Parisian manners that provided the most absorbing spectacle at the ballet premiere, that her ethnographic interest was drawn less to the exoticism of the dancers than to the remarkable behavior of the audience, a cultural performance equally as "extraordinary" as the strange species of ballet on the stage.

The behavior of audiences, in fact, is a favorite measure of manners in Wharton's novels. The first chapters of *The Age of Innocence* introduce the reader to elite New York society by presenting the opera-house decorum of an "exceptionally brilliant audience" – the proper carriages for transportation, the fashionable time for arrival, the seating arrangements within the opera box, the tacit rules for greetings and formal introductions. But as Wharton records these customs, we begin to see a second dimension of primitivism that is crucial to the structure of the narrative itself. The observances of opera decorum, for instance, are described as tributes paid to " 'Taste,' that far-off divinity" (1026). As this metaphor suggests, Wharton not only transcribes the manners of the New York elite but glosses them as the anthropological rites and religion of a "tribe." Manners and decorum "played as important a part in Newland Archer's New York as the inscrutable totem terrors that had ruled the destinies of his forefathers thousands of years ago" (1018). Wharton records the customs and manners of the rich as an avowed novelist-ethnographer, or a "drawing-room naturalist," to borrow her own phrase from *The House of Mirth*. Thus Wharton not only recognizes ethnography as a reflection of taste, she makes taste ethnographic – the New York tribal god of Taste. The method amounts to a superimposing of exotic and civilized manners, a technique Wharton employs at several levels. The device produces a deliberately whimsical effect, of course, but the implications are profound: far from subordinating the current interest in primitivism to a traditional form, Wharton invokes the exotic to refashion from within the established understanding of social form itself. Though affixed to a narrow axis of elite manners, Wharton's fiction delineates the broadest questions of culture addressed in early anthropology: what culture is, how it works, its power and its limits. In self-consciously exploring these questions, Wharton participated in the emergence of a whole "science of manners."[4]

That label, from Wharton's contemporary Marcel Mauss, describes the efforts of a wide range of contemporary writers and scientists to understand modern society through the lens of ethnographic estrangement, a reciprocal mirroring of exotic and European customs of the kind we have begun to see in Wharton's fiction. Thus what is a fictional technique for Wharton is a critical method for leading theorists: for Thorstein Veblen, who describes the practices of leisure-class "barbarians"; for Max Weber, who analyzes modern classes as "castes" modeled after ethnic groups and "anthropological types" (complete with their own "chiefs," "gods," and "laws of endogamy"); even for Freud, who used tribal "analogies" to describe the "pathology of cultural communities," as well as for a host of lesser-known names.[5] To place Wharton in this context is not to dispute that she is a novelist of manners; rather I aim to open the question of what it means to write about manners during this period. For Wharton, writing about manners had come to include work as different as portraits of small rural towns, essays on gardens and home interiors, eyewitness accounts of North African societies (including descriptions of a harem and the tribal blood rites of a Moroccan sect), even an unpublished erotic fragment that was composed for a project with the Conrad-like title "Powers of Darkness." What unifies this diverse range of Wharton materials is a disposition or posture of mind that anthropologist Ruth Benedict called "culture consciousness."[6]

"Culture" has long been one of our most overdetermined words, and the multiplication of its meanings began in earnest during just this era. Yet it is precisely the overtaxing of the concept that is instructive, for it points to new social contradictions that the idea of culture was called upon to suspend and mediate. In its multiple meanings, "culture" became a talisman for a transatlantic bourgeoisie that experienced a rapid growth of wealth at the same time that it faced a new and sometimes bewildering social heterogeneity in urban centers and colonial outposts. The culture consciousness articulated in Wharton's work, I shall argue, allows her writing both to critique and preserve the authority of the late-nineteenth-century elite class, a double strategy that finally serves to accommodate the very social changes that the class appeared to oppose. Like Benedict in her essay "The Science of Custom," Wharton presents culture as a "flexible instrument" for "divesting" a society of rigid absolutes while "reinstating and reshaping" the local values that sustain a particular social existence.[7] In this essay I trace some of the ways that Wharton's fiction embodies a new culture consciousness – not as a set of abstract axioms but as the intimate, subjective "feel" for the social that is fiction's most powerful resource. In turn, recognizing a historical context for contemporary concepts of manners and culture recasts many of the critical puzzles that still surround Wharton and her fiction: Is she an antimodernist or an innovator? a feminist or a strict social conservative? These debates, important as they are, cut us off from one of the fundamental achievements of her work. Wharton's fiction is neither culturally subversive nor apologist; rather it effects a new representation of the sphere of culture itself in order to articulate, circulate, and finally acculturate the shocks of the modern. We should not be surprised, in other words, that Wharton warmed to the "extraordinary" spectacle of *Le Sacre du Printemps,* nor that she replayed its sacrificial rites in her literature as the "New York way of taking life without the shedding of blood" (1282).[8]

"I go about this London hunting for the real." Written in a 1912 letter, Ezra Pound's striking description of "hunting for the real" echoes a sentiment expressed widely in this period. Dramatic social changes that were especially concentrated in cities had created a feeling of unreality for many writers and observers. Historian T. J. Jackson Lears has analyzed the sense of "weightlessness" and vertigo that began to appear in the writings of educated Americans as official creeds of optimism were broken up by fear of class and ethnic violence and by a changing urban landscape. For many, the sanctuaries of home and church were little protection against the "modern doubt" that, as one minister put it, "destroys the sense of reality" and "envelopes all things in its puzzle." "Reality itself began to seem problematic," Lears writes, "something to be sought rather than merely lived." What and where is the real? Many writers had taken these questions as a special challenge for art, and it was an era that saw frequent manifestos declaring literature an agent for discovering and exhibiting reality. Some novelists, for instance, claimed for their genre an unflinching scientific precision and power. Frank Norris called the novel an "instrument with which we may go straight through the clothes and tissues and wrappings of flesh down into the red, living heart of things."[9]

Norris discards as superfluous "wrappings" what had long been a dominant subject for the novel: manners, the imprint of history and locality on the individual, the social signatures of clothing, speech, posture, gestures. Gazing at the individual, the naturalist novel discovers mass animated by instinct; at its most extreme, as one critic writes, it performs "the extinction of the social, civilized self in a frenzy of sensation." And yet for other contemporary thinkers, it was exactly that social self that had become a new object of scientific interest. Patterns of social habit and convention emerged as a "second nature," a reality unable to be stripped away and awaiting its own yet to be discovered causal laws. "Not incidental or subordinate," wrote one scholar, manners are "supreme and controlling," the "dominating force in history." William James famously called habit the "fly-wheel of society." Seeking the real, many scholars looked to the conventional: the sphere of customs, folkways, social habits and usages. The professional study of culture was established during just this period in the disciplines of anthropology, sociology, and social psychology. John Dewey's declaration that "man is a creature of habit, not of reason nor yet of instinct" describes the new cultural view of the human animal, echoed decades later by Claude Lévi-Strauss: "There is no doubt that, between instincts inherited from our genotype and the rules inspired by reason, the mass of unconscious rules remain more important and more effective."[10]

In this way, customs and manners, long the province of letters – conduct books, the novel, the travel essay – came under the scrutiny of science. And during the same period, the traditional novel of manners acquired a scientific inflection. Unlike novelists such as Norris, Wharton retained the "social, civilized self" as her primary subject, but she made the world of drawing rooms, parlors, and theaters as much a field for "hunting for the real" as the cruder settings – the wilderness, the marketplace, the battlefield – of Norris, Jack London, or Stephen Crane. Like the naturalists, Wharton was fascinated by biology and evolutionism, reading deeply in Darwin, Huxley, Ernst Haeckel, and in current studies of heredity and Mendelism. Favorite anthropological texts included works by Herbert Spencer, Edward Westermarck (probably his *History of Primitive Marriage*), James Frazer's *Golden Bough,* and the "remarkable books on tribal life in Melanesia" by Bronislaw Malinowski, whom she came to know socially. To Wharton, scientific knowledge was indispensable for discovering our "inward relation to reality." But crucially, reality included not only material forces and human instincts but the irreducible reality of social forms. In Durkheim's words, "man is human only because he is socialised."[11]

And yet the reality of social convention, Wharton recognized, is always both essential and equivocal. For although there is no human life outside of a web of mutual relations, still no *particular* social feature – this form of marriage, that division of labor or gender roles – is in itself either necessary, unalterable, or permanent. *The Age of Innocence* explores precisely this tension between the real and the conventional – or between nature and culture, the submerged fault line that was also at the heart of anthropological studies. Until the arrival of Ellen Olenska, Newland Archer accepts even the most baroque observances and distinctions of his circle as a natural, almost "congenital" inheritance (1021). But when he falls in love with Ellen, the New York "tribal" customs and its rules of Taste begin to appear as an archaic formalism, a "parody of life." A gulf opens between the world of social convention and a private, alternative world he calls "reality":

he had built up within himself a kind of sanctuary in which she throned among his secret thoughts and longings. Little by little it became the scene of his real life, of his only rational activities. . . . Outside it, in the scene of his actual life, he moved with a growing sense of unreality and insufficiency, blundering against familiar prejudices and traditional points of view as an absent-minded man goes on bumping into the furniture of his own room.

(1224)

Newland's crisis is a personal and emotional one, of course, but its repercussions have the broadest possible social range. His illicit desire triggers an estrangement at the level of the smallest details of social life and spreads into the very "structure of his universe" (1097). And as the larger contours of the novel make clear, Newland's sense of "unreality" dramatizes the forces of dislocation pressuring a whole social era. The Archer family, for instance, feels keenly the changes in New York society, vigilantly tracing "each new crack in its surface" (1219). The novel provides hints about the sources of the ruptures: new technologies, a changing cityscape, novel ideas about women and marriage, the perception of "a country in possession of the bosses and the emigrant" (1115). The characters themselves, however, say almost nothing about these large-scale changes. Instead, they focus on small, discrete adjustments in their own social habits, a slight increase in "extravagance" of dress or a shift in the customary round of leisure entertainments. Yet as Pierre Bourdieu notes, the details of social manners in fact provide the most sensitive register of urban dislocations. The "development of cities," Bourdieu writes, "favours the confrontation of different cultural traditions, which tends to expose their arbitrariness practically, through first-hand experience, in the very heart of the routine of the everyday order." The effects of urban heterogeneity are felt most intimately in the imponderables of daily habits and ingrained cultural patterns. What is usually the unremarked "hum and buzz of implication" (as Lionel Trilling called manners) is thrown into relief, bringing, Bourdieu writes, "the undiscussed into discussion, the unformulated into formulation."[12]

Bourdieu describes this process as an "objective crisis" in the cognitive structures of an urban society. For the reigning clans of Old New York, though, social change and heterogeneity do not prompt a perceived erosion of reality, as they do for Newland. Instead, change is understood as an encroachment upon universal standards of propriety and taste. What is more, the elders absorb the very marks of change into their patterns of social custom: without fail Mrs. Archer will ceremoniously "enumerate the minute signs of disintegration" during the mid-October "household ritual" of assembling the proper carpets and curtains. Like the rector's jeremiad delivered every year at the Thanksgiving sermon, Mrs. Archer's laments about social decline become part of the linked institutions that actually foster continuity and strength for her social circle. On one side, therefore, even a crisis in manners becomes a process by which New York "managed its transitions" (1222). Social anxieties marshaled under the banner of Taste help to convert the very arbitrariness of manners into a continuing source of meaning and group cohesion.

On another side, however, exposing the arbitrariness of culture produces a different kind of social energy, a restlessness represented by Newland's agitated sense of unreality. For Newland, we have seen, manners are no longer a matter of natural decorum. Performing the round of social calls expected of a fiancé, he feels "trapped" as they "rolled from one tribal doorstep to another" and wonders if "his readings in anthropology caused him to take such a coarse view of what was after all a simple and natural demonstration of family feeling" (1069–70). Here anthropological allusions make vivid Newland's sense of estrangement; what was natural is now hollow, even coercive. "It is when the social world loses its character as a natural phenomena," Bourdieu writes, "that the question of the natural or conventional character (*phusei* or *nomo*) of social facts can be raised."[13] Newland seems to be directly at odds with his family on the question of social "form" and manners. Through ritual repetition, the Archers and their circle confirm their customs as a "natural demonstration" of feeling, whereas for Newland repetition serves to empty those customs of any inherent meaning. The novel stages a clash between two versions of culture: what we could call drawing-room culture ("decent people had to fall back on sport or culture," as one of the New York axioms has it), and anthropological culture ("culture in the wide ethnographic sense," as scholar E. B. Tylor announced in his *Primitive Culture*).[14] The conflict is between manners as inherent values of propriety and manners as relative local forms of human society – between, one could say, table manners and tribal manners. As different as these contrasting paradigms are, however, the conflict actually belongs to a larger solution to the novel's problem of social change. By displaying the tension, Wharton makes visible the particular "crisis of cultural authority" that Lears and others have identified among the educated classes of the late-century era.[15] At the same time, however, the tension itself is enlisted in the service of class continuity: by illuminating the difference between absolute and relative manners, the novel, as we shall see, imparts a heightened culture consciousness through which we observe a revitalized world of the Archers, a renewed social power for their kin and kind. Wharton introduces a cultural relativism into the novel of manners not as a sign of nihilistic decline but as a tool of social adaptation.

We can note first, however, that the culture consciousness articulated in anthropology relied upon the same tension between the arbitrariness and the positive meaning simultaneously present in cultural customs. Just as Wharton borrowed ethnographic tropes, anthropologists specifically called upon drawing-room manners to make visible that inherent doubleness. "The savage rules of etiquette are not only strict, but formidable," Robert Lowie wrote; "nevertheless to us their table manners are shocking." The image of "savage etiquette" drives home the point: what would be shocking in a genteel American dining room nevertheless can be culturally proper and even "strict." In his *Argonauts of the Western Pacific,* Malinowski mocks the colonial magistrate who, when "asked about the manners of the natives answered, 'Customs none, manners beastly.'" The joke enlists the reader's recognition that if misapplied the narrow definition of manners will be ridiculous. But Malinowski goes on to reclaim the idea of the quality and value of drawing-room manners when he argues that the Trobriand natives possess "excellent manners in the full meaning of this word"; that is, they possess not only distinct lifeways but internal codes of decorum, prestige, and glamour. It is in fact the "glamour" of the elaborate kula gift-exchange system that Malinowski is most concerned to convey and analyze, even as he concedes that the kula objects are, to European eyes, little more than "greasy trinkets." By drawing upon the disparity within the meaning of manners, Malinowski opens up a new way of representing the real: neither glamorous nor greasy *in reality,* the kula treasures belong to an "ethnographic reality" that is founded upon the difference between the two cultural perspectives. The "vital reality" of Trobriand objects and customs is "built up of tradition and personal experience," framed within the ethnographic realism of anthropology.[16]

Wharton's novel of manners presents a fictional version of this ethnographic or customary realism. What is real becomes intelligible precisely through a dialectic of the traditional and the personal, the arbitrary and the actual. And the medium for this dialectic is custom, the locally rooted but contingent forms which can be disowned or disobeyed but never transcended. When Newland Archer calls his very real passion for Ellen the "only reality," Ellen confronts him with the reality of bourgeois kinship terms: "Is it your idea, then, that I should live with you as your mistress – since I can't be your wife?" Newland's answer resists these social classifications: "I want somehow to get away with you into a world where words like that – categories like that – won't exist" (1245). But Ellen's reply, "Where is that country? Have you ever been there?" returns the novel to its foundation in the cultural: the variable but irreducible categories of countries, classes, regions, and urban castes. Ellen's response acknowledges both their mutual desire and their mutual relation to New York kinship (we are "Newland Archer, the husband of Ellen Olenska's cousin," she recounts for him, "and Ellen Olenska, the cousin of Newland Archer's wife") and the novel's poignancy comes from the tension between the conflicting realities of kinship and illicit passion. Wharton thus uses a love story to generate a drama of cultural consciousness, the same drama Malinowski discloses in Trobriand society, where he represents an ethnographic reality by narrating "the power of tribal law, and of the passions which work against and in spite of these."[17]

Wharton underscores this doubleness of culture, at once conventional and actual, in the scene that places Newland and Ellen within the "queer wilderness of cast-iron and encaustic tiles known as the Metropolitan Museum," in front of the glass cases housing the "Cesnola antiquities" (1261). The museum site is highly significant. As the lovers struggle with a painful recognition of the real force of New York kinship taboos, Wharton stages the scene before a setting symbolic of culture in Tylor's "wide" ethnographic sense, as represented by the exhibited fragments of a now-vanished ancient community. "Its glass shelves were crowded with small broken objects – hardly recognizable domestic utensils, ornaments and personal trifles – made of glass, of clay, of discoloured bronze and other time-blurred substances" (1262). Gazing on the display, Ellen points to the tension that Wharton has built into the novel as a whole, noting that these reified, frozen pieces of an exotic world carry a life and meaning now inaccessible but once as real as her own: "these little things, that used to be necessary and important to forgotten people, and now have to be guessed at under a magnifying glass and labeled: 'Use unknown.'" While Ellen dwells on the historical contingency of cultural experience, Archer returns the novel's dialectic to its opposite pole of immediacy – "meanwhile everything matters" – though this declaration is ultimately framed by a "vista of mummies and sarcophagi" (1263), another reminder of the mutability of cultures and their customs. Shifting rapidly back and forth between the two perspectives, Wharton creates a wider consciousness of culture out of the reader's heightened experience of cultural difference. Fragments of experience from disparate worlds are made to represent a new totality. By juxtaposing the exotic and the immediate, Wharton turns the "unreality" of the New York scene into the stable category of culture in its professional sense, merging a drawing-room crisis into the institutional authority of the museum (Wharton has

Newland announce proleptically the powerful prestige of civic museums like the Metropolitan: "Some day, I suppose, it will be a great Museum" [1262]). The "queer wilderness" of the museum becomes the field for hunting for the real in the territory of culture. And significantly, it is precisely the odd, organized eclecticism of the museum, holding together a varied range of customs and cultural objects, that here provides Wharton with a center of authority from which to recover the realism of manners for a society facing modernity.

This seeming paradox requires a closer examination. Like the strange wilderness of the Metropolitan juxtaposing Cesnola antiquities with Egyptian mummies, Wharton's fiction is a kind of textual museum that recasts elite manners by representing them as carefully preserved artifacts. But what exactly is to be gained from this defamiliarizing perspective? In seeking the real, why look to institutions like anthropology and museums and to what Paul Valéry called the "strange organized disorder" of disparate objects gathered and displayed in museum collections? Presenting a historical context for the large civic museums established in this era, Philip Fisher analyzes the role of the museum in institutionalizing forms of authenticity and cultural value for societies now fully committed to industrial production and bureaucratic systems. Museums, Fisher argues, are "counter-institutions to the factory":

> Museums became more and more central exactly in cultures touched most deeply by the modern system of mass-production. The British Museum in London and the Metropolitan Museum in New York represent a new kind of institution. No longer do they provide a visible history of the culture itself: that is, a display of objects rich with symbolic, local significance. Instead they are storage areas for authenticity and uniqueness per se, for objects from any culture or period whatever that were said to be irreplaceable.[18]

In modern museums, it is precisely the heterogeneity of varied artifacts – a medieval weapon, a tribal mask, an Impressionist painting – that guarantees authentic cultural value, for the museum exists to preserve and display what cannot be reproduced. A similar display of "relics" governs Wharton's fiction, allowing for the narrative juxtaposition of the manners of "Old New York" with prehistoric antiquities and tribal metaphors. Rather than amassing a rich surface of interlocking social details (the aim of earlier realists), Wharton creates a disjunctive view of manners. But this perspective in turn invokes an aura of authenticity out of the representation of mere fragments. A coherent narrative space unified under the concept of culture is produced from the very gaps between starkly different social worlds.

Wharton's 1924 work *Old New York* is instructive in this regard. As if to create her own museum "collection," Wharton issued the four novellas that form *Old New York* as a boxed set of volumes, together displaying the archaeological layers of a now "extinct" society. These stories are presented as representative fragments, each holding a metonymic glimpse of the endogamous "tribes" of the ruling classes of New York. The titles announce the stories as recovered artifacts displayed in chronological order: *False Dawn (The 'Forties); The Old Maid (The 'Fifties); The Spark (The 'Sixties);* and *New Year's Day (The 'Seventies).* Despite the labeling by decade, what binds these stories, the principles that give them a mutual resonance, are not historical but ethnological principles; that is, the narratives are not arranged as a New York history framing a homogenous span of time and interlocking events but as an ethnological collection, a record of meaningful details that invoke a sense of culture as E. B. Tylor defined it: culture as the "complex whole" of social life that unites the disparate materials of everyday life but is never representable except through selected fragments.[19] As in anthropology and museum displays, though, ordinary life in the stories is presented as something extraordinary, whether for its antiquity, rarity, or near extinction (in her memoir *A Backward Glance,* Wharton would claim all three for Old New York). Wharton's exotic tropes and allusions in the stories bestow the signature of culture in the wide ethnographic sense, allusions such as the description of the reigning matrons as "the female elders of the tribe" (431) in *The Old Maid* or the reference on the first page of *False Dawn* to the "bronze idols" (317) brought back from naval adventures, prefiguring the rare "Italian Primitives" that Lewis Raycie brings back from Europe. Framed as an ethnological culture, the genteel society of New York is recast as one of "the most totem-ridden of communities" (425). Paradoxically, then, Wharton's exotic misnomers are the most telling markers of Old New York's unique cultural value – not the value of a superior civility (for the stories uncover wounds and cruelties as often as gracious conduct) but an ethnological value that shares a structure of authenticity with museums and anthropological studies. The stories' disjunctive links between idols and Italian paintings, between tribal priestesses and wealthy matrons, like the noted disparities between New York society and ancient Cesnola in the Metropolitan, are marked gaps that presume a larger entity called "culture," the ultimate subject of both anthropology and Wharton's novellas.

It is not just the choice of the Metropolitan as a setting in *The Age of Innocence,* then, that links Wharton's fiction to the new institution of the museum. Many of Wharton's writings share the founding assumptions that made modern museums possible, assumptions that the authentic and the real are in some sense precarious, in need of preservation, and that they reveal their purest meaning in the form of special collections and related kinds of archival representation. Wharton is explicit about these assumptions in her memoir *A Backward Glance.* "The compact world of my youth has receded into a past from which it can only be dug up in bits by the assiduous relic-hunter," she writes, "and its smallest fragments begin to be worth collecting and putting together before the last of those who knew the live structure are swept away with it" (781). Conceived as "relics" and "fragments," the past is reassembled according to dual principles of worth: cultural wholeness and cultural extinction. On one hand she points to a "live structure" that is analogous to E. B. Tylor's definition of culture as a "complex whole," and on the other hand she records the loss of that living whole. Extinction is the ultimate source of cultural value: "The small society into which I was born was 'good' in the most prosaic sense of the term, and its only interest, for the generality of readers, lies in the fact of its sudden and total extinction, and for the imaginative few in the recognition of the moral treasures that went with it" (781). Once suitably collected and framed by the idea of cultural extinction, "moral treasures" are recovered and preserved.

In passages such as these Wharton expresses an elegiac protest against the rationalizing forces of modernity that seemed to erode civic traditions and impose a deadening order of standardized production and bureaucracy (what Wharton in a letter once called "Fordian culture"). She echoes an antimodernism that was one of the keynotes of the decades of American "incorporation."[20] It was an age when antimodernists like Henry Adams and G. Stanley Hall sought a renewed cultural vitality by looking to premodern worlds and tribal societies. Adams, a close friend of Wharton, immersed himself in medieval Catholic art and native Samoan life, two islands of an authenticity lost to the modern bureaucratized society. But the paradox of antimodernism was that its "backward glance" (to borrow Wharton's borrowing of Whitman) ultimately may have helped to accommodate the new forces of modernity that it appeared to oppose. Lears argues that "American antimodernism unknowingly provided part of the psychological foundation for a streamlined liberal culture appropriate to twentieth-century consumer capitalism" and its "therapeutic ethos."[21] It promoted psychic adjustments, cults of individual vitalism, and a privatized spirituality that helped to refashion modern citizens for new forms of bureaucratic authority. The turn to primitivism was a distinctly modern phenomenon that served a modern purpose. Whether or not this precise historical argument holds true, the ethnographic turn in Wharton's fiction does indeed show us a paradoxical modernity that could be represented through a backward glance to a "vanished" society.

In *The Age of Innocence*, for instance, a relativistic view of the rites and customs of Old New York eases the narrative transition to a modern society of technology and bureaucracy. The novel's final chapter, set twenty-six years later in Paris, reveals the full implications of Wharton's ethnographic approach to manners. The flexible lens through which the novel has viewed customs and culture allows for both a recovered sense of realism and an adaptation to social change. In modern Paris, Newland himself is now a relic ("Don't be prehistoric!" his son tells him). But it is precisely as an antiquarian object that Newland achieves a now-poignant sense of reality – though a reality now recognized as fragile, customary, and in need of preservation. Newland finds himself unable to cross the threshold to Ellen's apartment: " 'It's more real to me here than if I went up,' he suddenly heard himself say; and the fear lest that last shadow of reality should lose its edge kept him rooted to his seat as the minutes succeeded each other" (1302).

The moment is preserved in museumlike stillness. But with a precious sense of reality "rooted" with Archer in this scene, the chapter also embraces the opposing forces of modernity that had fostered the extinction of Old New York. Telephones and electric light, Roosevelt's new politics, and rapid overseas travel have been integrated into the lives of the next generation of leading New Yorkers. Even more important, the taboos against exogamous intermarriage with the sons and daughters of the worlds of business and politics have been lifted. Now society is a "huge kaleidoscope where all the social atoms spun around on the same plane" (1296), but the disorder is a vital energy harnessed by Archer's children. Wharton's portrait of a class that, while fearing decline, in fact retained and strengthened its claim to power through the tumultuous social changes of fin-de-siècle America is demographically correct. In spite of apprehension about receding WASP powers, the northeastern elite expanded its social influence and helped to smooth the transition to a new corporate society. In this sense the novel deploys an adaptive culture consciousness that helped to refashion the social authority of the leadership classes for modern conditions. Like Newland Archer's haunting sense of "unreality," the uneasiness of a generation in pursuit of the real finally helped to put in place a new social reality.

I have been arguing that Wharton's realism, like Benedict's culture concept, is a "flexible instrument" for negotiating the conflicts of an emergent modern world. The elegiac preservation of fragile cultural relics, however, is only one side of Wharton's fiction of manners. Her realism also includes a fascinated obsession with what seemed to be the vital energies of social aggression in primitive cultures. It is fitting that the first ethnographic museum (founded by the Englishman L. F. Pitt Rivers) began as a collection of weapons, for even at its professional peak the discipline of anthropology retained the early explorers' interest in what Malinowski called "crime and custom in savage society."[22] Any reader of *The Age of Innocence* will recognize this interest in Wharton, for the novel's final reconciliation comes only after a climactic scene of ritualized violence, a dinner party glossed as "a tribal rally around a kinswoman about to be eliminated from the tribe" (1281). The hunt for the real in Wharton's fiction of manners includes a complex attraction to contemporary notions of social coercion and power, and this romancing of aggression is equally important for understanding the workings of the culture concept in Wharton's fiction.

In *A Backward Glance,* Wharton writes that Charles Norton was "disturbed by my increasing realism." Norton had preferred the historical-romance genre of her first novel, *The Valley of Decision,* but afterward, Wharton notes, she had turned to "the life about me" for fictional material (900). That life was usually the world of cosmopolitan travel and the "best society" of New York and other capitals. But in her two tales of rural New England, *Ethan Frome* and *Summer,* the "increasing realism" is the product of what we could call Wharton's fieldwork. The novellas were "the result of explorations among villages still bedrowsed in a decaying rural existence, and sad slow-speaking people living in conditions hardly changed since their forebears held those villages against the Indians" (898). Wharton's "hill people" are New England primitives, a breed untouched by modernity, acting out their "savage tragedies" (1002) away from the sight of civilization. But unlike naturalist fictions, these tales do not strip away convention to reveal a coarse underside (though Wharton did challenge what she thought were "rose-coloured" portraits [1002] by writers like Mary Wilkins Freeman and Sarah Orne Jewett, who presented rural New England through the lens of a "soft primitivism," as historians have labeled the antiquarian idealizing of the preindustrial world). As in the New York fiction, these New England novellas still present a realism of custom, a dialectical movement between social forms and the volatile social energies that animate and sometimes alter them. Thus the rural culture of Wharton's New England is structured by the same "tense equilibrium" between custom and crisis that Malinowski discovered among the Trobrianders.[23]

For Malinowski, moments of violent crisis or "outbreak" provided an invaluable glimpse into the "riddles of Culture." Studying such conflicts "reveals to us the very nature of the social fabric."[24] Similarly, the crisis at the center of *Summer* anatomizes a system of cultural laws and transgressions that promise to unlock the "riddle" of the real. Charity Royall is caught between two forms of transgressive relations that define the limits of kinship and cultural law. The sexual overtures by Lawyer Royall, her legal guardian, present the threat of incest, a dangerous overlapping of social relations. By contrast, her affair with Lucius Harney poses the opposite threat: a sexual relation utterly divorced from any social institutions. Led by Lucius out of the town's library, guided past the visible forms of domesticity in his tours of rural house architecture, Charity eventually enters with him a merely pantomime marriage, the secret lovemaking in an abandoned shell of a home. But while she exchanges her (already tenuous) ties to the social world for a seeming reality of passion, she discovers that Lucius has remained rooted in a life of richly textured forms and established manners. In one glimpse of Lucius bending over an elegant woman, Charity discerns the larger social reality he inhabits, "his relations with other people – with other women – his opinions, his prejudices, his principles, the net of influences and interests and ambitions" (259) that are the real foundation of his life.

With this discovery, Charity has a painful recognition of her own place at the margins of his life and the life of North Dormer, and Wharton presents the crisis through ethnographic images that trace a compressed cultural evolution in the life of a single character. Charity's first response is an impulse of "savage" revolt: she "had never known how to adapt herself; she could only break and tear and destroy." Ashamed at "her own childish savagery, . . . she felt herself too unequally pitted against unknown forces," and "she could not imagine what a civilized person would have done in her place" (273). This internal crisis is played out in the plot as Charity returns to her origins among the "Mountain people," a return to the forces of sexuality and the danger of disordered "passive promiscuity" (294) (which echoes the theories of "primitive promiscuity" Wharton would have read about in Westermarck and others). The journey becomes a "tragic initiation" into social life. It is only by witnessing and passing through this primitive site that Charity comes to "adapt" herself to civilization and to contract a now-lawful marriage to Lawyer Royall.

This ending has puzzled some readers: why is the once abhorrent relationship with Royall now the ideal resolution? The transformation of incest into marriage, however, is a sign of the narrative's aspiration to uncover and master what anthropologists call the "deep structure" of culture, the rules and defining taboos that disclose the vital workings of a society. In *Summer,* Wharton stretches her realism of manners to include representation of the very origins of culture. The narrative thus enacts the search for sources of primitive social energies that was an obsession of fin-de-siècle intellectuals. Recovering the real, many believed, would require the exploration of terrible initiations and sacrifices that were the original animating forces of social life. *Le Sacre du Printemps* is an example of the widespread attempt in art and in social theory alike to seek out elemental powers of cultural life and renewal. This "fascination with primal, aggressive impulse," Lears suggests, helped to glamorize power for an elite apprehensive about its declining social power.[25] In this oddest of marriage stories, Charity's marriage represents not just a reconciliation of a narrative plot but a contemporary strategy for mastering the "riddles of Culture."

Like the rural setting of *Summer,* the world of fashion in Wharton's New York novels is organized around a hidden center of stark social appetites and energies. When Lily Bart in *The House of Mirth* reads a letter revealing the love affair of Selden and Bertha Dorset, she glimpses the powerful forces of collective taboo and revenge that will eventually destroy her: "Now the other side presented itself to Lily, the volcanic nether side of the surface over which conjecture and innuendo glide so lightly till the first fissure turns their whisper to a shriek" (109). Lily eventually dies as a martyr sacrificed to these volcanic energies. As materialistic and cruel as the fashionable world is shown to be, its powers define a vital reality that Lily cannot resist. In fact, the act of casting out Lily defines the boundaries of the real in *The House of Mirth.* As in *The Age of Innocence,* a new reality is constructed and confirmed by a violent social ceremony. Before an audience of restaurant diners, the usual rites of "leave-taking" turn into an expulsion of Lily from society: "Miss Bart is not going back to the yacht" (227), Bertha Dorset proclaims. The public confrontation is remarkably like the "chasing away" ceremony Malinowski records as the culminating act of a village crisis: "You are a stranger here. Go away! We chase you away! We chase you out of Omarakana." Once an offense is publicly charged and retribution publicly demanded, a new reality is collectively defined and accepted; the Trobriand chasing away ceremony, therefore, has "a binding force" on both the tribe members and the now-official "stranger." Similarly, a new truth is put in place by Bertha Dorset's lies in *The House of Mirth:* "the truth about any girl" (236), Lily tells Gerty Farish, is what is spoken publicly about her. Bertha's public scene acts as a kind of verbal magic, a force that requires "no direct bodily violence," as Malinowski writes of Trobriand spells, but which puts into place a new governing order.[26] *The House of Mirth* shows us a social reality that is inseparable from the power wielded through manners and customs. Like much contemporary naturalism, Wharton's fiction discovers a potential violence in everyday life, though in Wharton's world of customs and manners it is the subtlest shades of decorum that can contain the "gleam of a knife." Even as the novel condemns the cruelty and waste of the leisure class, it shows an ethnographer's fascination with a potential for defining and controlling social life through the coercive power of ritual and manners.

This ambivalence toward social power is even stronger when the protagonist is not the victim but the uncanny agent of it, as Undine Spragg is in *The Custom of the Country.* In this novel Wharton multiplies the crises that can occur in the sphere of manners and more openly displays the "weapons of aggression" (970) wielded there. Undine has an almost magical ability to imitate others' manners, a talent that allows her to enter and dominate virtually any exclusive circle she desires to join. But Undine also turns her power for assimilation against the very social worlds that embrace her. Each major episode in the novel culminates in the destruction she brings to some preserve of custom and values. Undine's resetting of the Marvell family jewels, which "destroy[s] the identity" (763) and tradition they contain, is replayed on a larger scale in her second marriage to a French nobleman. When Undine feels the "mysterious web of traditions, conventions, prohibitions" (961) close around her at Chelles, she commits one of her most shocking acts, selling the prized tapestries that represent the preserved accumulation of aristocratic culture. Undine's pursuit of social mobility and assimilation – what she calls her "inalienable right to 'go around'" (939) – thus comes into direct conflict with the culture of the museum world and its preservation of rare objects and values of the past.

But the novel gives an exhilarating power and glamour to Undine and her "weapons of aggression" at the same time as it shows that power at its most destructive. What are we to make of this mixture of attraction and repulsion? Unlike the ending of *The Age of Innocence,* the novel's resolution – the tapestries now displayed as spoils on the wall of Undine's mansion, with her desire and aggression still unsated – does not seem to promise an accommodation of tradition with the new forces of modernity. Undine, in fact, is "the monstrously perfect result" (759) of a new world of "unbounded material power" (802). But although Undine is monstrous, she is also the figure that exposes the weakness of the "aboriginal" tribes of New York, a social group which, like its foremost representative Ralph Marvell, is a vulnerable "archaic structure" of "rites and sanctions" (932) that are easily shattered. Ralph, it could be said, carries out the threat of "race suicide" that antimodernists worried was the fate of an enervated ruling class. In contrast, Undine embodies the personal and social force that fascinated writers such as Adams and Nietzsche, and her story points to the attempt, in Lears's words, to "re-create a problematic reality through aggressive action."[27] In *The Custom of the Country,* Undine is the monstrous Other that embodies threat and renewal alike, a necessary opponent through which an established order might revitalize its own cultural power. Hence Wharton might have had in mind a powerful antagonist like Undine when, in a 1918 notebook entry, she wrote, "I want the idols broken, but I want them broken by people who understand why they were made, and do not ascribe them to the deliberate malice of the augurs who may afterwards profit from them."[28]

Wharton's wish to see the "idols broken" by those who "understand" can be paired with another notebook inscription: "I foresee the day I shall be as lonely as an Etruscan museum."[29] The entries capture the mixed sentiment, a combination of anxiety and a sense of possession, that Wharton and many of her contemporaries expressed about their role as the custodians of culture. Yet, as I have been arguing, a dialectic of cultural anxiety and renewed authority finally served a single end, a process of accommodation to modernity. As much as Wharton dedicated herself to the preservation of the "relics" of traditional civilizations – including the seemingly fragile social forms of the wealthy nineteenth-century bourgeoisie – she was also prompted by feelings of the emptiness or insufficiency of those very traditions. An admirer of Nietzsche, Wharton was drawn to his iconoclastic assaults on the very cultural forms she most valued – and drawn, too, to his critique of value itself: "I think it salutary now and then, to be made to realize what he calls die Unwerthung aller Werthe [the valuelessness of all values]," Wharton wrote in a letter, "and really get back to a wholesome basis of naked instinct."[30] Like Malinowski, however, Wharton believed human instinct was expressed only in local forms of custom and ritual. Her pursuit of intense social experience led her to explore the tribal customs of the villages and palaces of Morocco, a world, she writes, that "still lacks a guide-book" (though, significantly, her personal hunt for the real is embodied in her own book, *In Morocco*).[31] Stepping outside of the preserves of museums and banal guidebooks, Wharton was transfixed by the rituals that seemed to display the live aggression at the root of culture. She watched the blood-rite dance of the Hamadchas, "in which blood flowed so freely that all the rocking feet were splashed with it," and Wharton's first impulse was to "fly from the repulsive scene." Yet even this scene of "horror" is not presented to us as a display of instinct but is reinscribed as cultural form – first as an "extravagantly staged ballet" (such as Nijinsky's?) and then as a rite "traced back to the depths of that ensanguined grove where Mr. Fraser [*sic*] plucked the Golden Bough." Represented in this way, the horror is "redeemed" by "beauty," and Wharton returns the reader to the ballet stage and to the science of manners, two European forms now revitalized through observation of the "nether" side of culture. What Wharton valued most about her trip to Morocco – that it was free from the "banalities and promiscuities of modern travel" – is precisely what she would help to damage, as her own volume represents a guidebook of sorts for an imminent wave of modern tourism.[32] Her book, along with the plans for new roads and archaeological projects the book describes, would become part of the network of travel, exchange, preservation, and bureaucratic administration that drew Morocco into the world that needs museums. The wider culture consciousness of Wharton's writings allowed her to embrace and identify with the premodern world. But that identification, quintessentially modern, carried with it the irresistible forces of modernization.

NOTES

1 Edith Wharton, Second Donnée Book, 8, in the Wharton Archives, Beinecke Library, Yale University. Wharton's response to the ballet is discussed in Cynthia Griffin Wolff, *A Feast of Words: The Triumph of Edith Wharton* (New York: Oxford University Press, 1977), 268–9.

2 R. W. B. Lewis, *Edith Wharton: A Biography* (New York: Fromm International, 1985), 108.

3 Edith Wharton, *The Age of Innocence,* in *Edith Wharton: Novels,* ed. R. W. B. Lewis (New York: Library of America, 1985), 1051. Quotations from Wharton's fiction and autobiography, subsequently included parenthetically in the text, will be drawn from this volume and the companion volume in the Library of America, *Edith Wharton: Novellas and Other Writings,* ed. Cynthia Griffin Wolff (New York: Library of America, 1990).

4 Marcel Mauss, *The Gift: Forms and Functions of Exchange in Archaic Societies,* trans. Ian Cunnison (1925; rpt. New York: Norton, 1967), 81.

5 Thorstein Veblen, *The Theory of the Leisure Class* (1899; rpt. New York: Viking, 1983), 1; Max Weber, "Class, Status, Party," in *From Max Weber,* ed. H. H. Gerth and C. Wright Mills (New York: Oxford University Press, 1958), 180–95; Sigmund Freud, *Civilization and Its Discontents,* trans. James Strachey (New York: Norton, 1961), 103.

6 The term appears in Ruth Benedict, "The Science of Custom: The Bearing of Anthropology on Contemporary Thought," *Century Magazine* 117 (April 1929), 641–9.

7 Benedict, "Science of Custom," 642, 658, 649.

8 Among the critics who have remarked upon Wharton's ethnographic interests and methods are James W. Tuttleton, "Edith Wharton: The Archaeological Motive," *Yale Review* 61 (1972), 562–74; Elizabeth Ammons, *Wharton's Argument with America* (Athens: University of Georgia Press, 1980); Mary Ellis Gibson,

"Edith Wharton and the Ethnography of Old New York," *Studies in American Fiction* 13 (1985), 57–69; and Katie Trumpener and James M. Nyce, "The Recovered Fragments: Archeological and Anthropological Perspectives in Edith Wharton's *The Age of Innocence*," in *Literary Anthropology: A New Interdisciplinary Approach to People, Signs and Literature,* ed. Fernando Poyatos (Philadelphia: Benjamins, 1988), 161–9. In addition to exploring Wharton's ethnographic diction, in this essay I attempt to situate her fiction in a historical context that included the rise of anthropology and a vogue for primitivism among the educated classes.

9   Ezra Pound, *Selected Letters, 1907–1914* (New York: 1971), 12; T. T. Munger, *The Appeal to Life* (Boston, 1887), 33–4; T. J. Jackson Lears, "From Salvation to Self-realization," in *The Culture of Consumption: Critical Essays in American History, 1880–1980,* ed. Richard Wight Fox and T. J. Jackson Lears (New York: Pantheon, 1983), 6, and Lears, *No Place of Grace: Antimodernism and the Transformation of American Culture, 1880–1920* (New York: Pantheon, 1981); Frank Norris, *Responsibilities of the Novelist* (New York: Doubleday, 1903), 7.

10 Eric J. Sundquist, "Introduction: The Country of the Blue," in *American Realism: New Essays,* ed. Eric J. Sundquist (Baltimore: Johns Hopkins University Press, 1982), 13; William Graham Sumner, *Folkways* (1907; rpt. New York: Arno, 1979), 36, 38; William James, *The Principles of Psychology,* vol. 1 (1890; rpt. New York: Dover, 1950), 121–2; John Dewey, *Human Nature and Conduct* (New York: Holt, 1922), 32; Claude Lévi-Strauss, "The Anthropologist and the Human Condition," in Claude Lévi-Strauss, *The View from Afar,* trans. Joachim Neugroschel (New York: Basic, 1985), 34.

11 On Wharton's reading, see Lewis, *Edith Wharton: A Biography,* 56, 108, 230, as well as *The Letters of Edith Wharton,* ed. R. W. B. Lewis and Nancy Lewis (New York: Simon & Schuster, 1988), 146, 15; Wharton's description of Malinowski's work and her comment on the "inward relation to reality" appear in *Letters,* 546 and 102; Emile Durkheim, *Selected Writings,* ed. and trans. Anthony Giddens (Cambridge: Cambridge University Press, 1972), 232.

12 Pierre Bourdieu, *Outline of a Theory of Practice,* trans. Richard Nice (New York: Cambridge University Press, 1977), 233, 168; Lionel Trilling's description of manners appears in "Manners, Morals, and the Novel," in Lionel Trilling, *The Liberal Imagination* (New York: Scribner, 1950), 206.

13 Bourdieu, *Outline of a Theory of Practice,* 169.

14 E. B. Tylor, *Primitive Culture,* vol. 1 (1871; rpt. New York: Putnam, 1920), 1.

15 See Lears, "Roots of Antimodernism: The Crisis of Cultural Authority during the Late Nineteenth Century," Chap. 1 in Lears, *No Place of Grace,* 4–58.

16 Robert Lowie, *Are We Civilized? Human Culture in Perspective* (New York: Harcourt, Brace, 1929), 48; Bronislaw Malinowski, *Argonauts of the Western Pacific* (1922; rpt. Prospect Heights, Ill.: Waveland, 1984), 10.

17 Bronislaw Malinowski, *The Sexual Lives of Savages in North-Western Melanesia* (1929; rpt. Boston: Beacon, 1987), 13.

18 Philip Fisher, *Making and Effacing Art: Modern American Art in a Culture of Museums* (New York: Oxford University Press, 1991), 29.

19 "Culture or Civilization, taken in its wide ethnographic sense, is that complex

whole which includes knowledge, belief, art, morals, law, custom, and any other capabilities and habits acquired by man as a member of society" (Tylor, *Primitive Culture*, vol. 1, p. 1).

20   *Letters of Edith Wharton*, 547; on the culture of incorporation, see Alan Trachtenberg, *The Incorporation of America: Culture and Society in the Gilded Age* (New York: Hill & Wang, 1982).

21   Lears, *No Place of Grace*, 6.

22   This is the title of one of Malinowski's monographs, which I cite in note 23.

23   Bronislaw Malinowski, *Crime and Custom in Savage Society* (1926; rpt. Totowa, N.J.: Rowman & Allanheld, 1985), 100.

24   Malinowski, *Crime and Custom*, 72, 100.

25   Lears, *No Place of Grace*, 137.

26   Malinowski, *Crime and Custom*, 103.

27   Lears, *No Place of Grace*, 137.

28   Wharton, manuscript, "Subjects and Notes (1918–1923)," 1, in the Wharton Archives, Beinecke Library, Yale University.

29   Wharton, First Donnée Book, 101, in the Wharton Archives, Beinecke Library, Yale University.

30   Wharton, quoted in *Letters of Edith Wharton*, 159.

31   Wharton, *In Morocco* (New York: Scribner, 1920), vii.

32   Wharton, *In Morocco*, 52–6.

3

ELIZABETH AMMONS

Edith Wharton and the Issue of Race

This chapter investigates two things. It looks at erasure of race in Wharton's writing, the ostensible nonexistence of race as a category despite the fact that Wharton lived at a time and led her life in such a way that racial difference was an inescapable part of life. Second, it is about the actual, important presence of race as a category in Wharton's work once we pay attention to her inclusion of color and, even more subtle, her representation of whiteness as racial. (That is, this essay asks readers to move beyond the dominant-culture practice of defining race only as that which belongs to nonwhites.) To paraphrase Toni Morrison in *Playing in the Dark: Whiteness and the Literary Imagination* (1992), my first concern might be expressed: What do we make of Edith Wharton's positing her "writerly self" as "unraced" – without racial signification – in a culture obsessed with racial designation?[1] My second might be phrased: How does our reading of Wharton and of Wharton texts change when we understand whiteness not as nothing, or as an absence, but as the presence of constructed racial meaning?

Because the topic I am addressing – the rhetoric and function of race in Edith Wharton's writing – is large and complex, I have not attempted an exhaustive analysis in this essay. Rather, my goal is to call attention to the need to examine the topic in Wharton. My overarching argument is that we must refuse to continue to approach her work as if race is not an operative category within it. To provide an example of where such investigation has led my own thoughts, I will focus on her published letters, her memoir *A Backward Glance* (1934), and three novels: *The House of Mirth* (1905), *Summer* (1917), and most briefly, *The Age of Innocence* (1920). But any text or groups of texts could be explored. Indeed, many studies are needed in order to bring fully to the surface the ways in which race functions in Wharton's fiction.

Wharton's published letters show that she agreed with the standard, white, racist generalizations and stereotypes of her day. Writing to Sara Norton in

1905 about her visit to the Vanderbilt mansion, the Biltmore, in Asheville, North Carolina, she remarks without a hint of disapproval: "Alas, that it is so far from everything & that beyond the park, as James said, there is only 'a vast niggery wilderness.' I hope you had a good Christmas, all of you, & that your father keeps well."[2] Equally blithe, in a 1914 letter to her friend Bernard Berenson she makes condescending reference to "the little Ctesse Kayserling, who seems a sweet ingenuous little philosopheress, with charming Chinese eyes" (*Letters*, 313). Her 1925 letter to F. Scott Fitzgerald praising his anti-Semitism in *The Great Gatsby* (1925) is well known: "It's enough to make this reader happy to have met your *perfect* Jew" (*Letters*, 482). Even in a volume known for its exclusion of her racism,[3] Wharton's letters display her easy comfort with dominant-culture racial attitudes.

In particular, Wharton's letters show the link between her casual racism and the colonial perspectives of her era. In addition to criticizing "stupid Italians" for not appreciating their own art and culture (*Letters*, 77), Wharton in several letters relies on tropes that draw their energy from common racializing theories contrasting the civilized with the uncivilized and white people with "natives." A love letter to Morton Fullerton in 1908, for example, casts erotic desire in a colonial metaphor of economic manipulation and exchange. Wharton compares herself to the "simple native" in contrast to her lover, the experienced white trader:

> And I'm so afraid that the treasures I long to unpack for you, that have come to me in magic ships from enchanted islands, are only, to you, the old familiar red calico & beads of the clever trader, who has had dealings in every latitude, & knows just what to carry in the hold to please the simple native – I'm so afraid of this, that often & often I stuff my shining treasures back into their boxes, lest I should see you smiling at them!   (*Letters*, 135)

Representing her own sexual desire as colonized – unsophisticated, vulnerable, laughable – Wharton uncritically reiterates empire's essential racist paradigm, that of the (dark) "simple," erotic, feminized "native" wishing to be dominated (sexually, economically) by the clever white man. Such images of orientalized sexuality perfectly illustrate Edward Said's argument about Orientalism as a constellation of values that are not authentically Eastern but reflect instead the West's exoticized fantasy creation of an "East" to serve its own racist agenda of promoting and supporting European dominance.[4] Wharton, for instance, reads Tunis in 1914 literally through the text of the *Arabian Nights:* "As for this place, it's a cauldron of 'louxoure' (as d'Annunzio says), & one can't take two steps in the native quarter, the amazing, unbelievable bazaars, without feeling one's self in an unexpurgated page of the Arabian Nights!" (*Letters*, 318). Boiling heat, luxurious-ness, "natives," sumptuous commercial exchange (the "unbelievable ba-zaars"), freedom from censorship (the "unexpurgated page"), and lush, erotic textuality (the *Arabian Nights*) merge in a stereotypic image of entic-ing, dark, slightly dangerous, racial space located in northern Africa – a region just outside the boundaries of cool, repressed, European culture, yet still under its command. Invoking similarly eroticized, racialized tropes in a letter from Tunis a few days later, Wharton exclaims about how much money she is spending on precious perfumes in the bazaar. She then says: "But that was nothing to our buying a so-called ambergris necklace from a 'coloured' prostitute in the bazaars at Sfax!! It appears that to be seen with one of these fragrant baubles in one's hands is to lose one's reputation forever. – When we came back I told Anna of my purchase, & said: 'These chaplets are said to make the negresses irresistible to the Arabs'" (*Letters*, 320). Associating herself imaginatively with the commercialized sexuality of black women that she has herself constructed (the representation of pros-titutes and "negresses" here is as much an act of fiction as any passage in one of her novels), Wharton both produces and consumes the thrill of vicarious sexual transgression. Projected, forbidden, erotic pleasure is cre-ated by stirring together totally predictable ingredients of culturally color-coded sex, gender, geography, and commerce.

Such passages in Wharton's letters, as well as in her travel narrative, *In Morocco* (1920), confirm that her world included people of color and that she was no different from most other white people of her generation in the racism she felt comfortable expressing. If her published letters betray rela-tively few expressions of crude bigotry, showing her more inclined to conde-scension and exoticizing, this may reflect her attitudes, or it may have to do with the Lewises' protective editing. In either case she embraced racist atti-tudes. That those attitudes appear to have been ordinary and nonobsessive simply suggests how "white" she chose to make her life, how deeply she immersed herself in a world of protective white privilege, heavily buttressed by class, that allowed her not to think much about race – even as she wrote about it.

That writing is my concern here: Wharton's construction of whiteness, in fiction after fiction, as the dominant racial category. What is the relation, for example, between *The House of Mirth*'s status as a best seller in 1905 and its intensely racial plot, in which the whitest of white women, literally named "Lily," whose task is to perform the beauty of Anglo-Saxonness in a tableau vivant, is better off dead than married to a Jew? Or, how do we read Wharton's rewrite of the same plot in *Summer* (1917), where the heroine is *not* the whitest of whites but, instead, a dark, sexual young woman literally from beyond the pale of civilization, who is forced into marriage against her will with an old white man (named "Royall") in whose custody she has lived and whom she hates? Or, in what ways is the exile of dark, "exotic" Ellen Olenska in *The Age of Innocence* (1920) a coded racial story about forbidden white male sexual desire during Reconstruction? Underlying such specific questions are sweeping ones. How does Wharton conceptualize and position whiteness and white privilege in her fiction? What political agendas do her scripts of overdetermined whiteness serve? Where does "color" occur? As a category, "whiteness" is meaningless without racialization of figures who do not fit the category and therefore set it in relief; so her fiction, we know, must inscribe the not-white. Where and how?

Before venturing answers, it is necessary to think about race in general. As contemporary theorists point out, race does not exist as a fixed, stable category or concept. It changes over time, plays different roles in different cultures and for different people within any given culture, and is invented to serve complex social and political ends. As Michael W. Apple explains, in summarizing the argument of Omi and Winant's *Racial Formation in the United States* (1986):

> Race is not an essence. It is not "something fixed, concrete and objective."
> Rather, race needs to be seen "as an unstable and 'decentered' complex of
> social meanings constantly being transformed by political struggle." The
> stress . . . on race not as thing but as a set of social meanings is key here.[5]

This emphasis on social construction is important to any thinking about race as a category of analysis. Race is a fiction, simply an idea, a human invention. At the same time, as Omi and Winant explain, dominant-culture racial mythology in the United States has a strong investment in calling race nothing but an idea and thereby denying its reality, saying – because it is "just" an idea – race does not really matter.

> The notion of a colorblind society where no special significance, rights or
> privileges attach to one's "race" makes for appealing ideology. . . . Yet even a
> cursory glance at American history reveals that far from being colorblind, the
> United States has been an extremely "color-conscious" society. From the very
> inception of the Republic to the present moment, race has been a profound
> determinant of one's political rights, one's location in the labor market, and
> indeed one's sense of "identity."[6]

Inherent in the very notion of "race" in the United States, in other words, is dominant-culture duplicity: denial of the importance of race, on the one hand, and, on the other, fierce investment in its maintenance as a fundamental category of difference. Precisely this doubleness, I will argue, is what we see in Wharton's fiction: denial and investment. Or, to phrase it differently, we repeatedly see in Wharton's work erasure camouflaging insistent reinscription.

Before turning to Wharton, however, let me emphasize that in any theorizing about race as an arbitrary construction and therefore itself a fiction, it is crucial to stress that the effects of the fiction of race are not fictitious but real. I underline this as a caution against academic theory, which can (or can seem to) reason away what actual people actually experience. The economic, psychological, emotional, and political effects of racism are everywhere present and felt in the United States. It does not matter that biological and other scientific attempts to define and therefore validate the physical reality of "race" all fail. Racialization as a social force still has real effects on real people's lives. Thus, even as theory identifies race, in the words of Henry Louis Gates, Jr., as "the ultimate trope of difference because it is so very arbitrary in its application" and so completely unverifiable in its alleged biological bases,[7] we need to bear in mind the following. Saying that race, like gender, is a "fiction" means it is a social invention. It does not mean that the felt effects of either are not real.[8]

Additionally, in order to think about the formation of racial identity in Edith Wharton's fiction, it is also important to think, even if very briefly, about textuality and contextuality. Whereas it used to be possible to conceptualize literary realism, the mode to which Edith Wharton was most drawn, as a fairly simple process of a text reflecting its world, that binary model – the world as stable and unitary, with fiction as a kind of equally stable and unitary mirror held up to it – has become profoundly complicated.[9] More persuasive today is the idea that literary realism creates the reality it then says it reflects. As Frederic Jameson puts it, the realistic novel engages in "the task of producing as though for the first time that very life world, that very 'referent' . . . of which this new narrative discourse will then claim to be the 'realistic' reflection."[10] Moreover, this textual production of a supposedly real world, as is true of any created text, is itself inseparable from what cultural studies, in the words of David Bathrick, describe as "a complex of differing histories": an almost impenetrable interrelationship among author, commerce, audience, text, literary tradition, popular ideology, and so forth.[11] The literary text we read, then, is not an isolated, coherent, self-contained, fictive "reflection" of the world. It is an unstable, interactive site of multiple cultural inscriptions and multiple interpretive possibilities, some traceable to an author's conscious "intentions" but others completely outside authorial control or even knowledge.

Approached from a cultural studies perspective, Edith Wharton's construction of whiteness in books such as *The House of Mirth, Summer,* and *The Age of Innocence* reveals her intense engagement with dominant-culture racial ideology in the early decades of the twentieth century. As Omi and Winant observe, "In each epoch of US history, a certain school of racial theory has been dominant, serving as the racial 'common sense' of its age. For much of our country's history, explicitly racist theories have played this role."[12] Certainly that was true at the turn of the century, when the explicitly racist theories in control were biologistic and imperialistic, and grew out of nineteenth-century social Darwinism and eugenics. Theorists applied Darwin's principle of natural selection to groups of people selected on the basis of skin color, geography, and culture, and to human civilizations. The conclusion they reached (which was also the premise, hence a nice tautology) was that some peoples and some civilizations had evolved more than others and were therefore superior. At the top of this hierarchical evolutionary ladder of "race" were, not surprisingly, in the scientific opinion of the Anglo-Saxon scientists producing the theory, Anglo-Saxons.

We know that Edith Wharton read and admired these social Darwinist race theorists. Writing about her earlier reading in her memoir *A Backward Glance,* she tells us that her friend Egerton Winthrop's "chief gift was to introduce me to the wonder-world of nineteenth century science. He it was who gave me Wallace's 'Darwin and Darwinism', and 'The Origin of Species', and made known to me Huxley, Herbert Spencer, Romanes, Haeckel, Westermarck, and the various popular exponents of the great evolutionary movement."[13] This list of scientists mixes elite and popular nineteenth-century race theorists who deployed Darwin's concept of evolution in analyses attempting to rank and categorize people according to some measurable physical sign of "race." The most famous, of course, was the man Wharton names second, Herbert Spencer, who argued that natural selection was "nature's indispensable method for producing superior men, superior nations, and superior races." Influenced by Spencer, other scientists tried to produce physical evidence to prove him right. When craniometry (measuring people's heads) failed, advocates such as Huxley and Haeckel, both of whom also show up on Wharton's list, studied human hair (which, of course, also failed).[14]

Despite material science's inability to corroborate social Darwinist racial theorizing, historical events by the turn of the century both displayed and were designed to produce precisely the kind of white supremacy that Spencer and his followers propounded. U.S. expansion in the nineteenth century (especially at the end of it) into Mexico, the Philippines, Native American lands, Puerto Rico, Hawaii, and Samoa exhibited, and at the same time constantly kept producing and reproducing, dominant-culture belief in western European, and more specifically Anglo-Saxon, racial superiority. Dark-skinned people, whether in traditional Lakota lands on the North American continent or on an island in the Pacific, fell under white, U.S., imperial rule because it was their manifest (racial) destiny to be defeated and then governed by whites. As the historian Thomas Gossett explains, "By the time of the Spanish-American War [1898], the idea of race superiority had deeply penetrated nearly every field – biology, sociology, history, literature, and political science. Then there was no doubt whatever concerning the name of the race. . . . Anglo-Saxon."[15] Although a few well-known white writers such as Mark Twain and William Dean Howells objected (rather quietly) to imperialist expansion, most white U.S. authors supported it, some, such as Frank Norris, Jack London, and Owen Wister, with great enthusiasm. And even among opponents, very few white people disputed its racist ideological foundation. From Theodore Roosevelt, president of the United States from 1901 to 1909 and an admired friend of Edith Wharton, to all the leading mainstream magazines of the time, several of which were Wharton's publishers – *Harper's, Scribner's, Century, Lippincott, McClure's* – U.S. imperialism based on the argument of Anglo-Saxon racial superiority was heartily embraced.[16] As Wharton's biographer R. W. B. Lewis notes, she was no exception. Wharton supported U.S. aggression in the Spanish-American War, regarded Theodore Roosevelt as "the model statesman," and despised Woodrow Wilson for his reluctance to involve the United States in the First World War.[17]

Although Wharton's participation in the racialized thinking of her era shows up in many places, perhaps none is more striking than her recollection, in *A Backward Glance,* of the two African American cooks employed by her parents when she was a little girl. The passage is remarkable because it so clearly shows how Wharton creates blackness in order to constitute whiteness. She visualizes very early in her remembered life and then in her autobiographical book the blackness that makes whiteness possible. Then, for the rest of the book, as in most of her writing, she can fall silent on the topic. Blackness having been invoked to establish whiteness, the representation of race is no longer needed; whiteness can be taken for granted. Additionally, the passage is important because it suggests how unquestioningly Wharton, from childhood on, linked whiteness, nationalism, and the beauty of privileged women in the West.

Wharton's description of the two African American cooks is an act of exoticizing, a rendering so exaggeratedly colorful that it vividly exemplifies what Toni Morrison calls "Africanism." Similar to Said's argument about Orientalism, Morrison's concept of Africanism refers to the West's creation of Africa out of its own imagined, psychologically and politically motivated need to have Africa be wildly different, "primitive," and subjugatable. Africanism has functioned for white people, in Morrison's view, reflexively: "It provided a way of contemplating chaos and civilization, desire and fear, and a mechanism for testing the problems and blessings of freedom."[18] Appearing in the third chapter of her memoir, Wharton's Africanism grounds the concept of whiteness, specifically Anglo-Saxonness, that defines her text. The two cooks function much as the black figures do in Manet's famous painting *Olympia* or Ingres's *L'Odalisque á L'Esclave,* in which a dimly visible black servant attends a prominently displayed white woman. That is: Without the presence of backgrounded "blackness," how could we see the foregrounded "whiteness"? How could we create and confirm hierarchy without both present? From an imperialist perspective, "white" as a meaningful social category demands the construction and social investment of "black" as its contrasting, subordinate category. (The same principle is at work in the production of gender or sexuality. What does "man" mean if we do not create the category "woman"? or "heterosexual" without "homosexual"?) The dominant culture must create and socially invest "black" (or "yellow" or "red" or "brown") as a significant racial category in order for "white" to carry meaning – as we see perfectly in Wharton's description of the cooks.

Worth providing in full, the passage begins toward the end of a paragraph about food. We meet the Jones family's

two famous negro cooks, Mary Johnson and Susan Minneman. These great artists stand out, brilliantly turbaned and ear-ringed, from a Snyders-like background of game, fish and vegetables transformed into a succession of succulent repasts by their indefatigable blue-nailed hands: Mary Johnson, a gaunt towering woman of a rich bronzy black, with huge golden hoops in her ears, and crisp African crinkles under vividly patterned kerchiefs; Susan Minneman, a small smiling mulatto, more quietly attired, but as great a cook as her predecessor.

Ah, what artists they were! How simple yet sure were their methods – the mere perfection of broiling, roasting and basting – and what an unexampled wealth of material, vegetable and animal, their genius had to draw upon! Who will ever again taste anything in the whole range of gastronomy to equal their corned beef, their boiled turkeys with stewed celery and oyster sauce, their fried chickens, broiled red-heads, corn fritters, stewed tomatoes, rice griddle cakes, strawberry short-cake and vanilla ices? I am now enumerating only our daily fare, that from which even my tender years did not exclude me; but when my parents "gave a dinner", and terrapin and canvas-back ducks, or (in their season) broiled Spanish mackerel, soft-shelled crabs with a mayonnaise of celery, and peach-fed Virginia hams cooked in champagne (I am no doubt confusing all the seasons in this allegoric evocation of their riches), lima-beans in cream, corn souffles and salads of oyster-crabs, poured in varied succulence from Mary Johnson's lifted cornucopia – ah, then, the *gourmet* of that long-lost day, when cream was cream and butter butter and coffee coffee, and meat fresh every day, and game hung just for the proper number of hours, might lean back in his chair and murmur "Fate cannot harm me" over his cup of Moka and his glass of authentic Chartreuse.

I have lingered over these details because they formed a part – a most important and honourable part – of that ancient curriculum of house-keeping which, at least in Anglo-Saxon countries, was soon to be swept aside by the "monstrous regiment" of the emancipated: young women taught by their elders to despise the kitchen and the linen room, and to substitute the acquiring of University degrees for the more complex art of civilized living. The movement began when I was young, and now that I am old, and have watched it and noted its results, I mourn more than ever the extinction of the household arts. Cold storage, deplorable as it is, has done far less harm to the home than the Higher Education.

And what of the guests who gathered at my father's table to enjoy the achievements of the Dark Ladies? I remember a mild blur of rosy and white-whiskered gentlemen, of ladies with bare sloping shoulders rising flower-like from voluminous skirts. . . . A great sense of leisure emanated from their kindly faces and voices. (*Backward Glance*, 829–30)

This "allegoric" passage merges Africanism, white privilege, antifeminism, and elite capitalist consumerism into one dense, literally delicious encomium to Anglo-Saxonism. Exoticized black women with their turbans and hoop earrings disappear into devourable food physically – their "blue-nailed hands" becoming hard to separate from the piles of edible flesh around them – and metaphorically: the catalog of recipes and dishes usurps their space in the text, takes over their place. In effect, they *become* the food. Or perhaps the food becomes them? In either case, black women are rendered consumables in this passage.

To be sure, Wharton's announced reason for including Mary Johnson and Susan Minneman in *A Backward Glance* is to memorialize their genius. In reading the passage we should not ignore that declared intention of praise nor the very real accomplishment of the two "real" women who worked for the Jones family. They no doubt were brilliant cooks, and Wharton no doubt genuinely loved eating their food. My point here has to do with the way Wharton uses them to racialize her text. Through her constructed version of the two women, Wharton produces a lavish, mouth-watering Africanism controlled and governed by elegant white women, whose "house-keeping" – the smallest social unit in the establishment of the idea of state or nation – she celebrates as the sine qua non of "Anglo-Saxon countries." Put another way, in this passage racism, antifeminism, and nationalism merge for Wharton in an allegory about well-fed, gorgeous, premodern childhood (her own) as a time of physical and aesthetic satiety provided by black women. Their labor (and it *was* labor to prepare all the food described by Wharton, especially in an era preceding modern conveniences) enables the leisure and grace – the decorative, kind-voiced, sweatless superiority – of the text's Anglo-Saxon elite. The black women's presence makes possible Wharton's rosy, white-whiskered gentlemen relaxing around her father's table in the company of their sloping-shouldered, flowerlike, white, female complements.

Wharton's representations of Mary Johnson and Susan Minneman appear early in *A Backward Glance* precisely so that they can disappear. Their visibility leads directly into an attack on "emancipation," literally translatable as women's liberation but also, because of the term chosen, evoking black freedom, which is inseparable from Wharton's constitution of whiteness. That is, Wharton's longing for the good old days of black women in the kitchen defines, in one important way, what her antifeminism is about. Conservative, dominant-culture ideologies of race, gender, and class synchronize to offer a seemingly effortless account of how natural, how spontaneous, how beautiful (recall those sloping shoulders) white privilege is. The Dark Ladies' job done – elite Anglo-Saxonness established – they and all references to people of color can, indeed must, disappear. White superiority having been constituted, it needs (from the white point of view) to dominate the text/the world invisibly and unchallenged.[19]

The black figures visible (even if only briefly) in *A Backward Glance* are the missing signifiers in *The House of Mirth*, the erased racial presences that Lily Bart's overdetermined whiteness can take for granted. This 1905 best seller does not need to show us the black women in the kitchen who make ultra-whiteness possible. Lily's name; her drastic difference from the "sallow-faced girls in preposterous hats" swarming through Grand Central Station ("Was it possible that she belonged to the same race?")[20]; her choosing to configure herself in a tableau vivant of a Sir Joshua Reynolds portrait; and, above all, her resistance to marrying a Jew, perform the crucial work of racializing her. All of these identify Lily Bart not simply as white, but *very* white – the apex of white, which is to say, in turn-of-the-century U.S. racial theory: Anglo-Saxon.

As an ideal, Anglo-Saxonness at the turn of the century had to surmount some resistance even among whites. As Gossett points out, before the Spanish-American War two wars with England had made most Americans and much American policy emphasize the differences between the two countries. But as England's imperial power began to weaken at the end of the nineteenth century, making alliance with America desirable, the United States, needing support in its confrontation with Spain, was equally eager for allies. Hence the British political leader Joseph Chamberlain's argument, in May 1898, for transatlantic Anglo-Saxon racial solidarity: "There is a powerful and generous nation, speaking our language, bred of our race, and having interests identical with ours. I would go so far as to say that, terrible as war may be, even war itself would be cheaply purchased if in a great and noble cause the Stars and Stripes and the Union Jack should wave together over an Anglo-Saxon alliance."[21] Endorsed on both side of the Atlantic, this idea of Anglo-Saxon unity, presupposing definition of the United States *as* Anglo-Saxon and tightly linking dreams of empire, theories of racial superiority, and definitions of U.S. nationhood – bore the imprimatur of the (aptly named) White House.[22]

Though unremarked in the criticism, the colonial subtext of *The House of Mirth,* published at the height of turn-of-the-century U.S. imperialist ambitions, should not surprise us. Although the story is American – Lily Bart and the other central characters are American – the book's stage is global. Lily and company are as at home in Europe as in the United States; Mrs. Gormer travels to Alaska; Lawrence Selden takes off for South America. Rich white people in Wharton's novel make not just the United States but the whole world their playground. They move about on their large map as if they own it all – which, of course, is the point. They do. Privileged, wealthy, white: most of the characters in *The House of Mirth* exhibit a casual, easy proprietorship toward any land they set foot on. They are psychologically entitled, by virtue of race and class privilege. The Trenors, Dorsets, and so on never question their right to sweep into any corner of the world, impose their notions of culture and civilization, buy off the locals, and set up temporary or permanent residence. As Edward Said has remarked: "Imperialism after all is an act of geographical violence through which virtually every space in the world is explored, charted, and finally brought under control."[23]

Against this backdrop of unlimited geographical access and control, *The House of Mirth* reiterates the standard, modern, patriarchal, Western, marriage plot, which is thrown into fierce internal conflict by Wharton's diametrically opposed allegiance to gender on the one hand and race on the other. As an economically independent woman writing during an intensely feminist era about the desire of a fictitious woman, Lily Bart, not to barter herself in marriage and thus become the human capital of a man, Wharton writes against the grain of the patriarchal master plot, repeatedly refusing to subject her heroine to marriage.[24] However, as a typically racist white person writing during a period of pronounced Anglo-Saxon hegemony, Wharton simultaneously inscribes a different and quite antiliberatory tale, one of Anglo-Saxon purity to the death (literally). The terrible fate escaped in this book, finally, is not marriage, but marriage to a Jew: the union of beautiful, pure, upper-class, Anglo-Saxon Lily Bart to the shiny, Semitic invader.

One of the most important signs of Lily's Anglo-Saxonness is the tableau vivant she chooses. At first she plans to pose as the eighteenth-century Italian artist Giovanni Battista Tiepolo's *Cleopatra*, the dark-haired North African ruler painted by him in the Palazzo Labia in Venice. But then she changes her mind; she decides to be Reynolds's *Mrs. Lloyd*, the significance of which lies both in the canvas and in the painter. Reynolds's Mrs. Lloyd, filmily clad and pictured in the act of writing her husband's name on a tree, arouses mingled fantasies of sexual desire and proprietorship in Lily's male voyeurs, especially Selden. Even more important, however, and totally unlike Cleopatra, whose sexual allure would be equally strong, Mrs. Lloyd (like her creator, Reynolds) is unquestionably, purely white. Indeed, she epitomizes Anglo-Saxonness.

The painter of *Mrs. Lloyd*, Sir Joshua Reynolds (1723–92), regarded English national virtues and universal human virtues as one and the same, a collapsed ethic neatly produced by and in turn reproducing Anglo-Saxon superiority.[25] Thus, evocation of his portrait in *The House of Mirth* both communicates and affirms whiteness as universal ideal humanness. The trope of Lily's tableau vivant fuses Anglo-Saxonness, nationalism, and universality into one breathtaking vision/version of racialized, idealized female beauty, perfectly figured by her displayed white flesh, of which we are permitted to see more in this scene than in any other in the book. Moreover, Lily does not merely impersonate *Mrs. Lloyd*; she *is* Reynolds's image. "She had shown her artistic intelligence in selecting a type so like her own that she could embody the person represented without ceasing to be herself. It was though she had stepped, not out of, but into, Reynolds's canvas, banishing the phantom of his dead beauty by the beams of her living grace" (*Mirth*, 141–2). What Reynolds's *Mrs. Lloyd* stands for – nationalized Anglo-Saxon "natural" dominance – Lily embodies. Expressly designed for the purpose, the tableau exhibits for the visual consumption of her audience both within and without the covers of the book Lily Bart's dazzling, overdetermined whiteness.

Diametrically opposed to this whiteness is the man who wishes to secure his position in the uppermost regions of the American upper class by possessing Lily, Simon Rosedale. Read racially, Lily's eluding his grasp – her not becoming his wife – is one driving force of Wharton's novel. The book is about the snow-white heroine, the flower of Anglo-Saxon womanhood, not ending up married to the invading Jew.

Wharton's characterization of Rosedale reproduces many of the standard stereotypes of Jews prevalent in the United States at the turn of the century.[26] He is shiny, ostentatious, intrusive, vulgar, and pushy. He first appears as "a small glossy-looking man with a gardenia in his coat" – the white flower on his lapel conveniently telegraphing his desire to acquire and display the human flower in the book – and his venality and acquisitiveness find rapid reinforcement in his ocular consumption of Lily: "Mr. Rosedale stood scanning her with interest and approval. He was a plump rosy man of the blond Jewish type, with smart London clothes fitting him like upholstery, and small sidelong eyes which gave him the air of appraising people as if they were bric-a-brac" (*Mirth*, 14). Drawing with ease on turn-of-the-century racializations that associated Jews with Asians, Wharton gives Rosedale "small sidelong eyes" (which she will later refer to as "small stocktaking eyes" [*Mirth* 268]),[27] and she repeatedly states that he is fat, showy, and "glossy" (14, 266, 304), referring to his "plump jewelled fingers" (266), "the pink fold of skin above his collar" (313), his conspicuous fur overcoat (304), and the way he impresses Lily as "gross, unscrupulous, rapacious" – like a "predatory creature" (261). This animalizing of Rosedale – the emphasis on his eager, fleshy, sexually predatory presence – taps anti-Semitic stereotypes *and* throws both Selden and Lily into lofty, hyper-Anglo-Saxon relief. In direct proportion to the extent to which Rosedale becomes greasy, hot, and sexually aggressive, they become cool, reserved, and sexually subtle. Rosedale operates much like the dark-backgrounded figures in the Manet and Ingres canvases. To rephrase the question I asked earlier about the two Africanized cooks in Wharton's memoir: How would we know just how white – how superwhite – Lily and Selden are without Rosedale to set off their sweatless pale perfection?

Rosedale's racial identity is explicitly referred to several times in *The House of Mirth*. We are told that he has the "mixture of artistic sensibility and business astuteness which characterizes his race" (17). We learn that he has "the instincts of his race" (127). We discover that he has "the tradition of his blood to accept what was conceded" (187). Clearly, his function in the book is to be the Jew. He is the outsider, the carrier of race whose presence sets in relief Anglo-Saxonness, showing us its supreme superiority, and his designs on Lily reveal what is at stake. Even though she decides late in the novel to marry this man, Wharton will not let that happen. She preserves the racialized master plot of white fiction (as opposed to the real-life plot of white society, which has practiced the opposite for centuries) that says death is preferable to interracial sex.

The House of Mirth's investment in white purity also gets underscored in the celebration of white motherhood with which the novel concludes. In addition to suggesting sororal bonds across class lines, the scene is heavily racially encoded, for procreation – imagining the next generation – is always what racial ideology comes down to. When Lily Bart dies holding to her breast a fantasy infant daughter she has invented out of her vision of Nettie Struther's maternity, the book not only declares her death beautiful, holy, pure; it also gives us a final vision of Lily as virgin white mother. Moreover, just before this death, Lily rearranges her trunk, laying her gauzy white Reynolds gown on top, thus reminding us again of the tableau, Anglo-Saxon to the core, that she so perfectly performed. Regardless of what Wharton's character might choose in a weak moment (Lily's offering herself to Rosedale as his wife), her plot, as we see in this highly staged finish, reiterates the fact that it is better – more beautiful, purer – to die than to end up married to a Jew. To do the latter, Lily would have to contaminate herself by committing an immoral act (using the letters to blackmail Bertha Dorset). Refusing, she dies uncorrupted in both senses; she does not use the letters, she does not make the marriage. Anglo-Saxon purity – unsullied virginal whiteness – is defended and preserved to the end.

The inversion of this plot, in *Summer,* only underscores how, when pushed to choose, Wharton's racial and class allegiances overpowered her gender ones. In this novel, published a dozen years after *The House of Mirth,* it is the heroine, Charity Royall, who is racialized as dark, wild, uncivilized, sexual, and in need, finally, of strong, white, Anglo-Saxon governance and control. Read only in terms of its gender configuration, the novel criticizes the dismal marriage into which Charity is forced. Wharton indicts the social structure that offers poor, uneducated, rural women few or no options for independence and self-determination.[28] Read in light of its racial implications, however, *Summer* tells a different tale. Competing against its feminist plot is a colonial one, a narrative in which the dark female from dangerous territory lying just outside the boundaries of white patriarchal control is brought under the white man's authority by completely ancient means. Lied to and impregnated by one privileged white man, Lucius Harney, Charity is forcibly married to the book's other powerful white male, the lawyer Royall. He personifies the ruling order, has been Charity's paternal guardian, once tried to rape her, has for all of her life been the man she loathed, and now will be her husband. Royall, in short, represents white authority, patriarchal tradition, and incest; and it is he, in the end, to whom Charity and the child to whom she will give birth are legally bound.

The difference in Wharton's treatment of her two heroines is dramatic: Lily, her Anglo-Saxon paragon, is not permitted to marry Simon Rosedale, a Jew; Charity, her swarthy sexual woman from "uncivilized" territory, is forced to marry the white lawyer Royall. Perhaps the difference is accidental. Or maybe it simply reflects a conservative shift in Wharton's attitudes between the early 1900s and the late teens about women and motherhood, particularly as a result of her experiences during the First World War.[29] But there is also a racial explanation. The difference between the two heroines' fates reflects consistency on Wharton's part. Refusal to marry her pure white Lily to an invading Jew and insistence on marrying her dark promiscuous Charity (case) to a great white father are flipsides of the same plot. Written during the First World War, a war about European borders but also about European colonial authority in other parts of the world, *Summer,* even more than *The House of Mirth,* participates in white colonial discourse. The book is about white law and order in the person of the old white man (*Royall*) finally gaining complete and supposedly benevolent control over the rebellious, sexual, dark young woman literally from a wild place (the Mountain) just beyond the borders of civilization. Surely Edith Wharton's enthusiastic response to a friend's praise of Royall – "I'm so particularly glad you like old man Royall. Of course, *he's* the book!" (*Letters,* 398) – reflects not merely class and age affinity (she was fifty-five when she published *Summer*) but also racial identification with this white man whose dominance (pathetic as it is) depends on mastery of someone darker.

Both of these novels assert and preserve white racial supremacy. In *The House of Mirth* the threatening orientalized male (Rosedale) is not allowed to invade Anglo-Saxon bloodlines and thus establish a paternity that is Semitic. In *Summer,* the threatening dark female (Charity) is not allowed to remain a single mother and therefore originate her own line but is, instead, forced to marry the most powerful white man around. In both books the hegemony of whiteness is displayed. In each, the heroine's tale takes second place, finally, to the narrative of race.

Other Wharton texts in which race constitutes an important, buried narrative suggest themselves. Approached racially, what significance might we find in the overdetermined darkness of Zeena Frome in *Ethan Frome?* Is her heavily orientalized name – Zenobia – simply ironic, or might it be a clue to this furious, powerful, destructive, dark woman's racialized negativity in

Wharton's famous horror story? Likewise, is the blatantly orientalized Ellen Olenska in *The Age of Innocence* (1920) – with her dark hair, sumptuous low-cut gowns, and seductively close, dim, draped rooms – ejected from the American leisure class not simply because she is female, artistic, and sexy but because she is *dark,* female, artistic, and sexy?[30] We can read Ellen's story, appearing as it does in a novel published one year after the terrible race riots of the summer of 1919 and set during the period all Americans knew as the Reconstruction, as a parable about white racist hysteria. As such, we might very well interpret it as a tale about the ruling class's refusal to let in a dark woman whose painful past, deep knowledge of human cruelty, and brilliant creativity threaten to shake the very foundations of white patriarchy. Moreover, I have to wonder: Does this hidden race narrative explain Martin Scorsese's otherwise inexplicable refusal, in 1993, to follow Wharton's color coding in his film of the novel, his willful casting of Ellen as a blond and May as dark-haired? Reversing Wharton's script, Scorsese effectively unwrites it, showing himself to be as frightened and resistant to its implied study of race – its tale of worn-out white power clinging to its exclusionary supremacy – as his utterly obedient pale hero, Newland.

I think that the importance of race in Wharton's writing has not received attention for at least two reasons. First, she herself masterfully created the fiction that race was not one of her subjects. Second, her critics – most of them, like her (and me), white people – have been happy to support that fiction. To do otherwise requires changing our perspective on Edith Wharton. We can no longer think of her as a major woman writer or major American writer or major novelist of manners but, instead, as a major white woman writer, white American writer, white novelist of manners. To return to Toni Morrison's concept: Edith Wharton wrote as a raced writer. That means, given her class, historical era, and personal values, that she enjoyed tremendous white privilege, which is inscribed in her texts, and that she is thoroughly implicated in standard turn-of-the-century racist and colonial attitudes and rhetorics, which also permeate her writing. Recognizing race as a subject in Edith Wharton's work – an inquiry which, I need to emphasize, this essay only begins – represents an important step (even if a disconcerting one to some readers) in redefining her within a multicultural U.S. literary-historical context.

NOTES

1 Morrison asks: "What does positing one's writerly self, in the wholly racialized society that is the United States, as unraced and all others as raced entail?"

Playing in the Dark: Whiteness and the Literary Imagination (Cambridge, Mass.: Harvard University Press, 1992), xii.

2 *The Letters of Edith Wharton,* ed. R. W. B. Lewis and Nancy Lewis (New York: Scribner, 1988), 101. Quotations from the letters in my essay are from this volume, cited hereafter in the text.

3 The Lewises, who selected for publication four hundred out of four thousand or more letters, decided to exclude letters with racist and anti-Semitic content, a choice which has been the subject of criticism. The following exchange is transcribed from a conference on Wharton letters:

R. W. B. LEWIS: We tried to be fair to her, to represent her life fully. Occasionally, she expressed some prejudices that we wish she didn't have. In a few of the letters we rejected, there are some racist or anti-Semitic remarks. There was one letter that we originally planned to include that did contain some vilely anti-Semitic comments.

NANCY LEWIS: Actually, the publisher persuaded us not to use the letter. Our editor contacted us and said that if we included this letter, it would be the only some [one] to get attention.

R. W. B. LEWIS: That's right. The publisher thought that letter would overshadow all the others in the media and that it would be wrong to include an atypical letter that could distort the public view of Wharton.

"Lewises Discuss the Letters: R. W. B. Lewis and Nancy Lewis on *The Letters of Edith Wharton,* Highlights from a Question and Answer Session," ed. Alfred Bendixen, *Edith Wharton Newsletter* 6 (Spring 1989), 1.

4 See Edward Said, *Orientalism* (New York: Random House, 1978).

5 Michael W. Apple, "Series Editor's Introduction" to Michael Omi and Howard Winant, *Racial Formation in the United States from the 1960s to the 1980s* (New York: Routledge, 1986), x.

6 Omi and Winant, *Racial Formation,* 1.

7 Henry Louis Gates, Jr., "Writing 'Race' and the Difference It Makes," *Critical Inquiry* 12 (Autumn 1985), 5.

8 As Diana Fuss states, "Clearly it is no more adequate to hold that 'race' is itself merely an empty effect than it is to insist that 'race' is solely a matter of skin color." Fuss then enjoins: "What is called for is a closer look at the production of racial subjects, at what forces organize, administer, and produce racial identities." See *Essentially Speaking: Feminism, Nature and Difference* (New York: Routledge, 1989), 92.

9 Good book-length discussion can be found in Amy Kaplan, *The Social Construction of American Realism* (Chicago: University of Chicago Press, 1988).

10 Frederic Jameson, *The Political Unconscious: Narrative as a Socially Symbolic Act* (Ithaca, N.Y.: Cornell University Press, 1981), 152.

11 David Bathrick, "Cultural Studies," *Introduction to Scholarship in Modern Languages and Literatures* (New York: Modern Language Association of America, 1992), 335.

12 Omi and Winant, *Racial Formation,* 5.

13 Edith Wharton, *A Backward Glance* (New York: Appleton-Century, 1934),

reprinted in *Edith Wharton: Novellas and Other Writings,* ed. Cynthia Griffin Wolff (New York: Library of America, 1990), 856. Hereafter cited in text.

14 Thomas F. Gossett, *Race: The History of an Idea in America* (Dallas: Southern Methodist University Press, 1963), 145.

15 Gossett, *Race,* 311.

16 For extended discussion see Gossett, *Race,* especially chapter 9. Also, informative discussion of turn-of-the-century racial attitudes and ideologies can be found in George Fredrickson, *The Black Image in the White Mind* (New York: Harper Collins, 1971), and James Kinney, *Amalgamation! Race, Sex, and Rhetoric in the Nineteenth-Century American Novel* (Westport, Conn.: Greenwood, 1985).

17 R. W. B. Lewis, *Edith Wharton: A Biography* (New York: Harper & Row, 1975), 139, 6, 329, 374.

18 Morrison, *Playing in the Dark,* 7.

19 Richard Dyer develops this idea at length in an excellent discussion of how the constituted invisibility of whiteness in film is strategic. As Dyer says, "the invisibility of whiteness . . . masks whiteness as itself a category. White domination is then hard to grasp in terms of the characteristics and practices of white people" (50). "White," *Screen* 29 (1988), 48–68.

20 Edith Wharton, *The House of Mirth* (New York: Scribner, 1905), reprinted in *Edith Wharton: Novels,* ed. R. W. B. Lewis (New York: Library of America, 1986), 5. Cited hereafter in text.

21 Gossett, *Race,* 324–5.

22 For extensive discussion, see Gossett, *Race,* especially chapter 13.

23 Edward Said, "Yeats and Decolonization," *Remaking History,* ed. Barbara Kruger and Phil Mariani (Seattle: Bay Press, 1989), 13.

24 I develop this argument about *The House of Mirth* at length in *Edith Wharton's Argument with America* (Athens, Ga.: University of Georgia Press, 1980); I discuss women writers in general, including Wharton, in *Conflicting Stories: American Women Writers at the Turn into the Twentieth Century* (New York: Oxford UP, 1991).

25 See John Barrell, "Sir Joshua Reynolds and the Englishness of English Art," *Nation and Narration,* ed. Homi K. Bhabha (New York: Routledge, 1990), 154–76.

26 See John Higham, *Send These to Me: Immigrants in Urban America,* 2nd ed. (Baltimore: Johns Hopkins University Press, 1984), or Michael N. Dobkowski, *The Tarnished Dream: The Basis of American Anti-Semitism* (Westport, Conn.: Greenwood, 1979).

27 For an excellent discussion of anti-Asian racism at the turn of the century, which included Jews among those identified as "yellow," see Susan S. Lanser, "Feminist Criticism, 'The Yellow Wallpaper,' and the Politics of Color in America," *Feminist Studies* 15 (1989), 415–41.

28 I argue this at length in *Edith Wharton's Argument with America,* chapter 5. I also discuss *Summer* in "The New Woman as Cultural Symbol and Social Reality: Six Women Writers' Perspectives," *1915: The Cultural Moment,* ed. Adele Heller and Lois Rudnick (New Brunswick, N.J.: Rutgers University Press, 1991), pp. 82–97; and I talk about Wharton's colonial outlook and racism in my introduction to the Penguin paperback edition of *Summer* (1993).

29 See Ammons, *Edith Wharton's Argument with America,* chapters 6 and 7.

30 I discuss Ellen as dark, sexual, and artistic – but do not think of her as a racialized character – in an earlier essay, "Cool Diana and the Blood-red Muse: Edith Wharton on Innocence and Art," *American Novelists Revisited: Essays in Feminist Criticism,* ed. Fritz Fleischmann (Boston: Hall, 1982), 209–24.

4

ELAINE SHOWALTER

Spragg: The Art of the Deal

No one knows where he comes from, but suddenly there he is in Apex, Kansas – first behind the counter at Luckabuck's Dollar Shoe Store, then at the office of the coal merchants, then at the Apex Water Works. Quickly he becomes "a leading figure in the youthful world of Apex," and, despite some scandals, he is clearly a man of destiny.[1] "Great men," as he notes, "always gravitate to the metropolis," (696), so, though he is red and glossy and balding and swaggering, he makes it to New York. His rise goes beyond the meteoric stage to a kind of stability:

> It was said that he had bought a house in Seventy-second Street, then that he meant to build near the Park; one or two people . . . had been to his flat in the Pactolus, to see his Chinese porcelains and Persian rugs; now and then he had a few important men to dine at a Fifth Avenue restaurant; his name began to appear in philanthropic reports and on municipal committees (there were even rumours of his having been put up at a well-known club); and the rector of a wealthy parish, who was raising funds for a chantry, was known to have met him at dinner and to have stated afterward that "the man was not wholly a materialist." (925)

As he becomes ever more successful, indeed a billionaire, he develops "a growing passion for pictures and furniture" and a burning "desire to form a collection which should be a great representative assemblage of unmatched specimens" (976). His goal is "to have the best . . . not just to get ahead of the other fellows, but because I know it when I see it" (976).

His wife is a fashion plate, with magnificent reddish-gold hair, who spends most of her time "in the scientific cultivation of her beauty" (980) and in patronizing the dressmakers, milliners, society artists, and jewelers. Her natural milieu is a hotel, whether the Nouveau Luxe in Paris or the Engadine Palace in Saint Moritz. For their wedding, he gives her a check for a million dollars and a ruby necklace and tiara that belonged to Marie Antoinette; they travel endlessly but live in a house on Fifth Avenue which is an exact copy of the Pitti Palace, and in a Paris hotel where hangs Van

Dyck's *Gray Boy* and the Louis Quinze tapestries from the Chateau at Saint Desert.

They could come from the "Style" section of the Sunday *New York Times* or from Donald Trump's first memoir and how-to-succeed-in-business guide, *Trump: The Art of the Deal,* but of course they are Elmer Moffatt and Undine Spragg, from *The Custom of the Country.* Set from about 1900 to 1912, Wharton's novel seems uncannily familiar as a portrait of the mythology of class in the American 1980s as well. Trump's very title seems Whartonesque, and for the literary critic it is a startling intertextual moment when he notes that "if you were going to make a career in business, Wharton was the place to go. . . . the real entrepreneurs all seemed to go to Wharton."[2]

The Art of the Deal reads like raw material for a Wharton novel. Here one finds made-to-order Wharton characters like Alice Mason, "the real estate broker who has managed to turn herself into a major socialite by getting the hottest people to come to her parties"; Trump's beauteous and competitive wife, who runs his chain of hotels and casinos without salary but for all the dresses she can buy; their Palm Beach estate, Mar-a-Lago, bought cheaply from the heiress Marjorie Merriweather Post, with its 118 rooms, 36,000 Spanish tiles, and Dorian marble walls; and Manhattan luxury skyscraper, Trump Tower, "as close as you're going to get, in the twentieth century, to the quality of Versailles." Trump is of course most eloquent on the subject of deal making: "Deals are my art form. Other people paint beautifully on canvas or write wonderful poetry. I like making deals, preferably big deals. That's how I get my kicks."[3]

The Custom of the Country is a book about the peculiar art of the American deal, from dilettantish aestheticism to blunt acquisitiveness, and its relations with other and more traditional forms of art. Elmer Moffatt, Ralph Marvell exclaims in a rare moment of insight, is "the kind of man who develops slowly, needs a big field, and perhaps makes some big mistakes, but gets where he wants in the end. Jove, I wish I could put him in a book! There's something epic about him – a kind of epic effrontery" (790). This is ironic, for Ralph is the least likely person in the novel to record the doings of an Elmer Moffatt, but Wharton is fascinated by Moffatt's art of the business deal and appreciates its heroic qualities. She calls him "Homeric" and compares him to Othello, and, although these references are perhaps more mock epic than genuine, they nonetheless imply respect. As Elizabeth Ammons says, *The Custom of the Country* is "one of America's great business novels,"[4] and Robert Caserio is correct when he claims that "the thoroughly amoral young financier Elmer Moffatt" is "Wharton's major contribution to the creation of the type of great financial and political man that dominates the heyday of American realism."[5]

In 1986, Wharton's Old New York and Trump's New New York came together at the John Singer Sargent exhibit at the Whitney Museum. The outer galleries were given over to the display of Sargent's large society portraits, usually of young women about to be married or exquisitely groomed matrons with their dogs or their children. Huge, glossy, filled with expensive objects, antique furniture, and elaborate clothes, the paintings are clearly about money, marriage, and ownership, and they were viewed by a fashionable New York crowd in Armani jackets and Lagerfeld furs who seemed to be their doubles and twins. Sargent's society painting is the literalized art of the deal, the representation of the moneyed and leisured worlds behind aesthetic appreciation.

Wharton knew Sargent well; he may have been the model for both the society painter Paul Morpeth, in *The House of Mirth,* and the more savagely depicted Claud Walsingham Popple, the "court" painter of Fifth Avenue in *The Custom of the Country.* Whereas Moffatt's deals depend on a psychological penetration that make him so much like a novelist that Ralph wonders "what intrinsic barrier divided the two arts" (795), Popple's "art" depends very much on the skills of the businessman and the restaurateur. Wharton describes Popple's work as "chafing-dish art" and his studio as "never too much encumbered with the attributes of his art to permit the installing . . . of an elaborately furnished tea-table" (745). Popple is the ideal society painter, for "the 'messy' element of production was no more visible in his expensively screened and tapestried studio than its results were perceptible in his painting" (745). Similarly, the dilettantish and dreamy Ralph, with his fantasies about writing poetry, begins to write only after he loses his illusions and learns how to get down to work.

The tough worldliness and unremitting satire of *The Custom of the Country* has always made it a difficult novel for Wharton's critics to accept. Harold Bloom, for example, although he calls *The Custom of the Country* "Wharton's strongest achievement," confesses that he finds it "rather an unpleasant novel to reread."[6] Janet Malcolm, describing the "satiric surrealism" of the novel, calls Wharton "an artist from whom we shrink a little."[7] Much of this critical revulsion centers on Wharton's antiheroine, Undine Spragg, rather than on the tycoons behind her. According to Cynthia Griffin Wolff, the women of this society could sell only their bodies and thus, in the eyes of the reader, "the women all seem more hideously disfigured than their male counterparts in the money game."[8] Undine seems far worse than Elmer, although his deals with "parties" and "shares" and shadowy victims are far more ruthless than hers. Similarly, Elizabeth Ammons notes, the female counterpart to the American robber baron is denied the battleground of Wall Street but "is given her own stock exchanged."[9]

It is in this regard that the discourse of gender in the book is most intriguing. Citing Wharton's analysis that Moffat "used life exactly as she [Undine] would have used it in his place," many feminist critics have argued that Undine is an Elmer manqué, or rather, that Elmer is what she might have become if she had been born male. Marilyn French calls him Undine's "alter ego, her male self," and argues that only the accident of being born female in a male-dominated society had held her back.[10] Wolff has argued that the very genre of Wharton's novel was a masculine one; "Horatio Alger's myth in all its manifestations was for men, not for women. The new captains of industry were men, and the literature that celebrated their conquest was a saga of active men and passive women."[11] She concludes that "this is an epic for men only and Undine cannot live it"; she has the energy "needed to conquer life" but "has been debarred from the victory by reasons of sex."[12] In her introduction to the novel, Wolff argues that "a woman almost never obtained success in business because the stock market was closed to her – corporate business of any kind was closed to her, as was business in general. It was unthinkable that a woman might match wits and stamina against men! Thus Undine Spragg with her restless, dissatisfied ambition and her independent, quick mind had no opportunity to exercise these attributes."[13] Wharton herself inscribes this ideology in her book, often through the remarks of the Marvell family friend, Mr. Bowen. "Why haven't we taught our women to take an interest in our work?" he asks. "Simply because we don't take enough interest in *them*" (757). If the men around her took more interest in women, critics suggest, Undine might learn how to function in the real, the business, world, and would not have to live vicariously through her marriages.

It is true that Undine feels that Elmer and she speak the same language, or at least that he understands *her*. "Here was some one," she thinks with relief at Saint Desert, "who spoke her language, who know her meanings, who understood instinctively all the deep-seated wants for which her acquired vocabulary had no terms" (975). In this novel, where Elmer and Undine finally run off together aboard the *Semantic,* sharing a common language means a great deal, and even if Undine does not follow all the details of Moffatt's plans, still "every Wall Street term had its equivalent in the language of Fifth Avenue" (976).

I would argue, nonetheless, that more than gender differentiates Undine Spragg from Elmer Moffatt, and that a male Undine Spragg would not be a great tycoon. First of all, despite Charles Bowen's speech and the many restrictions placed on women in the business world, in many respects Undine's American society is far more egalitarian with regard to gender than English or French society of the same period. In contrast, Rosamund Vincy in *Middlemarch,* an antiheroine of an earlier British society to whom Undine has been frequently compared, is thoroughly excluded from her husband's professional society and deliberately shielded from its financial side. Although Wharton tells us that the lives of women and men are very different, she depicts a world that is unusually heterosexual and heterosocial. The successful men in *The Custom of the Country* choose women as their friends and companions, rather than relying on Clubland, the masculine world of bonding and business that shuts women out. Ralph confides everything to his sister (who indeed controls most of the family's money) and to Clare Van Degen; Undine maintains friendships with a number of men which are much more lasting and substantive than her alliances with women.

On numerous occasions, men confide the details of their business transactions to women, and Undine is quick to catch on. She agrees to use her social connections to help Elmer Moffatt's career in exchange for his silence about their marriage and pays him off with a timely introduction to Ralph. She keeps quiet while Ralph gets involved in Elmer's shady real-estate deal, since the money will enable her to get to Paris to pursue Peter Van Degen. At Elmer's suggestion, she demands custody of her son Paul from Ralph, hoping that Ralph will buy her off with enough money to enable her to purchase a papal annulment and free her to marry Raymond de Chelles.

Moreover, Undine is a hard-headed pragmatist who quickly sizes up the realities of a situation. As Ralph perceives, when she suggests that he ask his sister for the money he needs, "it was always she who made the practical suggestion, hit the nail of expediency on the head. No sentimental scruple made the blow waver or deflected her resolute aim" (730–1). When Peter Van Degen refuses to marry Undine, she hocks his pearls to go after the next man. She negotiates a deal for the de Chelles tapestries – a deal Raymond must eventually accept – although, in the moral terms of the novel, this deal symbolizes her inability to understand the importance of French traditions and family honor.

Surely Undine is clever and ruthless, but cleverness and ruthlessness alone do not make the epic figure of the tycoon. We can see some of her limitations by comparing her to the heroine with whom she has most frequently been linked, Thackeray's Becky Sharp. Undine, writes Janet Malcolm, "is Becky Sharp stripped of all charm, spirit, and warmth, the adventuress pared down to her pathology, but a pathology that is invested with a kind of magical malignancy."[14] Harold Bloom notes that Undine, while "not quite of the eminence of Thackeray's Becky Sharp," has "an antithetical greatness about her," qualities of "force, drive, desire, and a cold splendor."[15] Cynthia Wolff is unusual in seeing Becky Sharp at a narrative disadvantage compared to Undine:

> The reader is meant to reject, perhaps even condemn, Becky Sharp's callous moral depravity, and by the end of the novel her sinfulness has been punished (she is left leading the sleazy life of a demi-mondaine); her moral opposites are Dobbin and Amelia, whose ultimate marriage marks the triumph of honor and goodness. By contrast, there is no moral center in *The Custom of the Country,* no major character who acts for goodness and righteousness. Certainly, there is no foil for Undine's terrific force.[16]

Indeed, Wharton was obviously influenced by *Vanity Fair.* She admired Thackeray and praised especially "the dense social turmoil of *Vanity Fair*" and the "dramatic intensity" of the triangle of Becky, Rawdon, and Lord Steyne, which "stands out from the rich populous pages, and gathers up into itself all their diffused significance."[17] The actress Minnie Maddern Fiske had a great success as Becky Sharp in the stage version that toured the United States in 1899, written by Langdon Mitchell, the son of Wharton's doctor, S. Weir Mitchell, and Paul Pickrel has observed that "no other novel of Victorian England has occupied as large a place in the American imagination as *Vanity Fair.*"[18] Wharton pays tribute to it in *The Custom of the Country,* especially with regard to Undine's treatment of her son and her triangle with Ralph Marvell and Peter Van Degen. But Wolff's comparison of Becky and Undine both overstates the degree to which the reader condemns Becky and ignores Thackeray's ironic treatment of Amelia and Dobbin, echoed in Wharton's novel by the more sentimentalized Ralph and Claire. Undine has many of Becky's worst qualities, but she lacks Becky's spirit, irreverence, and humor, and Wharton's novel as a whole lacks the social, ethnic, and racial density of Thackeray's. Similarly, in Margaret Mitchell's *Gone with the Wind,* a novel influenced by Wharton and Thackeray both, Scarlett O'Hara has a shrewd business sense and a capacity for hard work beyond anything Undine achieves. Unlike either Becky or Scarlett, Undine is never forced to confront real hardship or to fight for her survival. She is always a comic character, whose marriages, her "experiments in happiness" (939), allow Wharton to analyze the class systems and stratospheres of America and France.

Ultimately, in *The Custom of the Country,* both class and gender are determinants of survival at the top. Indeed, to cut your deal as a woman in Wharton's world, and to emerge with dignity, it is necessary to be an aristocrat. The Princess Estradina, another "Lili," chooses her lovers and her friends but maintains a fierce loyalty to family. In contrast to *The House of Mirth*, among others of Wharton's novels, *The Custom of the Country* has no sympathetic or even three-dimensional working-class women characters. The closest is Mrs. Heeney, the manicurist and masseuse. Mrs. Heeney is a likable Dickensian figure who also acts as a chorus to advance the plot, through her readings from the gossip columns, social notes from all over, and clippings from New York tabloids that she carries with her in a voluminous bag. But she is given no life or room of her own. Other parvenus and workers get even shorter shrift, especially if they are Jewish. Indeed, a kind of reflex anti-Semitism is one of the customs of the country that Undine never quite gets the hang of, although Wharton's irony falls upon her rather than upon the Old New Yorkers or French aristocrats who instruct her in it. Harry Lipscomb finds out that the handsome "Austrian" riding master who courts her in Central Park is really a Pole named Aaronson with a shady past in Cracow; Ralph is terribly agitated when Undine befriends "a Russian lady of cosmopolitan notoriety," whom she, in what he considers a vulgar lapse of etiquette, calls "the Baroness" but he, in a usage he evidently regards as well-bred, calls "the Adelschein" (726). Raymond de Chelles is mortally offended when Undine invites a "small swarthy" London art dealer named Fleischhauer to see the famous tapestries (971).

Unlike Becky Sharp or Elmer Moffatt, Undine does not see through the affectations and pointless snobbery of the world to which she aspires. Her first forays into New York society are intellectually embarrassing, as she displays her ignorance about painting and theater and praises "Sarah Burnhard" in "Fade" (645–6). But educating herself through newspapers like the *Radiator* and the *Town Talk* and through observing people at parties and concerts, Undine quickly realizes that "it's better to watch than to ask questions" (664). She rapidly discards Mabel Lipscomb's model of the nouveau riche, noticing that Mabel was "monumental and moulded while the fashionable were flexible and diaphanous, Mabel strident and explicit while they were subdued and allusive" (664). So too she discards and sees through other friends along her way without really developing a style of her own. At the end of the novel, Wharton writes that Undine "had everything she wanted, but she still felt, at times, that there were other things she might want if she knew about them" (1012). While Freud asks, "What do women want?", Wharton replies, "What have you got?" Undine's desire is a question of opportunity, exposure, and imitation.

In contrast, Elmer Moffatt projects "the sense of being detached from his life, in control of it, and able, without weakness or uncertainty, to choose which of its calls he should obey" (994). Wharton gives Elmer many qualities Undine does not share. In addition to a "large powerful" (796) intelligence, and "soaring self-confidence" (989), he has a genuine disdain for religious piety and social cant. His drunken performance at the Apex temperance supper and his cheerful disdain for its aftereffects are unequaled by anything Undine would ever contemplate. Elmer sees that the New Yorkers are also pretentious and self-congratulatory in their tastes, and he is tolerant of but basically bored by Undine's social ambitions. (In this respect, too, he sounds uncannily like the real thing – Donald Trump, who writes, in his second book, *The Art of Survival,* "In my opinion, the social scene – in New York, Palm Beach, or anywhere else, for that matter – is full of phonies and unattractive people who often have done nothing smarter than inherit somebody else's wealth – the Lucky Sperm Club, I call it.")[19] Moreover, Elmer has the capacity to respond with kindness to children, especially to male children, whereas Undine sees in her son only the signs of her own aging.

Most important of all, from Wharton's point of view, Elmer has an aesthetic sense that is more than restlessness, brute acquisitiveness, or greed. When Undine takes him around Paris to buy collectibles, she is aware that he has a sensual as well as a financial response to art: "The things he looked at moved him in a way she could not understand, and . . . the actual touching of rare textures – bronze or marble, or velvets flushed with the bloom of age – gave him sensations like those her own beauty had once roused in him" (994).

Undine herself is utterly without aesthetic sensibilities, and for Wharton this is the unpardonable sin. From the very beginning of the novel, Wharton satirizes Undine's fascination with the cheesy artistic pretensions and secondhand ideas of Claud Walsingham Popple: "His conversation struck her as intellectual, and his eagerness to have her share his thoughts was in flattering contrast to Ralph's growing tendency to keep his to himself" (747). Ralph Marvell seems to speak for Wharton when he patronizingly thinks that Undine's mind "was as destitute of beauty and mystery as the prairie schoolhouse in which she had been educated . . . and her ideals seemed to Ralph as pathetic as the ornaments made of corks and cigarbands with which her infant hands had been taught to adorn it" (718).

It was virtually impossible for Wharton to find anything beautiful that came from American culture. As she wrote to her friend Sara Norton, "My first few weeks in America are always miserable, because the tastes I am cursed with are all of a kind that cannot be gratified here, and I am not enough in sympathy with our 'gross public' to make up for the lack on the aesthetic side. . . . All of which outburst is due to my first sight of American streets, my first hearing of American voices, and the wild dishevelled back-woods look of everything when one first comes home!"[20] Indeed, Wharton has little but scorn for the possibilities of an American popular culture and national art. She is scathing about the efforts of the Marquise de Trezac (born Nettie Wincher) to cash in on Americanness by resuscitating Creole dishes and patronizing "negro melodists" (941); she mocks Undine's igno-rance in reading "When the Kissing Had to Stop" and enjoying the music hall but sees nothing comic in the New Yorkers' slavish adulation of Eu-ropean high culture. As with Ralph's thoughts, there is obviously much of Wharton's own prejudice in Raymond de Chelles's accusations of Undine's American barbarism: "You come from hotels as big as towns, and from towns as flimsy as paper, where the streets haven't had time to be named, and the buildings are demolished before they're dry, and the people are as proud of changing as we are of holding to what we have" (982).

But Wharton is much more tolerant of Elmer's backwoods grossness than of Undine's Midwest ignorance. She respects the ideals of the men – how-ever pretentious, grasping, impractical, derivative, or stale – much more than those of the middle-class women in the novel. Janet Malcolm has attributed this difference to Wharton's sheer dislike of women. In her essay "The Woman Who Hated Women," Malcolm declared that in Undine "Wharton takes her cold dislike of women to a height of venomousness previously unknown in American letters and probably never surpassed." In her view, Undine "inspires in her creator a kind of loathing that makes the reader nervous, even as it powerfully works on him."[21]

If so, Wharton may be repudiating in Undine something she recognized and feared in herself – perhaps even a naive and vigorous American self, who had to be buried in French phrases and a permanent exile. Created in 1913, the year of Wharton's divorce, Undine is Wharton's "anti-self," as R. W. B. Lewis observed:

> Edith's long yearning for psychological freedom is queerly reflected in Un-dine's discovery that each of her marriages is no more than another mode of imprisonment; and Undine's creator allows more than a hint that the young woman is as much a victim as an aggressor amid the assorted snobberies, tedium, and fossilized rules of conduct of American and, even more, French high society. Above all, Undine suggests what Edith Wharton might have been like if, by some dreadful miracle, all her best and most lovable and redeeming features had been suddenly cut away.[22]

Elizabeth Ammons also comments on the "buried affinity" between Whar-ton and Undine:

Wharton cast Undine as her opposite – ignorant, intrepid, unintrospective – yet also as her twin: Undine's energy, her anger and pride, her love of travel and gorgeous clothing and her impatience with failure and shabbiness – these, although exaggerated and simplified in the fictional character, do bring to mind the author herself.[23]

The opposite of Lily Bart, with her exquisite taste and refined moral sense, too scrupulous finally to survive in the crass social jungle, Undine has no ladylike instincts at all. Yet she and Lily are sisters under the skin, even if Undine's skin is thick and Lily's is thin. In killing Lily Bart, Wharton had killed off both the perfect lady and the "lady novelist" – the Ora Prance Chettle – in herself. It is striking that Undine, who is no lady, acts out many of the impulses that Lily rejects. Both Gus Trenor and Peter Van Degen demand sexual interest, an erotic installment on their loans to Lily and Undine. Yet it is Undine who, irrationally, goes off to live with Van Degen for several months. Again, Lily would literally rather die than blackmail Bertha, whereas Undine plays every card in her hand to get her husbands and to shed them.

As her discussions of Popple and Ralph Marvell make clear, Wharton had come to the point of recognizing that serious art must be messy and destructive, despite its superficial beauty and smoothness. She had found the courage to apply this lesson to her own life and to her writing, and although Undine Spragg Moffatt has to acknowledge that the role of ambassadress is closed to her because of her divorce, in the world of art Wharton had transcended such petty conventions. By this time in her life, she had come to terms with writing as a profession and had made a business of words, and in the dazzling and uncompromising words of *The Custom of the Country*, she inscribes her kinship with the country and countrymen she had left behind.

NOTES

1   *The Custom of the Country* in Edith Wharton, *Novels*, ed. R. W. B. Lewis (New York: Library of America, 1985), 985. All quotations cited in the text are from this edition.
2   Donald J. Trump with Tony Schwartz, *Trump: The Art of the Deal* (New York: Warner, 1987), 77.
3   Trump and Schwartz, *Trump*, 15, 41, 1.
4   Elizabeth Ammons, *Edith Wharton's Argument with America* (Athens: University of Georgia, 1980), 109.
5   Robert Caserio, "Edith Wharton and the Fiction of Public Commentary," *Western Humanities Review* 40 (1986), 191–2.
6   Harold Bloom, introduction to Bloom, *Edith Wharton* (New York: Chelsea, 1986), 1–3.

7   Janet Malcolm, "The Woman Who Hated Women," *New York Times Book Review* (November 16, 1986), 12.
8   Cynthia Griffin Wolff, *A Feast of Words* (New York: Oxford University Press, 1977), 249.
9   Ammons, *Argument,* 107.
10 Marilyn French, introduction to Edith Wharton, *The Custom of the Country* (New York: Berkley, 1981), xxvi.
11 Wolff, *Feast of Words,* 244.
12 Wolff, *Feast of Words,* 229–30.
13 Cynthia Griffin Wolff, introduction to Edith Wharton, *The Custom of the Country* (New York: Macmillan [Collier], 1987), xiii.
14 Malcolm, "Woman Who Hated Women," 12.
15 Bloom, introduction, 3.
16 Wolff, introduction, ix.
17 Edith Wharton, *The Writing of Fiction* (New York: Scribner, 1924), 143, 136.
18 Paul Pickrel, "Vanity Fair in America: *The House of Mirth* and *Gone with the Wind*," *American Literature* 59 (1987), 37.
19 Donald Trump with Charles Leershen, *Trump: The Art of Survival* (New York: Warner, 1990), 68.
20 *The Letters of Edith Wharton,* ed. R. W. B. Lewis and Nancy Lewis (New York: Scribner, 1980), 80.
21 Malcolm, "Woman Who Hated Women," 11.
22 R. W. B. Lewis, *Edith Wharton: A Biography* (New York: Harper & Row, 1975), 350.
23 Ammons, *Argument,* 98.

5

GLORIA C. ERLICH

The Female Conscience in Edith Wharton's Shorter Fiction: Domestic Angel or Inner Demon?

Despite apparent similarities, Edith Wharton's hyper-moral female characters differ in important ways from the domestic angels of sentimental fiction. That tradition, basically religious in origin, exalted woman as the finer sensibility and moral conscience of her family, an idealization that persisted well into the era of literary realism. It was still alive by the early twentieth century, when Edith Wharton was emerging as a novelist of manners – manners, that is, as indices of moral codes. Although Wharton retained the guardian role for wives, she did so for other than sentimental reasons. Indeed, the fanatically moral female characters that we examine here (primarily in *Sanctuary, The Touchstone,* "Bewitched," and "Afterward") seem more demonic than angelic. Wharton's representation of women as moral arbiters was doubtless supported by literary convention, but her tyrannical female consciences stem from a personal psychological source – the internalized voice of her own mother.[1]

The Whartonian conscience, both implacable and female, was what today might be called an "introject," or internalized image, of the "bad mother" of object relations theory. According to Melanie Klein, the founder of this school of psychoanalysis, an infant normally experiences its mother as split between the longed-for good mother, a source of infinite satisfaction, and the bad mother whose occasional unavailability generates infantile rage. In healthy development, the two polarized figures are eventually integrated into a single realistic image of a human mother containing both good and bad traits, one whose nurturance inevitably entails some degree of frustration. When this synthesis fails to occur, internalized mother figures may dominate the psyche with what feels like demonic power.[2]

When the normal intrapsychic "good mother–bad mother" split is ratified and intensified by real-life experience of mothering divided between two separate women, such as a mother and a nanny, the likelihood of later integration or synthesis of the sundered maternal attributes is greatly reduced. For many of those who experience divided mothering, the gentle nurturing qualities cluster permanently around one of the two mother fig-ures, the dangerous or threatening qualities around the other. In such cases, the polarized female attributes fail to fuse into a realistic image of mother as a whole woman with both positive and negative attributes.[3]

I believe that this is what happened with Edith Wharton. Her earliest attachments were split between a biological mother and a psychological mother, the latter being a loving Irish nanny named Hannah Doyle. A major contention here, more fully developed in my *Sexual Education of Edith Wharton,* is that the emotional split between mother and nanny initiated a fundamental and recalcitrant psychic split that was reflected not only in Edith Wharton's delayed sexual awakening and virtually celibate marriage but in her narrative structures as well. Even though nanny rearing was customary for a girl of Edith Wharton's time and social class, receiving primary care from a surrogate mother modifies a child's relationship to its biological mother. What is customary is not necessarily without signifi-cance.

In memoirs Wharton described her mother as cold, reproving, and re-mote, the nanny as benign and loving – the source of all warmth and comfort. This division between two actual mothering figures created a rift that left all the nurturant and positive aspects of mothering with the nanny, relegating to Lucretia Jones, the biological mother, only the negative aspects – domination, intrusiveness, power to injure. Once Lucretia Jones became inscribed in Edith's imagination as the bad mother, repair of the mother–daughter relationship seemed almost impossible.

Doyley's very virtues altered the balance of forces within the Jones family. She became a standard of comfort against which Lucretia Jones looked inadequate to her daughter. Responding with all her grateful love to Doy-ley's nurturance, young Edith must have failed to give Lucretia signals that would have stimulated her maternal impulses and elicited warmer re-sponses. A negative cycle was generated between mother and daughter, with the mother reacting to the child's rejection, the child allowing negative imagery to fill the sacred maternal space. Lucretia came to seem like the God of Calvinism – vigilant, omnipresent, and unappeasable. Edith felt a monumental need to placate her, a need so powerful that she offered up her own sexuality on the altar of this angry deity.

The fear of being thought unclean appears to have driven out whatever sexual knowledge Edith had picked up through her friends, her experience, and her extensive reading. She would not allow herself even to *think* what-ever her mother decreed to be "not nice." Believing that mother could monitor her most private thoughts, she effectively banished sexual knowledge from her mind. She convinced herself that "married people 'had children' because God saw the clergyman marrying them through the roof of the church!"[4] The illusion of maternal omniscience generated such exaggerated compliance, such extreme scrupulosity, that her entire sexual nature – feelings along with knowledge – was driven underground. As I argue more fully elsewhere, the kind of sexual ignorance that Wharton professes in the fragmentary memoir "Life and I" probably owes as much to her own repression as to her mother's prudery. Edith was exposed to the usual stimuli that arouse sexual inquiry, and she was too curious and intelligent not to have pieced together at least a rough idea of "the facts of life."

Despite maternal vigilance, Edith was able to pursue certain kinds of erotic activity outside of direct maternal surveillance. Discouraged from expressing her sexual curiosity, she conducted her own investigations, permitting herself a lively fantasy life that probably included incestuous yearnings and may have led to self-stimulation. Given the omniscience that she attributed to her mother, she must have felt that she was being observed even in the "secret garden" of her fantasy and judged herself guilty for any substitute erotic gratifications.

This guilt centered on a particular locale, her father's library, which was a typical Victorian gentleman's collection of classics in literature, philosophy, and travel. Here, sitting on her father's lap, she reveled in the rhythms of the poetry he read to her. Here, where she learned to read and later was free to range through all books except contemporary novels, young Edith sought knowledge that she could not get elsewhere, primarily sexual knowledge, that she was to hide from her mother and even from herself.

She developed a rapturous relationship to the written word, to which her beloved father had introduced her. His library became a "secret garden," a locus of virtually ecstatic experiences, from the sensuous pleasures of luxurious bindings to those of the expanding imagination.

> Whenever I try to recall my childhood it is in my father's library that it comes to life. I am squatting on the thick Turkey rug . . . dragging out book after book in a secret ecstasy of communion. . . . There was in me a secret retreat where I wished no one to intrude. (BG, 69–70)

And from young Edith's sexual exploration and sexual excitement in her father's library derives the centrality for her of the library as a locus of illumination about the forbidden aspects of life that she was later to banish from conscious awareness.

"Life and I" speaks of "excruciating moral tortures" (1072) as a principal characteristic of her childhood.

> I was never free from the oppressive sense that I had two absolutely inscruta-
> ble beings to please – God & my mother – who, while ostensibly upholding
> the same principles of behaviour, differed totally as to their application. And
> my mother was the most inscrutable of the two.   ("Life," 1074)

This image of her mother as a terrifying omnipresent power rendered the actual mother inaccessible for emotional support and ineffective in transmitting a model of capable femininity. Rejecting her mother, Edith willed herself to be unlike Lucretia Jones in important ways. She tried to emulate her mother's elegance but rejected her as model of an adult sexual being.

If her real mother was deceived by Edith's renunciations, the inner one, that Calvinistic god of her own creating, was not. It demanded atonement for her hidden pleasures, so that sexuality would never be possible for her without an element of guilt and punishment. That split-off maternal figure, augmented in power by the child's own self-recriminations, haunted Wharton for the rest of her life. Negotiations with morally exigent mother figures in novellas such as *The Touchstone* and *Sanctuary*, published just after Lucretia's death, are Edith Wharton's trial scripts for revising her relationship with the undying inner mother.

Even before Lucretia's death in 1901, the actual or historical mother had been split off from reality by physical and emotional distance, leaving full mythic potency to the internalized one. But Doyley, the good mother, had outer as well as inner representations. Throughout life Wharton kept by her side a series of beloved housekeepers, continuations of the benign figure of Doyley, that is, working-class women who provided her with reliable emotional support. Because her good-mother representation was thus tempered by reality, it was psychically less powerful than that of the bad mother, whose imago we are tracing here.[5]

Wharton's tendency to psychic splitting found literary expression in her polarization of female characters. On top of conventional fictional polarizations such as fair and dark women, good and bad ones, Wharton added, among others, verbally adept versus inarticulate, sexually ignorant versus sexually sophisticated, and biological versus psychological mothers, such as Charlotte and Delia in "The Old Maid." Most important for present purposes is the distinction between inner and outer mother, the internalized mother figure in contrast to the actual or historical mother.

It was not the historical Lucretia Jones (neither an exemplary mother nor a demonic one) who dominated Edith Wharton's psyche and exacerbated her moral sensibilities but the inner one, demonized by powerful psychic forces. The two novellas that Wharton wrote close to the time of her mother's death in 1901, *The Touchstone* and *Sanctuary,* show extraordinary awareness of this distinction between actual and inner mothers. From the omniscient inner mother who observed all missteps derived the tyrannical female conscience epitomized in *Sanctuary.* In this and other stories, women act as moral barometers whose intense scrutiny persecutes not daughters, as we might expect, but morally weak men. If, as I hypothesize, young Edith's psychic life had been dominated by a persecutory inner mother, we wonder why the author displaced this victimization onto weak-willed husbands and sons (a characterization Wharton applied to her husband Teddy as well as to her father). Quite possibly her way of combating her sense of psychic domination was to create powerful heroines who appropriate the mother's moral vigilance and direct it outward onto others, thereby gaining control of it.

Wharton's psychological and experiential predispositions thus fed into and intensified the received literary tradition of moral purity and produced the intense ethical dilemmas of her fiction. To appreciate this, we must see wherein she differed from her two main precursors in moralistic fiction, William Dean Howells and Henry James. Like them, Edith Wharton tried to distinguish her ethical concerns from the sentimental moralism of nineteenth-century domestic fiction. She too reexamined the ethic of self-renunciation and moral purity, challenging the popular assumption that self-denial is inherently superior to self-fulfillment. Wharton tended to follow Howells in repudiating the sentimental ideal of useless sacrifice in matters of love, but probably exceeded him in placing women in the position of guardian to men of less fastidious conscience and consciousness.

Although Henry James frequently concluded his plots with acts of renunciation, he did not tend to personify the conscience as female. Lambert Strether, in *The Ambassadors,* preserves his moral purity without the help of women, or in spite of them. When he renounces Europe and love, he does so in the belief that he can be "right" only by having "not, out of the whole affair, . . . got anything for myself." To this Maria Gostrey responds pragmatically, "But why should you be so dreadfully right?"[6] Although Kate Croy, in James's *Wings of the Dove,* is prepared to marry Merton Densher on Milly Theale's legacy, Densher keeps his hands clean by renouncing both the legacy and the marriage. In both instances, women operate from a pragmatic morality that contrasts with a male ethic of renunciation, although what these men perceive as ethical purity may be a cover for sexual panic.

Both Howells and Wharton pointedly differentiated their work from sentimental fiction by repudiating high-minded but useless self-sacrifice in favor of minimizing pain. In *The Rise of Silas Lapham,* Howells clearly denounces useless self-renunciation in matters of love by making it the ethic of an invented sentimental novel within the novel *Tears, Idle Tears,* discussion of which allows Howells's characters to debate the issue. But the power of sentimental ideology is such that even Penelope, who ridicules that novel as *Slop, Silly Slop,* has to fight past its ethic of self-denial to free herself to marry the man her sister loves.

Despite this fairly dogmatic dismissal of self-renunciation in love, Howells elevates strict purity where money is concerned. Silas Lapham's commonsense business ethic is insufficiently stringent for his wife Persis, who, with his permission and in accordance with social expectations, acts as his higher conscience. Persis is no better educated than Silas, but she has the female gift of a more refined, that is, more self-denying, ethic. As the higher conscience of the family, Persis holds Silas to a code of purity so excruciating that he must remove "the one spot – the one *speck* – off [him] that was ever there."[7] Doing so causes his financial ruin, but so much the better; the greater the price, the greater the purity. So exigent, so unrelenting, is this female conscience that when their expensive new house, Silas's pride, burns to the ground and she learns it was not insured, she exclaims, "Oh, thank the merciful Lord!" (258).

Where her daughters' marital choice is concerned, Persis Lapham's moral passion is occasionally overruled by her family, but in money matters her values seem generally exempt from the commonsense ethic of the novel. Despite expressions of irony about Persis's excesses, Howells appears to privilege the image of woman as the angelic sensibility and moral guardian of her husband and family. In a delicious piece of businessman's symbolism, Silas names his most refined line of house paint the "Persis brand."

Being a commonsense moralist as well as a connoisseur of renunciation, Edith Wharton sometimes lets this virtue prevail, but with a perceptible difference. In matters of sexual choice, she frequently echoes Howells's economy of pain principle, that is, her texts repudiate the useless sacrifice of one woman's love opportunities for the benefit of another. As a writer in the realist mode, she exposed the flaws of what she called "hopeless love and mute renunciation."[8] Thus, in "The Bunner Sisters" (1916), Ann Eliza's general selflessness and her renunciation of Mr. Ramy in deference to her sister's desire for him results ultimately in her sister's degradation and death. This lamentable outcome forced Ann Eliza to confront "the awful problem of the inutility of self-sacrifice."[9] In *The Mother's Recompense* (1925), Kate Clephane resolves her ethical crisis over her former lover's marriage to her daughter by stifling her revulsion in order to avoid what her minister calls "sterile pain."[10]

"Afterward" (1909), one of Wharton's best ghost stories, is built on an issue of business ethics resembling the moral crux of *The Rise of Silas Lapham*. In both, the husband's ethical lapse lies in taking advantage of a business opportunity that enriched him at another man's expense. An American couple, Ned and Mary Boyne, buy an English country house in the hope that it contains a ghost. It does, but in a most unexpected form. The ghost that eventually materializes is not a spirit connected with the house but one that the Boynes bring with them from their own past – Ned's concealed misdeeds and Mary's obliviousness of them. Ned had made his fortune in a mining speculation, "at the cost of 'getting ahead' of someone less alert . . . who had 'put him on to' " the opportunity. As a legal adviser comments, "I don't say it *wasn't straight,* and yet I don't say it *was* straight. It was business."[11] For this ambiguously crooked action, Ned Boyne is carried off forever by the ghost of the man who lost out in the transaction.

The tale exacts extreme retribution for an event that occurred prior to the narrative present, an act that may in this sense be called "prehistoric." "Afterward" connects to Wharton's moral preoccupations not through depiction of an exigent female conscience but through the author's decree of summary punishment for a prehistoric male misdeed. She renders this through the bewildered consciousness of a woman singularly ignorant of the realities of life. Like many of Wharton's fictional women, Mary Boyne had been so protected from the sordid ways of the world that she was unaware of her husband's business activities and the lawsuit concerning them. "Now, for the first time, it startled her a little to find how little she knew of the material foundation on which her happiness was built" (59). Viewed in this light, the ghost that appears "afterward," or belatedly, can be seen as the return of what Mary had repressed, some knowledge deemed unsuitable for young ladies. Here, as elsewhere in Wharton's fiction, economic ignorance can serve as metaphor for sexual ignorance.[12]

Mary Boyne's enlightenment is rendered in metaphors of illumination – usually of lamps being brought into that central scene of Wharton's consciousness, the library. The maid brings a letter about the controversial mine ownership into the dark library along with a lamp, which first illuminates Ned's face, then the "sharp stamp of worry between his brows." Ned, after reading his mail, which carries news of the dubious business affair, retreats into the shadow of the hearth. As his anxiety increases, the maid enters with a second lamp.

Mary Boyne sees by light delivered by others; she has no lamp of her own, nor does she ever have an opportunity to confront her husband or understand his situation. Instead, a ghostly stranger, the spirit of the wronged man, finds Ned Boyne in his library and leads him away forever. In that same library, Mary learns of her husband's dubious financial dealings from a visiting American lawyer. The library serves as witness to the story's central themes: the shadow of Ned's concealment, the darkness of Mary's ignorance, and her eventual illumination. This book-lined room is the emotional center of the story – the site of accumulated but withheld knowledge, retribution for secret male misdeeds, and a woman's belated education.

Had Ned Boyne returned, perhaps Mary would have joined the few wives to whom Wharton granted the pragmatic wisdom to accept the moral lapses of husbands they love, wives such as those in "The Lamp of Psyche" and "The Letters." More characteristic are women who emanate fierce mental purpose, or "intentionality," women such as Prudence Rutledge in "Bewitched." This wife calls in neighbors to demand the exorcism of a ghost that she insists is bewitching her husband.

"Bewitched" has interesting corollaries with *Ethan Frome* and "All Souls," Wharton's two other stories of lifelessness set in a snowy New England countryside. In all three, the agonized characters dwell remote from others in a frozen landscape. In both "Bewitched" and *Ethan Frome,* the nearest town is named "Starkfield," and the action is prompted by vigilant, almost omniscient, wives.[13] Loaded with images of death, "Bewitched" zooms inward from the frozen landscape of Hemlock County to the town of Ashmore, to the isolated house of Saul and Prudence Rutledge, to a parlor somewhat like a grave, "at once close and cold."[14]

Over the mantle a text declares, "The Soul That Sinneth It Shall Die," and the reader will be surprised to learn which soul incurs that penalty. Relentlessly, Mrs. Rutledge leads her three male guests to the idea that Sylvester Brand's deceased daughter, Ora, has been haunting her husband Saul. Ora had been the daughter of Sylvester Brand and his cousin, a marriage considered "too close" in blood by the rural community. Sylvester's wife wasted away and died, leaving him with two daughters. When Ora became engaged to Saul Rutledge, Brand sent her away in order to separate them. Returning several years later and finding Saul married to Prudence, Ora sickened and died, but Brand still had by his side his favorite daughter, Venny. On their way home the three men encounter the ghost of Ora Brand at the deserted farmhouse where it has been enticing Saul Rutledge for an unholy renewal of the love they had shared before her father drove them apart. Sylvester Brand shoots the specter of Ora, and promptly thereafter the other sister, Venny, dies of pulmonary disease.

In a perceptive reading of the subtext, Barbara A. White locates an analogy between "Bewitched" and the explicit depiction of father–daughter incest in the Beatrice Palmato fragment.[15] Reading one against the other, she argues, quite persuasively, that the hidden destroyer of women in "Bewitched" is the incestuous marriage of Sylvester Brand to his cousin, followed by incestuous relationships with his daughters. If, as Barbara White suggests, Brand was an incestuous father, one may suppose that Ora returns not only to dance with her lost fiancé but to come between her father and Venny, that is, to protect her sister from the abuse she herself had suffered. And because incest victims are usually forced to maintain silence about their abuse, perhaps Ora, whose name suggests "mouth," returns to make manifest, or "speak," the concealed abominations of her family history.[16]

As with other Wharton tales involving vengeance for hidden male misdeeds, the imputed crime is "prehistoric," that is, it occurs long before the narrative present, so long ago that it cannot be fully recovered or clearly represented. The sense of unspeakable prehistoric crimes or causations reinforces the speculation that I make tentatively in *The Sexual Education of Edith Wharton* and that Barbara White makes more positively throughout her study of Edith Wharton's short fiction, that the concealed male sins hovering in the background of many Wharton stories allude to a repressed history of incestuous abuse. Since White offers "Bewitched" and its parallels to the Palmato fragment as partial evidence for this theory, we should notice that Prudence Rutledge seeks vengeance not on her husband for consorting with the ghost of Ora Brand, nor on Sylvester Brand, the purported abuser of daughters, but on the ghost of Ora, the daughter and victim of the alleged abuse.

The atmosphere is a family one, "at once close and cold," in which a relentlessly persecuting wife uncovers a father's hidden sin and demands vengeance on a daughter. The frozen landscape could thus represent the silence surrounding such a sin, which even the story cannot name. We locate it only by following the pointing finger of the displaced and avenging wife. Orrin Bosworth, the story's "reflector" (Wharton's useful word for the character through whose sensibility the story is told) experiences Mrs. Rutledge as a prodigy of intentionality. She reminds him of his demented Aunt Cressidora, who years before had crushed a caged bird because its fluttering wings suggested a desire for freedom. Mrs. Rutledge's prominent eyes, at once sightless and all-seeing ("like the sightless orbs of a marble statue" [149]), are reminiscent of the destroyed eyes that mark the unspeakable insight of Oedipus. Her physiognomy of prominent brows "projecting roundly over pale spectacled eyes" (147) suggest the relentless, omniscient mother of Wharton's polarizing imagination. So, too, does Mrs. Rutledge's cold conviction that the daughter victimized by incest must be the one who pays; the victim is "the sinning soul that must die." The vindictive wife prevails; her ghostly rival is dispatched, releasing Saul into her appalling custody, much as Ethan Brand returns after a flutter of liberation into the custody of Zenobia.[17]

In Wharton's canon we find women endowed with moral passion even more exigent than that of Prudence Rutledge and Persis Lapham; they demand a dreadful "rightness" of their men – a superhuman purity, sometimes sexual, sometimes ethical. For example, in *The Reef,* Anna Leath, to whom renunciation comes all too easily, demands an unreasonable degree of sexual purity from the man she plans to marry. Learning that Darrow had diverted himself briefly with another woman while awaiting word from herself, Anna, who yearns to forgive, cannot do so and renounces her marriage plans. Finally, in comparing her own sexual renunciation to that of Sophy Viner, Anna discovers a distinction very important to Edith Wharton's morality, the difference between "renovating anguish" and "sterile misery."

The moral anguish that Edith Wharton experienced in childhood confrontations with her mother emerges with special power in the two novellas written at a time associated with the final illness and death of Lucretia Jones and after Edith's emotional collapse and treatment by the S. Weir Mitchell team.[18] Both stories give startling prominence to split-off mother figures who inhabit the psyches of morally weak young men. Although neither a great nor even a very good novella, *Sanctuary* provides Wharton's most overt depiction of a mother whom her son split between inner and outer: the internalized moral conscience experienced separately from, but simultaneously with, the actual mother of daily experience.[19]

In *The Touchstone,* written just before *Sanctuary,* Wharton divided the maternal figures between two women, a verbally gifted, psychically penetrating former lover and an inarticulate, gently guiding wife, both necessary for the young man's emotional maturation. Both novellas are awkward in structure. Neither observes the temporal unity or narrative inevitability that we have come to expect of Edith Wharton, unities she believed essential to short fiction.[20] Both tales involve major time gaps between the prehistory and the main action, which centers on concealed male misdeeds that are discovered by wives who must then bring about a moral resolution. In both, Wharton seems to be striving for deep religious resolutions that were beyond her fictional range but attains instead impressive insight into the psychology of guilt.

The Touchstone depicts the spiritual and emotional growth of an impoverished young lawyer, Stephen Glennard, who, needing money to marry a beautiful and equally impoverished young woman, surreptitiously sells the love letters written to him by Margaret Aubyn, a deceased novelist who had once loved him.[21] Only after Aubyn leaves Glennard behind and later dies does he realize to what extent she has infiltrated his soul. Guilt feelings over his betrayal of Aubyn's selfless love interfere with the marriage he funds with the proceeds from selling her letters.

His guilt has converted the memory of the dead novelist into the figure of an accusing mother whom he has wronged. Glennard finds himself imprisoned in "the windowless cell of . . . consciousness where self-criticism cowered."[22] His guilt for publishing Aubyn's love letters brings her back into his life more forcibly than if he had married her. Although distanced first by geography and later by death, Margaret Aubyn has achieved psychic omnipresence, a state more threatening to Glennard than physical proximity. He becomes furious at her, without having even a rational object for his rage.

> Anger against whom? . . . against that mute memory to which his own act had suddenly given a voice of accusation? Yes, that was it; and his punishment henceforth would be the presence, the inescapable presence, of the woman he had so persistently evaded. She would always be there now. It was as though he had married her instead of the other. It was what she had always wanted – to be with him – and she had gained her point at last.   (32)

In order to survive, Glennard must transmute this accusatory mother figure into an enabling one. With the guidance of his wife Alexa, Glennard learns how to transcend his guilt and accept the gifts Aubyn bequeathed to him. This agonizing process eventually frees Glennard from her psychic domination. In the fullness of time, after months of grinding anguish, he is released from her terrible grip and enabled to reincorporate her into his psychic system as a blessing.

Although *Sanctuary* (1903) appears to be working toward a similar transformation, its conclusion is obscured by a blurring of the authorial point of view. The moral agon occurs, not in the mind of the sinning male, but in that of an intrusive woman keeping guard over the consciences of two generations of male weaklings. Told by an omniscient narrator, this story of strange moral exaltation wavers between ironic distance from the heroine as an intrusive mother and rapt identification with her as a spiritual being and "moral barometer." The story has two parts widely separated in time, first the bliss and disillusionment of the newly engaged Kate Orme, second her widowhood and motherhood.

On the brink of her marriage, Kate Orme is a woman much like the young Edith Wharton – intense, extreme, endowed with "exploring susceptibilities" and a "tendency to seek out ultimate relations," yet ignorant of the economic and sexual realities of life.[23] This woman, whose nature "answered to the finest vibrations" (85), is filled with bliss at the prospect of marrying the somewhat obtuse Denis Peyton, whose mind is described as a "closed tunnel of incurious cheerfulness." Kate seems undaunted by Denis's inability to share her deepest thoughts or follow her onto hypothetical "pyres of self-immolation" (95).

Her unrealistic view of marriage reflects the sexual ignorance from which Edith Wharton tells us she herself suffered on the eve of marriage. Kate is a product of the same cult of female innocence, according to which "young girls should not be admitted to any open discussion of life" and "the blinds were drawn . . . on the ugly side of things" (88).

> Marriage had meant to her, as it means to girls brought up in ignorance of life, simply the prolongation of wooing. If she had looked beyond, to the vision of wider ties, it was as a traveler gazes over a land veiled in golden haze, and so far distant that the imagination delays to explore it.   (111–12)

Thus her disillusioning discovery of hidden corruption corresponds to the discovery of sexuality. Only Kate reacts with horror to the discovery of Arthur Peyton's secret marriage and paternity. Denis and her father are familiar with the wayward behavior of family black sheep and seek only to banish it from sight.

Sanctuary also refers to another aspect of Wharton's method of acquiring sexual education on her own, which was to make the most of whatever hints came her way. The first chapter of her memoir, *A Backward Glance,* concludes with the story of George Alfred, an outcast cousin on the paternal side, who strayed from respectability by associating with "some woman." The merest allusion by Edith's mother to George Alfred and his unmentionable woman "hinted at regions perilous, dark and yet lit with mysterious fires" (25). The language of the George Alfred passage echoes that of the famous wedding eve story from "Life and I" in which Edith begs her mother unsuccessfully for sexual enlightenment. Mamma was as evasive about George Alfred as she was reported to have been about conjugal relations, and the two subjects produced similar expressions of disgust. " 'But, Mamma, *what did he do?*' 'Some woman' – my mother muttered; and no one accustomed to the innocuous word as now used can imagine the shades of disapproval, scorn and yet excited curiosity, that 'some' could then connote on the lips of virtue."[24] From this mere hint her imagination could divine what her mother was trying to conceal, that sense of "regions perilous, dark and yet lit with mysterious fires, just outside the world of copy-book axioms, and the old obediences . . . and the hint was useful – for a novelist" (803).

Edith's cousin George Alfred becomes in *Sanctuary* Denis Peyton's half-brother Arthur, a wayward scion who died in disgrace, leaving behind a wife and child he never dared introduce to his family. Denis, knowing that his late brother Arthur had married secretly and fathered a child but that the widow could not prove it, accepts the inheritance of Arthur's fortune. When the widow comes to him to protest, Denis tries to buy her off. She rejects the bribe and drowns herself and her child in a lake near the Peyton estate. This event plunges Kate, Denis's fiancée, abruptly into knowledge of the sexual and economic underpinnings of life. She learns not only that men of good social position sometimes indulge in unsavory sexual adventures but that even her own fiancé was prepared to benefit from the widow's inability to prove her claim to his estate.

Kate reacts by probing into the facts of Arthur's death and of Denis's concealment of the marriage. Like Anna Leath in *The Reef,* she persists in investigating matters that jeopardize her marriage plans. Uncovering aspects of life long withheld from her, she demands that Denis make public expiation, but he refuses, on the grounds that no one will benefit from his sacrifice. His expedient ethical code reflects that of his mother, whose mind has "its blinds drawn down toward all the unpleasantness of life" (87). The senior Mrs. Peyton can justify any circumstance advantageous to Denis by the convenient dogma of divine providence. She views the deaths of her stepson Arthur and his wife and child as God's way of enriching Denis.

Kate's self-absorbed father represents the "consensus of respectable opinion" (109). His family, too, had a prodigal son, but managed to hush up the scandal. Thoroughly disillusioned by these glimpses of moral abysses "that men knew about" and accepted, Kate concludes that "the fair surface of life was honeycombed by a vast system of moral sewage" (110). All in all, the major players in this action represent a set of stereotyped attitudes toward opportunistic behavior, an allegorical patterning of characters and events that somehow fails to produce moral clarity.

Kate undergoes a crisis during which she must decide how her passage from ignorance to knowledge will affect her relationship to Denis. The opportunity to take over Denis's moral guidance provides her with a mission; by going ahead with the marriage, she can save Denis's potential offspring from the family's moral weakness. Knowing less of the real world than any other character in the story, she has appointed herself the moral barometer by which others shall be measured. Few readers can accept Kate's decision to marry a man for whom she feels contempt solely in order to save his potential offspring from moral error.

Kate falls into experience, not by sinning, but by taking on Denis's sin and extrapolating from it a conception of pervasive moral sewage that she alone can purify. She acquires knowledge of human iniquity simply by removing the tinted shades from the lamp by which she has always viewed experience. "No mask had been lifted from Denis's face: the pink shades had been lifted from the lamps, and she saw him for the first time in an unmitigated glare" (97). Now she can see that what had appeared to be "the curve of good nature" is really "the droop of slackness," the sign of his moral weakness (97).

Following this realization comes a "travail of the soul of which the deeper life is born. . . . Out of that dark vision light was to come, the shaft of cloud turning to the pillar of fire" (110–11). She has arrived at something heretofore unknown – knowledge of evil. Love as she had formerly conceived it will be converted into *caritas*, "something wider, deeper, more enduring than the selfish passion of a man and a woman" (111). With this exalted language, not noticeably ridiculed by the narrator, Kate is able to bypass the physical side of marriage and leap immediately to maternal *caritas*.

> What if she, who had had so exquisite a vision of wifehood, should reconstruct from its ruins this vision of protecting maternity – if her love for her lover should be, not lost, but transformed, enlarged, into this passion of charity for his race? . . . something had cleft the surface of self, and there welled up the mysterious primal influences, the sacrificial instinct of her sex, a passion of spiritual motherhood. (113)

This spiritualization of love allows Kate to skip from husband to child, transferring and displacing passion. By this leap beyond marriage into motherhood Kate short-circuits the sexual education begun by her glimpse into the abyss. The virginal unity of her selfhood will be cloven not by penetration but by a mystical form of parthenogenesis.

In the second part of *Sanctuary*, Kate is already a widow with a grown son who is on the verge of marriage. Denis has died after seven years of marriage (the biblical period of bondage), during which, with Kate's complicity, he squandered his ill-gotten fortune. One could well imagine that Denis simply withered away beneath the scorn heaped upon him by his high-minded wife. As Mrs. Peyton, Kate has dedicated herself almost exclusively to the professional, esthetic, and moral rearing of their son Dick, who is now an architect. She has accompanied him at every stage of his life, even taking an apartment in Paris on the Rue de Varennes while Dick attended the Beaux Arts. Up to this point Denis had been enjoying a "romantic friendship" with his mother, a degree of attachment criticized by Kate's friends. For Kate the "intimacy with her son was the one need of her life that she had, with infinite tact and discretion, but with equal persistency, clung to every step of his growth, dissembling herself, adapting herself, rejuvenating herself in the passionate effort to be always within reach, but never in the way" (115).

In accord with the assumptions of the story regarding heredity, Dick Peyton has inherited his mother's "naturally exalted temperament" and his father's weakness of resolve. Embodying the extremes that went into his making, he is a moral battlefield that his mother, intensely alert to every reminder of the paternal heritage, is determined to conquer. Weak willed like his father, Dick is wavering, easily discouraged, and in need of praise if he is to persevere in anything. Having taught him to favor ideal rewards over material ones, Kate now asks whether his idealism may be "but a shifting of the danger-point on which her fears had always hung? She trembled to think how little love and a lifelong vigilance had availed in the deflecting of inherited tendencies" (117–18).

Having for so long maintained complete management of Dick's soul, Kate naturally fears his impending marriage, especially since it is to Clemence Verney, a young woman whose ethical principle is expedience. Clemence would justify any opportunistic move on Dick's part by her own variety of social Darwinism. She believes in taking what one can get, or, more pertinently, encouraging the actions of men who can procure what she wants. Clemence will give herself only to a man who is a winner, a success. Dick's hold on her, as well as his professional commitment, seem to depend on his winning a major architectural competition.

Although Kate ostensibly denigrates such worldly trophies, she resents the fact that Dick's talented friend Darrow intends to compete for the same prize and may stand in the path of her own boy's success. Darrow, who is dying, has completed a splendid set of drawings, and, on learning from Kate how greatly Dick needs the victory, he offers Dick the use of his architectural plans in a deathbed letter.

The story of Kate's fight for the soul of her son is plotted as a complete analogue of his father's moral temptation, with past events and personages either replicated or reversed. Dick's temptation, which is the crux of Kate's struggle for the boy's soul, was unconsciously engineered by his mother, who let the visibly ill Darrow know how much depended on Dick's winning the competition. When she sees that the idea she had planted in Darrow's mind had flowered into this offer, "the thought scorched her to the soul" (132). Now she must by indirection reach into Dick's mind and prevent him from succumbing to the temptation that she herself has constructed. She seems to have instigated the crisis in which Dick will face a moral trial like that of his father and pass it honorably as a result of her influence.

This moral crisis is not unconnected to the life cycle crisis of Dick's passing out of Kate's control into that of another woman. She clearly would not be sorry if Dick's refusal to commit professional plagiarism should also shake him loose from Clemence. As a desperate gamble that might accomplish both goals, she stoops to manipulating Clemence by telling her of Darrow's offer so that Clemence can, by arguing in favor of the plagiarism, reveal her crass opportunism and incur Dick's distaste. Each seeing herself as the curator of Dick's "frail scruples" (141), the two women fight for control.

Kate's confusion of moral passion with her unacknowledged agendas such as rivalry with Clemence and worldly ambition for Dick casts doubt on the purity of her motives and her capacity to be anyone's moral sanctuary. At a moment of self-questioning, even she sees that her supposed selflessness on Dick's behalf is really "a kind of extended egotism" (131), but by now she is too obsessed to desist.

So closely attuned are mother and son that Kate believes herself clairvoyant about his intentions. Believing that Dick will succumb to temptation, Kate persists in trying to manipulate his mind. She tries telepathically to "hover on the edge of his thoughts" while appearing to stand back and let him make his own decisions. As Dick begins to retreat from her intensity, she becomes so obsessed with reading and moving his mind that she bursts into his office, where he has fallen asleep over his abandoned drawings. He announces that he has given up the competition and "much more," presumably Clemence, all, he avers victoriously, because of Kate's having established just the right degree of distance and nearness. The actual mother, he believes, has maintained a discreet distance, whereas the inner one held fast despite his resistance. He had grown weary of arguing with this inner mother and wanted to be let alone to

> work out my own theory of things. If you'd said a word – if you'd tried to influence me – the spell would have been broken. But just because the actual *you* kept apart and didn't meddle or pry, the other, the you in my heart, seemed to get a tighter hold on me. [Without success he had tried to resist the pressure.] I fought it off till tonight, but when I came back to finish the work

there you were again – and suddenly, I don't know how, you weren't an obstacle any longer, but a refuge – and I crawled into your arms as I used to when things went against me at school. . . . If you had let go for an instant I should have gone under – and if I'd gone under I should never have come up again alive. (162)

Most readers will rejoice that Dick chooses not to seek professional eminence using someone else's ideas but they may be less sure that this very act of renunciation was not someone else's idea. The young man's moral battle is fought for him in his mother's mind. He has resisted his mother and yielded, rather than wrestling with her imago and transforming it, as did Stephen Glennard. Dick's renunciation of what should never have seriously tempted him in the first place speaks less of moral growth than of passive resignation.

Thus the story's triumphant conclusion misfires. The *Pietà*-like tableau of Dick limp in the arms of his mother recalls the final moment of James's *Turn of the Screw,* in which the governess holds the lifeless body of the boy for whose soul she believed she had been fighting. Kate Peyton has exorcised from her son his paternal heritage and the influence of his fiancée, but has she helped him become a man or retained him as a boy? Has this psychically powerful mother become a functioning conscience or a persecuting demon? Although *Sanctuary* is less successful a tale than *Turn of the Screw,* it has, I believe, occult analogies to its powerful predecessor in the literature of psychic domination.

Edith Wharton's moral preoccupations, although culturally connected, have a psychological genesis. Viewing *The Touchstone* and *Sanctuary* as paired stories written out of childhood experience that was revived by the death of the author's mother allows us to see how Edith Wharton split female characters into polar opposites and how the imago of Lucretia Jones came to inhabit female characters such as Prudence Rutledge, Margaret Aubyn, and Kate Orme. What differentiates Wharton's fanatically moral women from the angelic moral guardians of domestic fiction is the prodigious psychic power that installs them, immortal and untransmuted, into the minds of others.

NOTES

1   The following discussion of Edith Wharton's relationship with her fashionable socialite mother is condensed from my book *The Sexual Education of Edith Wharton* (Berkeley and Los Angeles: University of California Press, 1992).
2   See *The Writings of Melanie Klein,* ed. R. E. Money-Kyrle in collaboration with B. Joseph, E. O'Shaugnessy, and H. Segal, 4 vols. (New York: Free Press, 1984).

3 Of course, the consequences vary according to countless circumstances, such as personality, gender, social class, and the age of the child when the nurse enters its life. The earlier in infancy the surrogate situation is established, the more marked are the consequences.

4 "Life and I," p. 1087, manuscript version of part of *A Backward Glance,* now printed as an appendix to *Edith Wharton: Novellas and Other Writings,* ed. Cynthia Griffin Wolff (New York: Library of America, 1990), which also contains *A Backward Glance.* Subsequent references are cited parenthetically in the text (as "Life" and *BG,* respectively).

5 Doyley figures appear occasionally in Wharton's fiction, particularly the governess in *The Buccaneers.*

6 Henry James, *The Ambassadors* (New York: Harper, 1930), 432.

7 William Dean Howells, *The Rise of Silas Lapham* (Cambridge, Mass.: Riverside, 1957), 107. Subsequent references are cited parenthetically in the text.

8 Edith Wharton, *The Writing of Fiction* (New York: Scribner, 1925), 3.

9 "The Bunner Sisters," in Wharton, *Madame de Treymes and Others: Four Novelettes* (New York: Scribner, 1970), 303.

10 Edith Wharton, *The Mother's Recompense* (New York: Library of America, 1990), 715. This scene is reminiscent of the ministerial consultation in *Lapham,* in which the authors use the ministers as mouthpieces to express the ethic of economy of pain to resolve moral crises created by the code of self-renunciation.

11 "Afterward." In *The Ghost Stories of Edith Wharton,* illustrated by Laszlo Kubinyi (New York: Scribner, Sons, 1973), p. 73. Subsequent references are cited parenthetically in the text.

12 Compare, for example, Lily Bart's radical innocence of both sexual and economic realities, and the way the two are intertwined in her disastrous loan from Gus Trenor.

13 Like The Mount, Wharton's Berkshire estate, the house of Prudence Rutledge and that of Sara Clayburn in "All Souls" have carefully noted white gateposts, an unusual architectural feature in that locality.

14 "Bewitched," in *Ghost Stories of Edith Wharton,* 148. Subsequent references are cited parenthetically in the text.

15 Barbara A. White, *Edith Wharton: A Study of the Short Fiction* (New York: Twayne, 1991). The Palmato plot summary and the erotic "Unpublishable Fragment" were found among Wharton's papers at the Beinecke Library at Yale. Although never published by Wharton, they can now be found in several biographical-critical works, including those by R. W. B. Lewis, Cynthia Griffin Wolff, and my *Sexual Education of Edith Wharton.*

In his essay "Edith Wharton," Louis Auchincloss has ventured the intriguing but unlikely idea that Venny Brand had been masquerading as the ghost of her dead sister. In Auchincloss, *Pioneers and Caretakers: A Study of Nine American Women Novelists* (New York: Dell, 1965), 35.

16 Considering that Edith Wharton was very attentive to the naming of characters, it is surprising that in one short tale she has a ghost named "Ora" and also a reflector named "Orrin" (Bosworth), who vibrates sympathetically to the uncanny occurrences. The name Ora also has sexual connotations that may be

pertinent. Wharton's use of two names well known from Hawthorne's work, "Brand" and "Hibben," is also worth noting.

17 This bizarre practice had a historical precedent with which Wharton may have been acquainted. Recent research by Paul S. Sledzik into vampire-killing rituals in New England reveals that corpses of victims of tuberculosis were unearthed and mutilated as late as 1893, to prevent their "sucking the life force from the living." "New Englanders 'Killed' Corpses, Experts Say," *New York Times,* October 31, 1993, 36.

18 As Cynthia Griffin Wolff makes clear in *A Feast of Words: The Triumph of Edith Wharton* (New York: Oxford University Press, 1977, 85–6), Wharton suffered severe emotional anguish after the publication of her first collection of short stories and underwent the Mitchell treatment from October 1898 to January 1899. Her mother died in 1901.

19 *Sanctuary* has received comparatively little critical attention. The most extensive recent treatment is by Lev Raphael in *Prisoner of Shame* (New York: St. Martin's, 1991), which recognizes that Kate Orme's vicarious fall into experience is somehow a sexual education from which she shrinks. But Raphael's single-minded insistence on shame as the hitherto unperceived key that redeems a faulty story from absurdity ignores too much of the story's content and texture. It also relies on an interpretation of Kate's childhood that Wharton neither states nor implies. In my view, Kate's choice to live in and through her son is not self-effacement due to shame but appropriation of another person's life. The psychological picture is much richer than Raphael's explanation suggests.

20 Wharton said, with respect to unity of time in short fiction, "Nothing is more retarding than the marking of a time interval long enough to suggest modification in the personages of the tale," although greater leeway is allowable in the long short story, or novella. *Writing of Fiction,* 44.

21 For a fuller discussion of *The Touchstone,* see chapter 2 of my *Sexual Education of Edith Wharton* or an earlier version of it in *Literature and Psychology* 36, nos. 1–2 (1990), 26–49.

22 *The Touchstone,* in Wharton, *Madame de Treymes and Others,* 32. Subsequent references are cited parenthetically in the text.

23 Edith Wharton, *Sanctuary,* in *Madame de Treymes and Others,* 93. Subsequent references are cited parenthetically in the text.

24 Edith Wharton, *A Backward Glance,* in *Edith Wharton: Novellas and Other Writings,* ed. Wolff, 803. The italics in the quotation are Wharton's.

6

RHONDA SKILLERN

Becoming a "Good Girl": Law, Language, and Ritual in Edith Wharton's *Summer*

At first glance, *Summer* (1917) does not seem to fit the mold of the novel of manners, the genre usually associated with Edith Wharton. This short novel primarily involves people of a lower class than is typical of the genre: there are no salons, grand balls, vast estates, sparkling wordplay, no meddling mother trying to marry off her daughter, no comic relief. Still, the story does involve a marriageable yet resistant young woman who must come to terms with the symbolic order (which can be thought of as the sociocultural matrix by which things and actions are interpreted) through courtship, social ritual, and, finally, marriage. But the foregrounding of Charity Royall's resistance to this incorporation on the one hand, and her apparent final capitulation to it on the other, has led readers of *Summer* down two different interpretive paths.

In brief, the plot of *Summer* revolves around Charity Royall, a young woman of obscure parentage who has been reared by two foster parents, Lawyer and Mrs. Royall. Mrs. Royall has been dead a few years when the narrative begins. Charity still lives with Lawyer Royall in a small Massachusetts town called North Dormer; although she yearns to escape, we learn that she has recently turned down a chance to attend boarding school because she feels obligated to Lawyer Royall, who would be "too lonesome" without her. However, Royall eventually tries to seduce his foster daughter, then twice asks her to be his wife: Charity is revolted. She instead falls in love with a visitor to North Dormer, an urbane young architect named Lucius Harney. As Charity becomes more sexually experienced through her affair with Harney, her interest in her own origins grows. She eventually becomes pregnant with Harney's child, only to learn that he has been previously betrothed to a girl of his own, more privileged, class. In desperation, Charity seeks her own mother, who lives with a clan of outlaws on "the Mountain," but her mother dies before the two can be reconciled. Charity assists the local minister at a nightmarish burial, spends one night on the mountain, then leaves, hungry, cold, and distraught. While making her weary way down the mountain, she encounters Lawyer Royall, who, knowing she is pregnant, immediately takes her to a nearby city and marries her. "You're a good girl," Royall tells Charity the day after their marriage; "I guess you're good, too," she responds, thankful that he had at least spent their wedding night in a chair and not in bed with her.[1] As the novel closes, Charity returns with Royall to his red house in North Dormer, the very place that she had dreamed of escaping, married to the only father she has ever known.

Marilyn French, Cynthia Griffin Wolff, Barbara A. White, and Candace Waid all but throw rice on this marriage. In *A Feast of Words,* Wolff declares that "the incest motif per se does not figure prominently in *Summer;* it is not a 'bad' thing that Charity eventually marries Lawyer Royall. Quite the contrary." White calls Royall "a prince" and "the only choice for Charity." More recently, Candace Waid has argued that Royall "has saved Charity from reliving the (prostitute's) life of her mother"; Royall "serves as a representative of the paternal hierarchies that are designed to protect women and the young."[2] On the other hand, Elizabeth Ammons views *Summer* as Wharton's most open criticism of America's patriarchal sexual economy, and Lev Raphael agrees, illustrating that Royall gains control of Charity only through tactics of humiliation.[3]

The more positive interpretations place too much emphasis on the last chapter of the novel, that is, on closure, while ignoring the points of resistance and the subtly shifting perspectives that occur along the way. Even though Marilyn French and Barbara White do detect a doubleness in the structure of the novel, their analysis of this feature does not extend very far and in fact does more to support their "happy-ending" readings than anything else. French perceives optimism in the cyclic seasons as they wheel in counterpoint with the linear requirements of plot; White describes the doubleness as a matter between an immature, emotional ("feminine"?) inner scene and a more intelligent, realistic ("masculine"?) outer scene. But because neither takes into account the ongoing, conflicting, gender-based responses to the dominant ideology, both readings collapse the apparent doubleness into the dominant ideological stance, which says that *it is a good thing* that nature gives way to civilization, heart gives way to head, woman to man. In other words, both French and White trace the doubleness to oppositions which structure the phallogocentrism that, I will argue, *Summer* challenges. In the end, French, Wolff, and White seem convinced by the word "good" that echoes in the last chapter of the work. But the word is Lawyer Royall's, and surely by the end of the novella the partiality (in the sense of both bias and incompleteness) of his authority has been exposed. As readers of this conflicted text, we should be wary of placing so much confidence in seemingly closed linguistic and ritualistic systems, especially since the structural doubleness of the novel exposes the inadequacy of traditional patriarchal representations.

When Wharton explains in her autobiography, *A Backward Glance,* that while writing *Summer* she did "not remember ever visualizing with more intensity the inner scene, or the creatures peopling it" (356), she probably had in mind something more akin to Julia Kristeva's semiotic or Mikhail Bakhtin's "internal polemic" than the seasons or raw emotions; in other words, she may have been referring to a site of feminine resistance that the prevailing modes of representation (the external scene) tend to foreclose.[4] The Lewises' edition of Wharton's letters reveals that during 1916 (while writing *Summer*), she certainly was in a position to be responsive to anomalous expressions of anger and despair: in the space of about a year, three of her closest friends – Henry James, Anna Bahlman, and Egerton Winthrop – died; Wharton characterized them as some of the few who were "not haunted by conventional humbug."[5] She was managing six charity hostels in France, where 750 children and 150 elderly were seeking refuge from the dislocations of World War I; in fact, she cautioned her friends to read *Summer* "with indulgence, for it was done in fits and starts because of the refugees."[6] Additionally, she resented the United States' refusal to enter the war: like James, she was "outraged by the divergence between act and utterance which has come to be a matter of course for the new America."[7] Her divorce from her husband and her affair with Morton Fullerton were both distant enough by then for her to analyze them as failures partially produced by the repression of (her own) female sexuality.[8]

But if Wharton incorporated a language of resistance into *Summer,* we must be able to read it. As Elaine Showalter cautions in "Feminist Criticism in the Wilderness," "muted groups must mediate their beliefs through the allowable forms of dominant structures. . . . [Because language can present problems,] women's beliefs find expression through ritual and art, expressions which can be deciphered by [those] who are willing to make the effort to perceive beyond the screens of the dominant structure."[9] A multilayered analysis, one that draws from literary theory, gender studies, semiotics, and anthropology, can help us attend to the resisting voices and gestures in *Summer.* Such an approach allows us not only to trace the process by which Charity Royall, who represents the resisting feminine, is drawn into the symbolic order of North Dormer and pressed into becoming a "good girl," but also to find that Charity Royall does manage to express her resistance to the symbolic order throughout the novella.

As the novella opens, she stands on the threshold of a new consciousness regarding her situation: "A girl came out of Lawyer Royall's house, at the end of the one street of North Dormer, and stood on the doorstep" (159). Seeing Lucius Harney laugh "with all his teeth" as he chases his hat only throws into relief her own miserableness and prompts her to shrink back into Lawyer Royall's house. She detests her isolation and her forced dependence on her foster father, Lawyer Royall. "How I hate everything!" she murmurs to herself (159). These are the first words she utters; thereafter, Charity remains in opposition to the accepted modes of operation in North Dormer.

As a daughter of outlaws from the Mountain, Charity was literally born into rebellion. According to Lucius Harney's description, the Mountain folk form "a queer colony up there, . . . a little independent kingdom. . . . They have nothing to do with the people in the valleys – rather look down on them, in fact" (190). Harney notes that "they seem to be quite outside the jurisdiction of the valleys. No school, no church – and no sheriff ever goes up to see what they're about" (191). The preacher is called up for funerals, but not for christenings or marriages, because the Mountain people dismiss such ceremonies: they remain outside the symbolic order. At this point, Charity only knows that the Mountain "was a bad place, and a shame to have come from, and that, whatever befell her in North Dormer, she ought, as Miss Hatchard had once reminded her, to remember that she had been brought down from there, and hold her tongue and be thankful" (161). North Dormer represents "all the blessings of the most refined civilization," compared to the place she had come from (161).

As the novel more powerfully suggests, Charity is also born into rebellion by virtue of her gender. In fact, the Mountain is repeatedly associated with the feminine in general and with female sexuality in particular.[10] At the beginning of Charity's secret involvement with Harney, stories concerning her relatives seem to be "the clue to her own revolts and defiances" (190); her curiosity about the Mountain intensifies as she becomes more sexually active; and after she becomes pregnant, Charity consistently conflates "going to the Mountain" with going to see her mother, a woman who was once a prostitute. But when Charity finally discovers her dead mother's body, she finds a present absence, an absent presence, a mother whose mouth is open but who cannot speak, a woman both inside and outside of representational systems. Whatever answer, comfort, or community Charity hoped to find is denied.

The novella can be seen as an expression of the problem of feminine representation and subjecthood; that is, the story addresses the question of whether a woman can act, think, create, or even exist in ways that are not defined and interpreted by the patriarchal symbolic order. One of the most remarkable features of Charity Royall is her inarticulateness and her unfamiliarity with various modes of cultural representation. She regards the books in the Hatchard Memorial Library in North Dormer (where she works) as artifacts only, not as texts that have anything to do with her; she is "confused" by a lecture explaining pictures of the Holy Land; she does not know what "architecture" means, when Lucius Harney asks for a book on the subject; when Harney sends her a letter, she finds its beautiful expressions "almost as difficult to understand as the gentleman's explanation of the Bible pictures at Nettleton" (278). Late in the novel, after Harney has left for New York, Charity twice tries to write him but, finding no words to describe her feelings and thoughts, she can only send a signed picture postcard of Creston Falls: "She felt the pitiful inadequacy of this, and understood, with a sense of despair, that in her inability to express herself she must give him an impression of coldness and reluctance; but she could not help it" (270). Often she cannot even represent her own thoughts to herself; all that she registers is a vague sense of rebellion, of being wronged, of desolation and betrayal. Apparently she can somehow sense her thoughts, but not necessarily in language: "At night she planned many things . . . it was then she wrote to Harney. But the letters were never put on paper, for she did not know how to express what she wanted to tell him. So she waited" (273; Wharton's ellipsis). As a Mountain native, Charity in some measure embodies the noncodified "feminine" that is incorporated into the Law of the Father (the male-centered system of representation).

To illustrate this fact in miniature, let us consider Charity Royall and her name, a name that is not legally but only provisionally "Charity Royall" throughout most of the book. Charity's quest for her mother – and her mother's name, and hence her own birth name (which is never spoken) – becomes more intense as her desire to escape Royall and North Dormer grows. In her introduction to *The Kristeva Reader*, Toril Moi describes Kristeva's feminine as "different or other in relation to language and meaning, but nevertheless only thinkable within the symbolic [system], and therefore also necessarily subject to the Law,"[11] and it is just this position that Charity occupies relative to her social surroundings: she is different, other, and in opposition to them. During the course of the novella, however, she is initiated into the symbolic order of North Dormer.[12] Four rituals structure her initiation: a Fourth of July celebration, an Old Home Week ceremony, her mother's funeral, and her own wedding. Each step marks a struggle in which Charity attempts to resist or appropriate the ceremonies for her own ends, while simultaneously she becomes more and more socially inscribed. Finally, she returns "home," married to the law that is her father, "legally" Charity Royall. But by this time, and this is a most important point, she has undermined the unity of the system which holds her, *for her child will still be illegitimate even though legally "fathered" by Lawyer Royall.* In the end, Charity Royall exposes the gaps and discrepancies inherent in the accepted modes of representation and marks the "space-off" of a different, provisionally uncontained, feminine site of experience.[13]

Charity also suggests the "unrepresentable" feminine in Wharton's own experience of sexuality. In her autobiographical "A Little Girl's New York," Wharton describes an incident that occurred when she was seventeen: she and her mother passed a woman sitting in a canary-yellow carriage and wearing a hat "lined with cherry color, which shed a lovely glow on her cheeks": when the captivated young Edith asked her mother, "Do you know the lady?", Lucretia Jones replied with a "stern order not to stare at strange people" and instructed Edith to turn her head toward the other window whenever their carriage passed the yellow one. They had encountered New York's "first fashionable hetaera." Years later, Wharton commented that "in the impoverished emotional atmosphere of old New York such a glimpse was like the mirage of palm trees in the desert."[14] In some measure, Wharton recovers that woman as Charity Royall, who wears a white hat with "cherry-colored lining" and red roses on the brim to, fittingly, an Independence Day celebration. Given this context, the scarlet-lined bonnet connotes Charity's budding sexuality, an aspect of the feminine that may be present but cannot be publicly recognized or inscribed in discourse without being violently distorted by the available modes of (male-referenced) signification. Intuitively, Charity recognizes this fact: "To avoid attracting notice, she carried her new hat carefully wrapped up, and had thrown a long grey veil of Mrs. Royall's over the new white muslin dress which Ally's clever fingers had made for her" (223). Once outside the gaze of Lawyer Royall and the other townsfolk, however, Charity proudly wears the hat to the Independence Day festivities.

Susan G. Davis's *Parades and Power* (1986), which discusses the socio-historical symbolism of parades and other patriotic celebrations, sheds light on the significance of the Fourth of July celebration. In early modern Europe, only the authorities of church and the state could appropriate the power of processional display. The tradition of processionals was later transferred to America, where issues of equality eventually made the public sphere a more problematic area; street performance often proved dangerous for those who were not white and not male. Still, the participants in parades and other ceremonies attempted to portray the public arenas as neutral ground and their orations as expressions of universal values. But, as Davis cautions, the public arenas were and are contested terrain. Certain groups were intentionally denied access to the street: working-class festivities were condemned as debaucheries; women made themselves "women of the streets" when they ventured too far out of the private sphere and into the public arena.[15]

But Charity Royall is "determined to assert her independence" (222), so she has lied to Lawyer Royall, telling him that she is going alone to "the Band of Hope picnic at Hepburn" rather than the Fourth of July festivities in Nettleton. Like Lily Bart, she unfortunately accepts as universal the idea of independence, not realizing until too late its particular application to a certain class and a certain gender.

That class is an issue is evidenced by Lucius Harney's disdain for the "descending mob" of rural and town folk attending the celebration. Until this point, Harney has "never put his arm about [Charity], or sought to betray her into any sudden caress. . . . His reserve did not suggest coldness, but the deference due to a girl of his own class" (223–4). But in Nettleton, Charity's apparent lack of aesthetic discrimination foregrounds their class differences: she thinks that not "Springfield or even Boston had anything grander to show" than "the noise and colour of this holiday vision" in Nettleton (225); she prefers sarsaparilla to the French wine he orders; she admires a gaudy lily-of-the-valley brooch instead of the elegant blue one that Harney eventually buys her. And when she gasps in ecstasy over the fireworks and a "Washington Crossing the Delaware" pageant on a lake, Harney takes the opportunity to kiss her hard on the mouth. Under the symbolic auspices of the golden "Father of Our Country," Lucius Harney can assume a sort of self-government by virtue of his gender and class, liberties not generalizable to others less fortunately male.

As the abortion clinic and Lawyer Royall are soon to remind her, such sexual and social independence are for men of means only. While waiting at the wharf, on their return from the lake, Charity and Harney encounter drunken Lawyer Royall in the company of Julia Hawes, a "bad girl" from North Dormer who has resorted to prostitution in Nettleton. When Julia declares, "Here's grandpa's little daughter come to take him home," Charity notices that Royall's "face, a livid brown, with red blotches of anger and lips sunken in like a old man's, was a lamentable ruin in the searching glare" (235). Jealous of Harney and infuriated at Charity's public exhibition of sensuality and independence, Lawyer Royall twice shouts, "you whore – you damn – bare-headed whore, you!" Suddenly Charity "has a vision of herself – hatless, dishevelled, with a man's arm about her. . . . The picture filled her with shame" (235). For anyone familiar with *Ethan Frome,* the white hat with the cherry-colored lining is the vulval equivalent to the phallic red pickle dish of that earlier work: as Lawyer Royall interprets the scene, she has lost her virginity. Thus begins Charity's initiation into the symbolic order, "The Law of the Father," which both elicits female independence and sexuality and denounces its potential.[16] Heretofore, Charity has viewed her body as her own, as living with Royall but not "belonging" to him legally. From now on, her body will be the site of struggle between her own desire and pleasure and the law.

The humiliating scene with Royall prompts Charity to leave North Dormer and to seek a life elsewhere. She plans to return to the Mountain:

> She had never really meant it before; but now . . . no other course seemed open. She had never learned any trade that would have given her independence in a strange place, and she knew no one in the big towns of the valley. . . . Her dream of comradeship was over, and the scene on the wharf – vile and disgraceful as it had been – had after all shed the light of truth on her minute of madness. It was as if her guardian's words had stripped her bare in the face of the grinning crowd and proclaimed to the world the secret admonitions of her conscience. (239)

According to Michel Foucault, Western culture has actually constructed the concept of "sexuality" as "a way of 'policing' society through procedures of normalization rather than prohibition. Discourses are themselves acts of power, acts of division and exclusion, which give themselves as knowledge." Repression, then, is not "the secret about ourselves, but our possible subjection to surveillance."[17] In the Fourth of July festivities and their aftermath, we see both the partial construction of Charity's "conscience" and her discovery of this "secret" about herself: that she is a "whore" for publicly displaying her sexuality. At the same time, though, she resists interpellation (the process by which a social representation is internalized by an individual as her own representation): she realizes that the "scandal of the wharf" has already been made into "a story, exaggerated and distorted" (237). She decides to seek a suitable place outside of North Dormer, where those outside the law (and signification) abide.

At this point, though, Charity does not go all the way to the Mountain; she will wait until she is carrying her illegitimate child before she joins the outlaws. During this early foray, she is stopped by an evangelist who emerges from a gospel tent: "Sister, your Saviour knows everything. Won't you come in and lay your guilt before Him?", he asks "insinuatingly, putting his hand on her arm." Charity retorts, "I on'y wish I had any to lay"

(241). Charity is obviously vacillating about her "guilt": she is still "betwixt and between" categories, to use Victor Turner's phrase.[18] Not yet convinced of the law's (Royall's) and the church's (the evangelist's) arguments concerning the evil nature of women's sexuality, she has yet to follow her rebellious impulse to its conclusion; that is, she has yet to go to the Mountain.

During this betwixt and between time, Charity unexpectedly encounters Harney, who beseeches her to return to North Dormer. In an effort to explain her desperation, Charity blurts out that she "know[s] about men" and believes that Royall would not have insulted her if he "hadn't wanted [her] to be like those other girls. . . . So's he wouldn't have to go out" (244). Harney reacts by exclaiming, "The damned hound! The villainous low hound! . . . I never dreamed – good God, it's too vile." Charity immediately feels "a flush of shame" for having spoken "of such things" (244). Proper unmarried women, even those of North Dormer, are not supposed to know about, much less articulate, sexual matters; even Harney's elderly unmarried aunt must "be talked to like a baby" about sex, Charity discovers (171). Again, in patriarchal systems of representation, the female form may be infused with sexuality, but ownership of that sexuality belongs to a man (her father or husband), which is why she may not speak or "know" of it, although he may. If she does "know" of her own desire, the woman runs into the double bind of either (1) not being able to cast it outside of male-centered representations or (2) casting it in available modes of (male-centered) representations, which distort feminine sexuality into shame. The fact that Charity does "know" leads Harney to make advances, for her knowledge declasses and devalues her. The narrative abruptly breaks: Charity and Harney become lovers in a little abandoned house nearby, we learn as the narrative picks up weeks later.

It would be too easy to conclude that Harney seduces Charity when she is most vulnerable, although her circumstances may have convinced him that he no longer needed to treat her with the deference due a woman of his class. But this is not Harney's story. Charity longs for him, and the thing that makes her desire different from that portrayed in most male-authored novels is that she manages to keep it apart from the cultural imaging of feminine desire. She does not expect their romance to last forever; she does not consider sex a reason for marriage; and ironically, after actually having sex, she is no longer ashamed of herself. To this degree Charity resists a value system not her own.

When her affair with Harney is about six weeks old, Charity and the other young women of North Dormer are pressed into making decorations for North Dormer's Old Home Week celebration. It has been noted by several anthropologists that, although women often make most of the preparations for festivals, they are not allowed to assume any of the main performative roles during ceremonies. So it is here. Once again, the "speaking parts" go to Reverend Miles and Lawyer Royall, the church and the law. The young women who have spent weeks fashioning flags and weaving garlands are consigned to the background where, arrayed in white dresses and veils, they sing "Home, Sweet Home." But once again Charity subverts the meanings culturally assigned to the "virgin whiteness" of the dresses and the song: "she no longer had such visions [of marrying Harney] . . . warmer splendors had replaced them" (255). Nor, of course, is she a virgin. And when the girls intone the paean to domesticity, we discover that

> it was a joy for Charity to sing: it seemed as though, for the first time, her secret rapture might burst from her and flash its defiance at the world. All the glow in her blood, the breath of the summer earth, the rustle of the forest, the fresh call of birds at sunrise, and the brooding midday languors, seemed to pass into her untrained voice, lifted and led by the sustaining chorus.   (256)

Her song is decidedly *undomestic*. Like the sixteenth-century Native Americans whom Michel de Certeau describes as making of "the rituals, representations, and laws imposed on them something quite different from what their [Spanish] conquerors had in mind," Charity uses the occasion for her own "ends and references foreign to the system [she has] no choice but to accept."[19] Charity's defiant rendition of the song underscores her oppositional position within the social system: she was taken from her original home (the Mountain), and the home she has known has not been particularly sweet. But the song is an ironically appropriate one for this scene because the four walls she has dreamed of escaping soon figuratively close in on her: Lawyer Royall delivers a rousing speech about "coming home for good" (a bit hypocritical, considering that he has always regretted living in North Dormer); Charity spies Harney sitting next to the affluent Annabel Balch, to whom, she realizes, he is betrothed; and as Reverend Miles extols the purity of the virginal choir, Charity succumbs to a fainting spell brought on by her pregnancy. The circumstances emerge that will keep her home for good.

Suspicious that she and Harney are enjoying a sexual liaison, Lawyer Royall soon tries to regulate their relationship by coercing Harney into marrying Charity. When he surprises them at their trysting place, a disintegrating house furnished with a mattress and a few pretty trifles, he again takes the opportunity to humiliate his foster daughter. He turns to Harney and snarls:

you know why you ain't asked her to marry you, and why you don't mean to. It's because you hadn't need to; nor any other man either. I'm the only one that was fool enough not to know that. . . . They all know what she is, and what she came from. They all know her mother was a woman of the town from Nettleton, that followed one of those Mountain fellows up to his place and lived there with him like a heathen. . . . I went to save her from the kind of life her mother was leading – but I'd better have left her in the kennel she came from. (266)

We must recall that until this point, Charity has learned very little direct information about her mother, but, according to the law of the father, Charity is a "what" born of a "what," a dog from a bitch in a "kennel." Yet we (and Charity) know that Mr. Royall himself attempted to seduce her before proposing and that he seeks the services of prostitute Julia Hawes. This knowledge undercuts the unity of his words and points not only to the double standard but also to the gaps in the symbolic order represented by Royall.

To understand Royall's virulence about Charity's affair and Charity's confused anger about his reaction, it is helpful here to turn to Gayle Rubin's essay "The Traffic in Women" (1975), which combines the anthropological theories of Claude Lévi-Strauss with the psychological schema of Sigmund Freud. Lévi-Strauss suggested that the essence of kinship systems in both capitalist and noncapitalist societies was the exchange of women: men marry women, in other words, to gain more male alliances. For Rubin, the incest taboo can be understood as a way to ensure that exchanges of women take place between men, extending their kinship. Rubin claims further that, given this social relation, men have rights to their female kin, whereas women do not have the same rights to their male kin or to themselves.[20] But Charity has already been given away by her father, a jailed outlaw who, co-opted by the law, decided he wanted his daughter to be "brought down and reared like a Christian" (194). She has already been given to Royall, who apparently thinks he should be able to keep her even though, *from Charity's point of view, Royall is her father,* and thus should not be able to keep her. He has already discouraged her from pursuing one means of independence (education), and now he is incensed that she might discover another – through her desire for someone other than himself.

Rubin notes that the theories of Freud and Jacques Lacan account for the ways in which a child is prepared for life within the prevailing sex/gender system. Indeed, Charity's situation can be read as a sort of parable dramatizing the girl-child's struggle with the oedipal stage of development. Freud argued that, in order for children to develop normally, they must adequately resolve the oedipal crisis by rejecting the mother, identifying with the father, and thereby internalizing the symbolic order which structures their consciousness. Before the oedipal phase, the child's sexuality is unstructured and nongendered; when the oedipal crisis has been resolved, Gayle Rubin explains, the child's gender has been constructed by the rules of the culture "nurturing" it. In exchange for his mother, the boy child is given the phallus, with which he will later get a woman. (The phallus can be thought of as a metaphor of representational power within patriarchy.) But the girl's experience is more complex: since she cannot obtain the phallus from her mother, the girl turns to her father because it is through him that she can enter the symbolic exchange system and thereby gain the dubious power of serving as an exchange object.[21] Such relative feminine powerlessness compels the girl to renounce her mother in order to choose the father as the love object.

Lacan, who bases his theory of language acquisition on Freud, uses the Freudian oedipal paradigm as a sort of metaphor that explains the symbolic order. Lacan argues that after resolving the oedipal crisis, the child enters the symbolic order, founded on the Law of the Father, which includes not only language, but signs, roles and rituals – in short, representations. The negotiation proves especially difficult for females because they must internalize masculine structures (which they do by turning to the father and entering the symbolic exchange system) and repress or reject feminine ones (which they do by rejecting the mother). Consequently, feminine "representations" cannot come into being; any potential has already been foreclosed, since the mother has already been incorporated into the male symbolic system. Excluded from the symbolic order, then, the feminine exists only as a potential opposition to the phallogocentrism of the patriarchy.[22] Still, the "feminine" can and does disrupt the unity of the Law of the Father (the symbolic order) by revealing its contradictions, its gaps, and its incompleteness.

It can be argued that before she marries Lawyer Royall, Charity Royall (that is not yet her legal name; i.e., she is incompletely inscribed) is in the last stages of an oedipal crisis. (Although she may appear to be a bit old for this phase, it must be remembered that Oedipus was, too.) Like Oedipus, Charity's resolution has been deferred because she was taken away from her mother as an infant. The threshold imagery so prominent at the beginning of the novel suggests that Charity is betwixt and between categories, in a liminal space between girl and (socially inscribed) woman. That she has earlier stopped Lawyer Royall on the threshold of her bedroom, saying, "This ain't your wife's room any longer" (170), suggests that she has not yet rejected her mother and "allowed in" the phallus-bearing father. Not surprisingly, it is during this state that she is most rebellious and contemptuous of North Dormer. Her aforementioned inarticulateness underscores the fact that she has not subscribed to the patriarchal system of representation.

But Lucius Harney, an architect who is more familiar with established social structures (and who, because of class and gender, has less to lose in them), reluctantly agrees to marry Charity as soon as he "arrange[s] some things" out of town, although he does not know of her pregnancy when he departs. Convinced that marriage to Harney would be disastrous and that she cannot stay with Royall, whom she now loathes, Charity decides that she can seek out her mother on the Mountain or become a prostitute like Julia Hawes, "only – was there no alternative but Julia's? . . . In the established order of things as she knew them she saw no place for her individual adventure" (281). Of course, she would still be part of the "established order of things" were she to become a prostitute.

Seeking a place for her individual feminine adventure, Charity decides to flee to the Mountain, to her mother's place. Charity "supposed it was something in her blood that made the Mountain the only answer to her questioning, the inevitable escape from all that hemmed her in and beset her" (282). On the most literal level, Charity is simply looking for comfort among her own kind; in addition, like so many of Wharton's most memorable characters, Charity also seeks a space beyond the confines of the exchange market, away from a system of representation that not only fails to represent her but that renders her own desires virtually unrepresentable. In the established order of things as she knows them, there is no place for her individual adventures. Perhaps there is another way of knowing and another order of things: she will try to find out.

Charity's quest for alternative signification begins with her acceptance of her desire. According to Luce Irigaray, any possible attempt at defining woman outside of the established symbolic order would have to start with *jouissance,* or feminine sexual pleasure, because the woman's experience of her own body lies beyond phallic description and representations. Irigaray even equates the clue to woman's desire with discovering an ancient maternal civilization.[23] To reach her mother, Charity has to "retrace the road over which she had so often flown to her lover" (283). The landscape of *Summer* is highly suggestive, and so it is fitting that, in her search for another way of knowing and thinking about herself, Charity must "retrace" – reconfigurate – her desire. Charity has already gotten beyond conventional thinking about her state: she recalls "her start of involuntary terror when the fat evangelist" had said, "Your saviour knows everything. Come and confess your guilt"; however, "there was no sense of guilt in her now . . . only a desperate desire to defend her secret from irreverent eyes, and begin life again among people to whom the harsh code of the village was unknown" (283). What is a secret but something kept out of the circulating symbolic order, often because one fears misinterpretation if the secret is known – sometimes, in fact, because the symbolic order cannot accurately represent the secret? Charity seeks a maternal place where she can live according to a different code, one in which her baby will be received and not delegitimized, where she can represent herself and her experiences without being expected to feel shame and regret.

But patriarchal law and Christian religion prove, in the end, too powerful for Charity and her quest for nonpatriarchal representation. Irigaray and other scholars suggest that the clue to a feminine language lies in an ancient civilization: it probably does, in the ancient pre-Judeo-Christian civilizations of the Neolithic period (9000 B.C.), or possibly even the Upper Paleolithic (up to 25,000 B.C.), when goddesses were worshiped in Europe and the Middle East. Many of these societies were matrilocal (the man moved to live with the woman's family) and matrilineal (the children took the mother's name). Women had rights to themselves, were artists and held the highest religious positions: they could, and did, have powers of representation. But eventually tribes worshiping the newer male deities persecuted and suppressed goddess-worshipping ones, and consequently women lost status, lost rights, lost the power of representation. A brief survey of Judeo-Christian history reveals what ensued: women were supposedly cursed with subservience to men and pain in childbirth because of Eve's transgressions (Genesis 2). Women became property – although a father could sell sexual access to his daughter and then later marry her off, a woman who "gave her self away," thereby depriving her father of a fee, was stoned to death (Deuteronomy 22:20–2). Hebraic law reveals a phobic attitude toward women's sexuality, perhaps in response to the ritual sex associated with worship of the Great Mother, Yahweh's early competition. This fear of women's contaminating power, manifested in their flesh, continued to be expressed in the Christian teachings of Paul, Saint Augustine, Thomas Aquinas, Sprenger and Kramer (authors of the infamous *Malleus Maleficarum,* 1486), and even Pope John Paul II, who suggested as late as 1980 that a man who took pleasure in looking at his wife's body committed a sin. In such a patriarchal religion, women are portrayed as necessary for procreation, but otherwise morally weak, infectious to men, and consequently in need of suppression.[24]

Historically, then, the church has buried the Great Mother and her progeny, woman (I use the lower-cased term here as a metaphor for all that patriarchal representation has left out of its conception of "Woman"), marking the grave with the dual image of the virgin and the whore, the very dichotomy that Charity Royall wishes to escape by uncovering her mother. So it is fitting that a man of the church is the one to say "Your mother is *dead,* Charity; you'd *better come with me*" (288; my emphasis): something is better than nothing. Indeed, Charity does go with Mr. Miles, following his lead throughout the nightmarish burial scene, viewing her mother's body by the light that he casts upon it:

> they stood before a mattress on the floor in a corner of the room. A woman lay on it, but she did not look like a dead woman; she seemed to have fallen across her squalid bed in a drunken sleep, and to have been left lying where she fell, in her ragged disordered clothes. One arm was flung above her head, one leg drawn up under a torn skirt that left the other bare to the knee: a swollen glistening leg with a ragged stocking rolled down about the ankle. The woman lay on her back, her eyes staring up unblinkingly at the candle that trembled in Mr. Miles's hand. . . .
>   He knelt down by the mattress, and pressed the lids over the dead woman's eyes. Charity, trembling and sick, knelt beside him, and tried to compose her mother's body. She drew the skirt down to the battered upturned boots. As she did so, she looked at her mother's face, thin yet swollen, with lips parted in a frozen gasp above the broken teeth. There was no sign in it of anything human: she lay there like a dog in a ditch.   (289–90)

Supine on a seamy mattress, sweaty legs apart, swollen mouth open, Mary Hyatt's body is revolting, frozen in a kind of horrific ecstasy like a backwoods Bernini *Saint Theresa.* Yet because of her overt corporeality, she does not look human by the light of Reverend Miles's candle or his religion: "human" women should not look so – well, nasty. But clearly she is a woman – too much of a woman to be human, perhaps, so that according to patriarchal thought she spills over into the animal category, just as "kennel"-begotten Charity did when Lawyer Royall caught her on a mattress with Lucius Harney.

On a literal level, Charity helps Mr. Miles bury her mother, but on a psychological level Reverend Miles (and all that he represents) helps Charity repress her own desires, including her desire for her mother (a metaphor for non-patriarchal representations). For the moment, Charity is comforted by Mr. Miles's "mighty words" that have the power of "soothing the horror, subduing the tumult, [and] mastering her":

> "Through our Lord Jesus Christ, who shall change our vile body that it may be like unto His glorious body, according to the mighty working, whereby He is able to subdue all things unto Himself. . . ." The last spadeful of earth fell on the vile body of Mary Hyatt.   (292; Wharton's ellipsis)

In many ways, this ritual signals the turning point for Charity Royall, the point at which she has internalized the symbolic order that is based upon the repression of the mother. It is, in the narrator's words, Charity's "tragic initiation" (294). Charity will hereafter find it impossible to sustain her resistance because she has found no way to adequately represent it. "He is able to subdue all things unto Himself": potential polyphony is subdued by monologism; a unifying masculine voice covers over feminine difference. The mother's body, a potential power source for women, is buried beneath the word "vile."

Charity had turned to her mother for another system of thought and expression, but her mother's open mouth could utter nothing. The operating system of representation necessitates her repression. Variations of this scene recur in women's fiction, as Margaret Homans's *Bearing the Word* (1986) and Deborah Kelly Kloepfer's *The Unspeakable Mother* (1990) illustrate. Margaret Homans has argued, "Women's place in language, from the perspective of an androcentric literary tradition (and the psycholinguistic theory it generates), is with the literal, the silent object of representation, the dead mother, the absent referent."[25] Kloepfer, in her discussions of Jean Rhys and H.D., discovers that "a dead mother is a trope for textlessness, a way of speaking the unspeakable, a way of inscribing a silencing, a failure, or a repression of the female speaking subject."[26]

Still, Charity tries to "*compose* her mother's body" (289, my emphasis) – to arrange it not only for burial, but to *give it form* for remembering. She succeeds to some degree. Although Charity never discovers an external place for her individual adventure, she does find a place in her own psyche for her experience of her mother. Her quest for her maternal home at least enables her to challenge Lawyer's Royall's version of her own history:

> she remembered what Mr. Royall had said in telling her story to Lucius Harney: "Yes, there was a mother; but she was glad to have the child go. She'd have given her to anybody. . . ."
>   Well! after all, was her mother so much to blame? Charity, since that day, had always thought of her as destitute of all human feeling; now she seemed merely pitiful. What mother would not want to save her child from such a life? Charity thought of her own child, and tears welled into her aching eyes, and ran down over her face. If she had been less exhausted, less burdened with his weight, she would have sprung up then and there and fled away. . . .
>   (295; Wharton's ellipses)

She recognizes what her mother must have known: that the maternal community has neither sustained economic power nor representational power. Mary Hyatt was not an evil mother; she was simply a mother caught in the same dilemma as all mothers. In an essay about another Mary, entitled "Stabat Mater," Kristeva explains that mothers in particular engage in the masochistic behavior of erasing themselves for the sake of their children's socialization, for the sake of continuity, for the sake of law.[27] Determined not to "add another life to the nest of misery on the Mountain" (296), and yet equally resolved that "she could not remain at North Dormer, and the sooner she got away from it the better" (297), Charity decides to return to the established of things a whore: masochistically, she accepts this fate as the only one that will provide financial support for her baby.

As Charity leaves the Mountain, she is physically and emotionally exhausted, a state Royall takes advantage of when he takes her into town for marriage. It is only under coercion that she submits to the ritual that will mark her final capitulation to the Law of the Father. Indeed, during the wedding ritual, she no longer even controls her own voice or body; she merely repeats what she is told to say, and the minister's wife places her hand in Royall's. While it can be argued that Royall proves extremely kind and understanding in his willingness to marry a woman impregnated by another man (although this view would only be produced in patriarchy), we must wonder at his haste: undoubtedly he senses that Charity's resistance is down.

Gayle Rubin, echoing Freud, explains that a girl's turning away from her mother to her father is marked by an "ascendancy of passivity" because she is aware of "the futility of realizing her active desire, and of the unequal terms of the struggle."[28] Before and during the ceremony in which Charity marries Royall, she is described as "confused" and "dazed"; she follows Mr. Royall "as passively as a tired child" (302). In fact, Charity neither agrees to marry him nor actively participates in the ritual that will bind her to him for life:

> The clergyman began to read, and on her dazed mind there rose the memory of Mr. Miles, standing the night before in the desolate house on the Mountain, and reading out of the same book words that had the same dread sound of finality. . . .
>
> She was so busy trying to understand the gestures that the clergyman was signalling to her that she no longer heard what was being said. After another interval the lady on the bench stood up, and taking her hand put it in Mr. Royall's. It lay enclosed in his strong palm and she felt a ring that was too big for her being slipped on her thin finger. She understood then that she was married. (304–5)

Thus Charity emerges with a legal identity based on the rejection of the mother. According to the traditional marriage ceremony, the "two become

one," the provisional maiden name gives way to permanent masculine no-
menclature, the semiotic succumbs to the symbolic, difference consolidates
into unity under the power of the closed system of word and symbol. Were
this truly to happen, death – absolute stasis – would result, as suggested by
the fact that this ceremony reminds Charity of her mother's funeral.

But in what is basically a coda to *Summer,* we find that marriage has not,
as the traditional novel of manners would have it, resolved all differences.
This marriage signals both Charity's capitulation to the Law of the Father
and her subversion of it: the two newlyweds have not (yet) become one in
the wedding bed; moreover, the child made legitimate by this union also
exposes the fictionality of that legitimacy and that unity. And though Royall
tries to tempt Charity into becoming an object for display, giving her forty
dollars for clothes that "will beat 'em [all the other girls] hollow," Charity
resists (308). She may wear a wedding ring – a public symbol – on her
finger, but she uses the forty dollars to recuperate a private sign of her
mother's rebellion and her own feminine desire, a brooch with a stone as
blue as a mountain lake ("mountain" suggests her mother, while "lake" –
like the brooch itself – is reminiscent of her Independence Day excursion
with Harney). Charity's decision to recuperate the brooch suggests that she
has preserved a space within herself that neither Lawyer Royall nor the Law
of the Father can invade.

Helene Cixous writes that "the feminine cannot be expressed within
closed structures."[29] It is interesting to note that Edith Wharton wrote
Summer while trying to complete *Literature,* a book about the art of writing
that, incidentally, she never finished. *Summer* is at least in part about opening up existing structures, about the problem of putting the unrepresented
feminine into the text. Images of half-structures abound: the Hatchard Memorial Library, described as a mausoleum, must be ventilated (the roof
opened up) if the books are to survive; the only house conducive to love
seems to be the partially dilapidated one where the lovers tryst. Wharton,
like Kristeva, seems to imply that for art and love to occur, the *"au delà*
dream side of things and the *netteté,* the line" need to be acknowledged.[30]

NOTES

1   Edith Wharton, *Summer,* in *Edith Wharton: Novellas and Other Writings,* ed.
    Cynthia Griffin Wolff (New York: Library of America, 1990), p. 311. Quota-
    tions cited parenthetically in the text are from this edition.
2   See Marilyn French, introduction to Edith Wharton's *Summer* (New York:
    Berkley, 1981), pp. i–xlix; Cynthia Griffin Wolff, *A Feast of Words: The Tri-
    umph of Edith Wharton* (New York: Oxford University Press, 1977); Barbara

A. White, "Edith Wharton's *Summer* and 'Women's Fiction,' " *Essays in Literature* 11.2, 223–35; Candace Waid, *Edith Wharton's Letters from the Underworld: Fictions of Women and Writing* (Chapel Hill: University of North Carolina Press, 1991).

3 Elizabeth Ammons, *Edith Wharton's Argument with America* (Athens: University of Georgia Press, 1980); Lev Raphael, *Edith Wharton's Prisoners of Shame* (New York: St. Martin's, 1991).

4 See Toril Moi, ed., *The Kristeva Reader* (Oxford: Blackwell, 1986); Mikhail Bakhtin, *The Dialogic Imagination,* ed. and trans. Michael Holquist (Austin: University of Texas Press, 1981).

5 *The Letters of Edith Wharton,* ed. R. W. B. Lewis and Nancy Lewis (New York: Scribner, 1988), p. 379.

6 *Letters,* p. 397.

7 *Letters,* p. 379.

8 Wharton was estranged from Teddy Wharton for years before she divorced him in 1913. Her affair with Morton Fullerton, an American *London Times* correspondent, lasted from about 1908 to 1911, although they remained friends thereafter.

9 Elaine Showalter, "Feminist Criticism in the Wilderness," *Feminist Criticism: Essays on Women, Literature and Theory,* ed. Elaine Showalter (New York: Pantheon, 1985), p. 261.

10 Monika M. Ebert, among others, makes this point in "The Politics of Maternality in *Summer,*" *Edith Wharton Review* 7.2 (Winter 1990); 4–9, 24. However, using a blend of materialism and essentialism, Ebert claims that Charity Royall renounces "the primeval mother within her" because she "has sold into the consumer society produced by men" (p. 9). It is difficult to view Charity as a narcissist who revels in luxury, as Ebert suggests. Surely her refusal to spend the forty dollars that Royall gives her on "beating all the other girls hollow" indicates her rejection of the woman-as-conspicuous-consumer role.

11 Toril Moi, introduction to *Kristeva Reader,* p. 11.

12 Since "Dormer" seems cognate to "dormant," the book suggests that women initiated into the symbolic order are inducted into a kind of sleep.

13 In her *Technologies of Gender* (Bloomington: Indiana University Press, 1987), Teresa de Lauretis borrows the term "space-off" from film studies: it refers to the space "off" camera that is nonetheless implied by what is *in* the frame of the camera. De Lauretis uses space-off as a metaphor for the space where the unrepresentable feminine can operate.

14 Edith Wharton, "A Little Girl's New York," *Harper's* (August 1938), 357.

15 See Susan G. Davis, *Parades and Power: Street Theater in Nineteenth-Century Philadelphia* (Philadelphia: Temple University Press, 1986), pp. 13–47.

16 See de Lauretis, *Technologies of Gender,* p. 14, for a discussion of the social construction of female sexuality: although located in the woman, female sexuality is seen as "belonging to" the man.

17 Michel Foucault, *Power / Knowledge,* ed. and trans. Colin Gordon (New York: Pantheon, 1980), p. 108.

18 For a fuller discussion of liminality, see Victor Turner, *The Ritual Process: Structure and Anti-Structure* (Chicago: Aldine, 1969).

19 Michel de Certeau, *The Practice of Everyday Life,* trans. Steven F. Rendeall (Berkeley and Los Angeles: University of California Press, 1984), p. xiii.

20 Gayle Rubin, "The Traffic in Women," *Toward an Anthropology of Women,* ed. Rayna R. Reiter (New York: Monthly Review Press, 1975), pp. 177–82.

21 Rubin, "Traffic in Women," pp. 194–5.

22 For an accessible discussion of Jacques Lacan's contribution to neo-Freudian psychology and French feminism, see Elizabeth Grosz, *Sexual Subversions: Three French Feminists* (Sydney: Allen & Unwin, 1989), pp. 16–25.

23 Luce Irigaray, *The Sex Which Is Not One,* trans. Catherine Porter (Ithaca, N.Y.: Cornell University Press, 1985), pp. 15–25.

24 Many social, historical, and feminist studies make this point. See, for instance, Elizabeth R. Allgeier and Albert R. Allgeier, *Sexual Interactions* (Lexington, Mass.: Heath, 1984), chaps. 1–3.

25 Margaret Homans, *Bearing the Word: Language and Female Experience in Nineteenth-Century Women's Writing* (Chicago: University of Chicago Press, 1986), p. 32.

26 Deborah Kelly Kloepfer, *The Unspeakable Mother: Forbidden Discourse in Jean Rhys and H.D.* (Ithaca, N.Y.: Cornell University Press, 1989), p. 15.

27 Julia Kristeva, "Stabat Mater," in *Kristeva Reader.*

28 Rubin, "Traffic in Women," p. 195.

29 Helene Cixous, "Rethinking Differences: An Interview," trans. Isabelle de Courtivron, in *Homosexualities and French Literature,* ed. George Stambolian and Elaine Marks (Ithaca, N.Y.: Cornell University Press, 1979), p. 71.

30 This is a line from Wharton to her companion and lover, Morton Fullerton. *Letters,* p. 151. R. W. B. Lewis and Nancy Lewis surmise it was written in 1908.

7

MAUREEN HOWARD

The Bachelor and the Baby:
The House of Mirth

What a book a devil's chaplain might write on the clumsy, wasteful,
blundering, low and horribly cruel works of nature!

– Charles Darwin

It will soon be ninety years since Edith Wharton made her agreement with
Scribner's Magazine to finish, and publish in serial form, a work which she
had found troubling. *The House of Mirth* is a novel of New York society,
the world she never completely discarded, though she declared she had
given it up. Henry James, while praising the historical reenactments and
Italian setting of Wharton's first novel, *The Valley of Decision,* crisply
advised her "in favor of an American subject."[1] The Master proposed she
"*Do New York,*"[2] and Mrs. Wharton proceeded to deal it out to a society
she understood to be a narrow slice of the American scene. From Lawrence
Selden's opening encounter with Miss Lily Bart in Grand Central Station,
we anticipate that the novel will occupy the familiar territory of custom and
constraint that amused and angered Wharton. But the precision of Selden's
view of Lily Bart "as wearing a mask of irresolution which might . . . be the
mask of a very definite purpose,"[3] and Lily's shrewd use of him – "What
luck! . . . How nice of you to come to my rescue!" (4) – sets in motion a
game of hide-and-seek that these two will play to the bitter, open end. *The
House of Mirth* is a novel of concealment and revelation, of what is presumed socially and what must be discovered – morally and emotionally –
by both of its principals, and what remains unknowable to them.

The novel also reveals Wharton in the act of discovery, distancing herself
from Lily Bart, who portrays the social creature the novelist was once
destined to be. Both Lily and her maker were women in transition; Wharton
consciously evolving from a literary notoriety to a novelist of the first rank;
Lily failing as an ornament of the privileged, fumbling toward an imagined
view of herself in a larger society. If Wharton was troubled when she went
back to the novel, it may have been that early on she understood her heroine
could not be dismissed as the tarnished beauty in a comedy of manners, nor
would pure melodrama serve for her demise. In *The House of Mirth,* she
made use of both genres, then, with growing artistic confidence moved on to

the unlikely territory of American naturalism that would deepen her best work. Wharton did not accept the Social Darwinism of the naturalists, but found, in writing this novel, a Darwinian view that supported her belief in individual adaptation. Lily Bart's death, which follows close upon the revelation that one may choose to live with purpose, is clumsy, wasteful, blundering – unwilled. The novelist's moves are chosen, productive, skillful – a triumph of her will.

It is as a privileged guide that Wharton first presents herself in *The House of Mirth* knowing that the exact details of the trivial society in which she displayed her irresolute heroine had enormous appeal to the uninvited, not only to the masses who followed the tattle of scandal and excess in high places but to the more discreet readers of *Scribner's*. Beginning with the serialization (1905) and publication of the novel, she found a large audience who enjoyed such disclosures by the ultimate insider and who were to find it in *The Custom of the Country, The Age of Innocence, Old New York,* and in many of her finest stories: "The Other Two," "The Long Run," "Autre Temps."

The House of Mirth was a contemporary work, scoring off the new entrepreneurial society of the new century, a society of getting and spending and then getting more. What Edith Wharton knew with surprising assurance from her beginnings as a writer of social satire was the importance of particulars, that each amusing detail must carry more than its apparent weight. Thus, the inappropriateness of an unmarried woman like Lily taking tea with a man at Sherry's leads Selden to invite her to his rooms. Her acceptance is Lily's first risk. And as she looks over his bookshelves, it is "the ripe tints of good tooling and old morocco" that her eyes linger on, "with the pleasure in agreeable tones and textures that was one of her inmost susceptibilities" (10). Surfaces, decor will attract or repel her throughout the novel. Looking down upon the sumptuous hall at Bellomont, her spirit is restored: "There were moments when such scenes delighted Lily, when they gratified her sense of beauty and her craving for the external finish of life; there were others when they gave a sharper edge to the meagerness of her own opportunities" (26). Although her manner is grand, her sense of personal worth is so frail that all settings in the novel, including the warm domesticity of Nettie Struther's tenement kitchen, enrich or diminish her, and she is ever conscious of her own decorative value, estimating the inevitably dwindling capital of her face and figure.

That she is between trains at the outset of her story is appropriate, for Lily is eminently transient, without a setting of her own. In the cozy surround of Selden's bachelor digs, she connects the freedom of having one's own place with the possibility of goodness: "If I could only do over my aunt's drawing-room I know I should be a better woman" (7). However casually delivered, the line is an admission of her rootlessness and her self-doubt. The wit as well as the moral confusion of this statement are not unrecognized by her, neither are they fully understood. She will not speak plainly, with insight and direction, until her next visit to Selden's library, at the end of the novel. It should be noted that Edith Wharton had recently "done over" her mother's stuffed and stuffy parlors, not literally but in writing (with Ogden Codman) *The Decoration of Houses.*[4] The novelist, who continued to be much taken with the esthetics of her domestic life, was able to distinguish between interior decoration and social values; her heroine, homeless to the end, comes to a personal and social enlightenment on the city streets and in a boardinghouse in this very "housey" novel.

As she leaves Selden's apartment for the next exhausting social venture, Lily encounters Mr. Rosedale:

> "The Benedick?" She looked gently puzzled. "Is that the name of this building?"
>
> "Yes, that's the name: I believe it's an old word for bachelor, isn't it? I happen to own the building – that's the way I know." (15)

Wharton, who felt that she'd got hold of what it was to write a novel in writing this one, an early work and her finest, understood that simply having Lily break the rule by taking tea in Selden's rooms was not enough, nor was it enough for her readers to draw in their breath when she is discovered there, nor enough to catch Lily out in a lie. The allusion to Benedick, the confirmed bachelor of Shakespeare's *Much Ado,* was not lost on the *Scribner's* audience, nor is it lost on Lily. That she is "gently puzzled" has to do with her mere concealment of fact – she had noted the name of The Benedick – and with her manipulation of Rosedale. For all her expertise – she is worldly in the ways of women of her class – there will be much she doesn't know: specifics about money and property lead the list, dollar-and-cents facts dealt with by the men of her class, expertly dealt with by Mr. Rosedale. Her puzzlement, though feigned, is also moral. She has, indeed, been to a forbidden place. Might there be consequences? Rosedale asking her to verify the literary reference tops this exchange. She is Miss Lily Bart, possessed of culture. That Simon Rosedale knows "it's an old word for bachelor" only because he owns the building is a clever introduction to the theme of cultural possession – the getting of rare books, paintings, jewels, boxes at the opera, houses and horses – all for display. And the getting of beautiful women, for as we watch Lily display herself we understand that she is intended for further display as cultural artifact/wife. But the uncaring act of cultural possession has already been addressed in the matter of Americana, which Lily is curious about. Selden informs her that those who can afford to collect rare books which relate to our history, the likes of Percy Gryce, don't personally savor them, while he collects first editions he is fond of. It is a first edition of La Bruyère, who recorded the manners of his day with scathing accuracy in portraits and maxims, that Lily sets back on his shelf where the novelist placed it.

When one comes to the last page of *The House of Mirth*, it is as instructive to reread its opening chapter as it is, say, to turn back to the first pages of *Emma* or *The Great Gatsby,* both novels of manners, more or less. More than novels of manners is what we believe these works to be, as though they must satisfy us by transcending the amusements and comforts of that genre, as indeed they do with a breadth of implications in their first pages: Emma's managerial deployment of servants and friends, Nick Carraway's lofty dissertation on his heritage and class. The brightness with which Lily and Selden play against each other was, to Wharton and her audience, recognizable drawing-room comedy, but their repartee, if we listen carefully, has as desperate an undertow as the immensely clever exchanges in Oscar Wilde – brittle words. Their speech is mannered, fluent, flirtatious to an end that is self-defining, determinedly unphysical, protective.

The heavy hand of melodrama, that pop Victorian genre, is parodied in Lily's meetings with, first, the charwoman, whom she finds physically distasteful, and then Mr. Rosedale, the landlord of The Benedick. The plight of the underclasses and the power of the landlord were abundantly noted in penny dreadfuls and stage thrillers of the day. For a moment, as Lily takes leave of the first chapter, it is as though our heroine, practiced in verbal maneuvers and social calculations, finds herself within the wrong script. She does, in fact, stammer as she extricates herself from Rosedale. That faltering is essential to our understanding that there may be more to Lily than meets Selden's (or Rosedale's) eye and that Wharton, writing what she understood to be her first serious novel, found that she could not depend on formulaic moves.

What we may also note, in the intricate and deft opening of the novel, are the chance meetings – there are three; the risks – Lily's innocent adventure in going to Selden's rooms; and the shame – slight, passing – of her obvious, self-incriminating lie. Wharton plays with melodramatic prescriptions in depicting Lily Bart playing at melodrama, for in being buffeted by the hoi polloi in Grand Central she is a maiden in blatantly minor distress. She is delighted to be rescued by Selden, who will prove incapable of rescuing her when she is truly in need. Yet as she springs into a hansom to catch the next train to the next social obligation, she feels herself rescued *from* Rosedale, a man who is willing to help her in the end. Our expectations of a real save, the reward of melodrama, have been disappointed long before the end of the novel, when Lily dreams herself to death.

So much is suggested in mock melodrama as the curtain goes up on the drama of the poor little rich girl, whose maid has gone ahead to the Trenor's estate up the Hudson, that we are lured, like the readers of *Scribner's*, to the pleasant complications of the next installment, the weekend at Bellomont – then the next, the Van Osburgh wedding – and so on. The tone of the old cliff-hangers allows Wharton to pose the bald question at the end of each installment: Whatever will become of our heroine?

Lily's opening line – "Mr. Selden – what good luck!" (3) launches the imagery of chance, risk, fate, gambling, calculation which runs throughout the novel and which will connect Edith Wharton's turn upon an evolutionary theme in which heritage is not destiny. Fate, as in the old one-reelers (or nineteenth-century melodramas), appears with the sensational rescue of a telegram, a letter, a check, a chance meeting, the deal of a hand. Whether Lily loses or wins at cards, she understands that she must play the social game. That she plays cards for money becomes one of her aunt's main complaints against her. She wins on the market, a game she does not understand, for it entails a debt to Gus Trenor, her financial savior and would-be seducer, yet another man to be rescued *from*.

The ingenue of melodrama must be unsullied and young, but Lily Bart lives at the edge of permissible behavior. A great calculator of her advantages, she is hardly an innocent. Her fate would not concern us if she were. *The House of Mirth* becomes a forceful moral tale because Wharton reveals Lily as conventionally corrupt, jaded, snobbish, aging, yet an exceptionally beautiful and quirky product of her society. A sport of nature, she is just unconventional enough in her self-awareness, and her contempt for the pleasurable life she is addicted to, not to consolidate her gains, consistently revealing her flaw of irresolution. Lily Bart is unwise and uncertain in estimating her worth, investing heavily in the ornamental woman she was fated to be, given the accident of her birth, placing little value on the useful woman she might have chosen to be against the odds.

The quest for Lily's character and for her own identity as more than a passing literary fancy drew Wharton away from the solutions of melodrama and the satisfying end games of social comedy. Perhaps that is why Henry James found *The House of Mirth* to be "two novels and too confused."[5] But if we understand that the novel is purposely rent in two, the confusion, if there is any, can be seen as the insoluble dilemma of Lily Bart. She is in transit, literally – between trains, house parties, friends and false friends, high life, low life. Wharton was also on the move, and in writing *The House of Mirth,* she found that there was no prefab house of fiction, social satire or deterministic naturalism, that would accommodate Lily, a modern heroine. I read Wharton's novel as a modernist work which denies the comforts of genre and its available views. In fact, the novel denies the assumptions of genre twice, for after abandoning the novel of manners and melodramatic effects, Wharton turns away from the predetermined closure of naturalism to the romantic and ambiguous death of Lily and the mock-romantic spectacle of Selden at her bier.

The two works that inform us in reading the novel, and that, I believe, informed Wharton in the writing, are Jane Austen's *Emma* and Theodore Dreiser's *Sister Carrie.* We can turn again to the opening chapter of *The House of Mirth* to discover the wit of a marriage novel of manners in the broad play of Selden and Lily's banter and to observe an initial glimpse of the naturalistic in the "dull tints of the crowd" (3), the teeming masses of Grand Central, and, of course, in Gertie Farish's good works and Lily's uncharitable looking down on Mrs. Haffen, the charwoman.

Edith Wharton's debt to Jane Austen has often been noted. *Emma,* in particular, haunts the pages of *The House of Mirth.* Only Emma Woodhouse, appealing and willful, can be seen as a nearly antipodean model for Lily Bart. In the first sentence of *Emma,* Austen's heroine is "handsome, clever, and rich, with a comfortable home and happy disposition" having lived nearly "twenty one years in the world with very little to distress or vex her."[6] The dissimilarity of Wharton's heroine is surely intentional: Lily, though handsome and clever enough, is impoverished, homeless, twenty-nine, and, though it is passed off lightly at first, somewhat vexed. In both novels, money and marriage are on the table. In Austen, marriage is an institution within a stable world. Unwed, Emma Woodhouse has power, delights in it, misuses it. She does not need marriage, until she discovers that love's advantage may be in having no predictable advantage. In Lily Bart's unstable society, marriage has already become at best a flimsy institution in which to house one's ambitions. *The House of Mirth* may be read as a perverse marriage novel, for if we track Lily's business, the business of getting married, she is, at twenty-nine, a failure. And, what is most evident, she has no inner desire to be wed. The pressures are all external. While she understands the material advantages of marriage, the comfort zone, she is never interested in the power of marriage, though she observes the use of that power by her friend Judy Trenor and her adversary Bertha Dorset. The more her financial and social circumstances demand marriage, any marriage – to George Dorset, to Simon Rosedale – the less responsive Lily is. At times she is careless to the point of self-destruction; as she misses catching Percy Gryce or listens to the marital woes of George Dorset, Lily seems not to fancy the scene she finds herself in, feels her position in regard to these men absurd, even morally repellent. It is not fate, after all, but a fastidious irresolution: she defaults in the marriage game, finding it insufficient, much as Mrs. Wharton did in abandoning the smart comedy of manners, but the novelist's move was by choice, a testing of her strength as a serious writer.

Austen and Wharton share the skills of good gossips. The forward movement of *Emma* depends largely on the propagation of gossip and on conjecture, on the uses and misuses of information. In *The House of Mirth* we understand that chatter is self-serving, destructive. The reader is privy to what is said of Lily Bart before the compromising news reaches her, a stage-worn device that co-opts us, makes us seemingly wiser. But Wharton is up to a more engaged use of Lily's reputation: Selden's first assessment of Lily Bart is in the nature of gossip. Throughout their story, insofar as it is ever *their* story, he will allow his estimate of her conduct to be adjusted by what is said of her. His tracking of events – ". . . had she indeed reached the nine-and-twentieth birthday with which her rivals credited her?" – is gossip, cutely retold, secondhand. The rhetorical question does not let him off the hook: what people say matters to Selden. A woman may be victimized by prattle; but a man may not. It is Selden who let on to the readers of the first installment in *Scribner's* that "there is nothing new about Lily Bart" (3), a comment not on her age but on her as news – old news. In the last scene of the novel, as he views her in death, he is, for a moment, ready to accuse her of "the old hints and rumors" (347) that she had taken money from Gus Trenor. Sad as that scene may be, the final irony, even the final smile given the reader, is his admission that he must come up with explanations about Lily's settling of accounts "out of the very insinuations he had feared to probe" (347). It might be said that Selden is left behind in the novel of manners which Wharton abandoned, more a victim of his literary heritage than Lily Bart.

Wharton was critical of James in his late novels for copping out on his characters' backgrounds. Whence their money? What place have his travelers left? The novelist who had come alive in Wharton understood that the family histories of Lily and Selden, both orphans, would sit heavily in the first chapter as rationale. She is careful to give us their heritage at some delay, for a time concealing Lily's bitter, ambitious mother, who saw her daughter as the "last asset of their fortunes" (35), and the feckless father, whose financial ruin precipitated a "slow and difficult dying." "To his wife he no longer counted: he had become extinct when he ceased to fulfill his purpose" (34). Lily's mother, a devil's chaplain of Darwin's note on the cruelty of nature, discards the weak husband and selects her daughter's beauty as the dominant strain for survival. Selden's heritage is not revealed until we are well into the plotting of Lily's fall from society's grace. It is in one of his moments of belief in her, even in a passing thought of love beyond the sentimental, that we learn of his mother's "values" (161). (The quotation marks are Wharton's.) Selden has inherited "the stoic's carelessness of material things, combined with the Epicurean's pleasure in them . . . and nowhere was the blending of the two ingredients so essential as in the character of a pretty woman." What does that make Lily? An aesthetic object of desire. Selden constantly aestheticizes his view of Lily at the expense of her humanity and his. Lily exists for his contemplated pleasure, for her mother's gain.

Wharton suggests more problematic questions of heritage that had already become a major concern in her work. In the extraordinary opening chapters of *The House of Mirth*, she presented a specimen case of evolutionary metaphors. About the matter of Lily's costly breeding, Selden senses "how highly specialized she was" (5). We soon learn that Rosedale is "still at a stage in his social ascent" (6). Percy Gryce, the rich mama's boy, feels in Lily's ministrations "the confused titillation with which the lower organisms welcome the gratification of their needs" (21). At Bellomont she glimpses the "laboratory where Selden's faiths are born" (73) on the very morning when she chooses not to go to church. Selden, ever vigilant as counselor in his own defense, does not doubt the "spontaneity of her liking" (71) but cannot see himself as "the unforeseen element in a career so accurately planned [that it] was stimulating even to a man who had renounced sentimental experiments" (72). These allusions toy with the evolutionary concerns of the day. As we read *The House of Mirth*, we must always allow for Wharton's wit. Her readers were familiar with the popularized versions of Herbert Spencer's adaptation of Darwinian theory to philosophical and social thought. Richard Hofstadter's *Social Darwinism in America* still stands as the most useful discussion of Spencer's lectures in America (1882), which influenced American thought before the Gilded Age and into the first decade of the twentieth century. Spencer's evolutionary theory accommodated both theist and atheist[7] and was clearly and simply tied to the concept of progress, an upbeat notion tailor-made for the colossal figures of American industry, the millionaires, new and old, of Mrs. Wharton's New York. Andrew Carnegie was one of Spencer's chief supporters, but then so was

Henry Ward Beecher. Half read or misread, Spencer's obliging view of evolutionary theory was in the common domain.

Writing in *A Backward Glance* many years later of her introduction to
"the various popular exponents of the great evolutionary movement,"[8]
Wallace, Spencer, and Huxley among them, Wharton speaks of "the first
overwhelming sense of cosmic vastness which such 'magic casements' let
into our little geocentric universe."[9] In the 1890s Wharton copied into her
Daybook passages from Spencer's *First Principles* and *Principles of Ethics*.[10] By 1903, when she was plotting the doomed life of Lily Bart, a
reductionist genetics was a familiar theme in the work of William Dean
Howells and Theodore Dreiser and in the manifestos by Frank Norris.
Couched in terms of a simple Social Darwinism, heredity was taken to be
destiny – life in a test tube. Wharton was playful in her use of the evolutionary metaphor in her fiction, yet also seriously committed to an understanding of evolution's complex relation to individual hereditary development
and choice. By the time Edith Wharton came to write *The House of Mirth*,
William James had been lecturing for years at Harvard against Spencer's
vague, all-accommodating views, finding them passive, mechanistic. Gerald
Myers conveys James's tone, often one of dismissive mockery in dealing
with Spencer: "He [James] could accept apes as ancestors, but he could not
abide dogmatic extensions of Darwinism which denied free will, the efficacy
of consciousness, or the value of the individual."[11] We may be certain that
Wharton's youthful enthusiasm for the popularizers of evolutionary theory
had been updated. She had already alluded to scientific fashion with high
irony in a volume of stories just published, *The Descent of Man* (1904). In
the title story a scientist sells out, lets his writing be vulgarized, lends himself
to celebrity. It is a variant of the idea of scientist turned entertainer –
perhaps glancing at Oliver Wendell Holmes, eminent doctor, lecturer, and
author of *The Autocrat of the Breakfast Table* or the Harvard professors,
Edward Youmans and John Fiske, who made an industry of Spencer.

Wharton, whose productivity must give us pause, had recently published
Sanctuary (1903), a programmatic novella in which a woman marries a
weak man so that his child will not "be born with some hidden physical
taint," as though her strength and her "vision of protecting maternity"[12]
may genetically block any unfortunate hereditary trait. In a deflated happy
ending, the ambitious son, an architect, does not claim as his own the work
of a more talented friend. Before and after writing *The House of Mirth*,
Wharton was obsessed with problems of intellectual and artistic honesty. It
would remain one of her compelling themes, but the poor little rich girl
doing her New York felt the pressure of her own heritage as she developed

Lily Bart. In writing, she transgressed, invited herself into the gentleman's library, where she would do more than admire bindings. In her earliest work – the anecdotal and often heavily melodramatic stories, the travel books, her work on Italian gardens, and on interior decoration (one of her inmost susceptibilities as well as Lily's), the dutifully researched "romantic chronicle,"[13] *The Valley of Decision* – she hid behind writerly scrims. In *A Backward Glance* she acknowledged that she had become a "professional," dangerous word for a writer, a term that can be seen to encompass her magazine fiction, potboilers and serious efforts alike. For all her fluency, the role of professional writer was willed in Wharton, and she constantly reworked themes of artistic integrity. She had forged her identity as a writer, but still felt that it was not her natural inheritance. Her concern with heritage, its imprint or possible erasure, can be seen most clearly in her finest work. *Summer*, in particular, deals with the painful recognition of parentage. Charity Royall has much in common with Lily Bart, who reviews her family history one final time before her death. The imprint of the overcivilized life Lily had been made for, one of transient exhibition, is as defining as the degraded scene of Charity's birth. Historical, even genetic facts are inescapable, but not the final determinant of human possibility.

The challenge for Mrs. Wharton in writing *The House of Mirth* was to write beyond the brightly stated themes in the opening installments, which from the start of reworking the book implied a sober intention beyond doing her New York. What, for instance, might she manage with types like the spinster, Gerty Farish, with her dowdy good works; or Mrs. Haffen, a grotesque; or the caricature of the millionaire Jew? Having saddled her American subject with American themes of the new century – Selden's spurious freedom, Lily's hereditary baggage, greed and social responsibility – how was Wharton to mine the evolutionary trope so that her readers might see Lily with her nonadaptive traits: her useless hands, the contempt she has for her own species, her flaw of irresolution? (It might be said that she is made to die prematurely, rather than breed unto the next generation.) And how to make clear that Selden's "republic of the spirit" is glib, tag-end romanticism, a place of such idealized freedom that he admits no like soul? And, we may well ask, as we observe his exquisite moral choices, freedom for what? How was the novelist, hitting her stride, to move her readers beyond laughter at Lily's affectations and disapproval of her overrefined taste, to pity – and even terror – as the impoverished, aging "girl" embraced her fate? Above all, how were the joyless spectacles of The Gormer's rise, Bertha Dorset's further infidelities, Rosedale's step up the social ladder, to play with the gritty background of naturalism which Wharton discovered to be suitable for Lily's descent?

She came upon a device to arrest the giddy action in the scene of tableaux vivants in which Lily poses as Sir Joshua Reynolds' portrait *Mrs. Lloyd*. Life imitates art in the living picture which must be voiceless, still. As an art form, tableau vivant is at once naive and decadent – pageant posing of *The Nativity*, or *Washington Crossing the Delaware*. In the later nineteenth century it was a staple of the *entr'acte* in popular French theater.[14] Tableau vivant both devaluates human gesture and, in the frozen stance the *pose plastique*, reduces the historic or painted moment to childish iconography, an obliteration of the brushstroke of artistic achievement. Wharton instructs her readers: "To unfurnished minds they remain, in spite of every enchantment of art, only a superior kind of wax works; but to the responsive fancy they may give magic glimpses of the boundary world between fact and imagination. Selden's mind was of this order: he could yield to vision-making influences as completely as a child to the spell of fairy tale" (140–1).

We must catch the novelist's tone. She is sending up the whole frivolous enterprise of the evening's entertainment while placing Selden, who constantly frames and distances experience: "for the first time he seemed to see before him the real Lily Bart, divested of the trivialities of her little world, and catching for a moment a note of the eternal harmony of which her beauty was a part" (142). On the other hand, Lily understands that the unanimous "OH!" of the spectators has been called forth "by herself, and not the picture she impersonated" (143). In playing the parlor game, she has given life to the lifeless medium and is "intoxicated," senses her "recovered power." Posing as *Mrs. Lloyd* is the culmination of her training in self-presentation. Her triumph is as transitory as the reaction to the tableau vivant: the thrill of a moment.

In that exemplary first chapter, Selden sees Lily as "a captured dryad" and reflects "that it was the same streak of sylvan freedom in her nature that lent such savour to her artificiality" (13). It is a sentiment that might run as a caption to the Reynolds portrait. *Mrs. Lloyd* is an inspired choice on the part of novelist and heroine. It is one of his portraits of a classically costumed lady posed in a stagy natural setting. "Lily," we recall from her Bellomont tryst with Selden, "had no real intimacy with nature, but she had a passion for the appropriate and could be keenly sensitive to a scene which was the fitting background of her own sensations" (66). What is not acknowledged in the novel is that in the painting Mrs. Lloyd is carving the name of her future husband on a tree – as lovers were wont to do in Tasso, in Ariosto's *Orlando Furioso*, often a subject in Italian baroque art,[15] and, of course, in *As You Like It,* Orlando being the youth who "abuses our young plants by carving Rosalind on their barks, hangs odes upon Hawthornes, and elegies upon brambles." Lily Bart has no husband, no lover. The letters inscribed on nature in the portrait must be *un*written by Wharton, so that every man at the entertainment may carve his initials in. Promiscuity, as well as idealization, is in the eyes of the beholder. In *Bodyworks: Objects of Desire in Modern Narrative,* Peter Brooks says that Emma Bovary has no body of her own. "Her body is the social and phantasmiatic construction of the men who look at her."[16] Unlike Madame Bovary, Lily constructs herself; she wants to be viewed, framed as a society woman in staged nature. She underestimates the risk.

In the Reynolds portrait, the sculptural bust is cut off from the animated lower body. The head is stiff as a cameo profile, a reference to classical art and cultural artifacts much in vogue, collectors of the eighteenth century buying up the revered culture of a revered past, much as the newly rich of Wharton's novel were buying up Renaissance masters. Mrs. Lloyd's bust is half shadowed, but her inner thighs are selected, illuminated by a bold triangular shaft of light. The focus is an erotic choice, not as dramatic as mannerist lighting of partial bodies, nor as shocking as Courbet's *Origin of the World* or Magritte's *Representation,*[17] but, in its early Royal Academy way, *Mrs. Lloyd* is startling. We cannot know what lighting effects were available in 1904 at the Wellington Brys', but Lily Bart, a foolish virgin, in confused innocence, surely drew attention to her sexuality. She seems to have read the Reynolds painting not as bisected woman but as a neoclassical unity, for after all, Mrs. Lloyd has one hand on nature, one on the manmade plinth.[18]

Cynthia Griffin Wolff reads Wharton's title of her most Jamesian novel, *The Age of Innocence,* drawn from the famous Reynolds portrait of a little girl, as a private pun upon herself as novice and the Master's great work, *Portrait of a Lady.* But her first use of a Reynolds, in *The House of Mirth,* seems more significant: it is a reification of James's title. Isabel Archer, in *The Portrait of a Lady,* is never painted. She marries disastrously. Like Emma and other Austen heroines, she is valued for her mind. Lily Bart is not. What Wharton made of her heroine's mind is interesting: Lily fears introspection, which becomes unavoidable as her life closes in. It must have amused the readers of *Scribner's,* in 1904, that Lily always traveled with her *Rubaiyat,* and when she feels pursued by the Furies, Wharton makes it clear that she has just read Euripides in a volume found on a guest-room shelf. The mind–body problem, the draw to surfaces rather than meaning, is suggested by Lily's appropriate yet unwitting choice of *Mrs. Lloyd:* and by the novelist's use of the painting – "I will give you my portrait of a lady, what it means to be a lady in this society," says Mrs. Wharton to Henry James. The audience at the de Brys would have known this Reynolds portrait, and so would many of Wharton's readers, not perhaps as readily as *The Age of Innocence*, but reproductions were part of the culture of culture. Cheap mezzotints and lithographs hung in every parlor; "great art" was poorly reproduced in the tony monthly magazines. The guessing game of tableau vivant can only be played through reenactments. In her appropriation of that entertainment and further appropriation of *Mrs. Lloyd*, Wharton was setting her readers up for a conditioned response. Like Manet in his repaintings of Watteau and in his theatrical rendering of costumed models, Wharton expected her audience (both within and without the novel) to partake of a prepared vision that she then refocused in order that we may experience the danger and triumph of Lily's artistic moment.

I was drawn to rereading *The House of Mirth* some years ago, while doing research on the Chicago Exposition of 1894. In *Scribner's,* along with an admiring editorial on The Great White Way, there appeared an early sonnet by Edith Wharton, "Life/Art" (that dichotomy again), and an article "Working Girls Clubs" by Sarah Sidney Davidge. "The clubs are drawn from those employed in trades and business," Mrs. Davidge wrote, "the groups so aggregated and gathered, not by any extraneous force or influence, but by a system of natural selection." The article goes on to report that women of privilege have established proper living quarters for working girls where improving talks are given – "Should women be allowed to vote?" "How to tell a real lady." The final illustration shows young women being instructed in trimming hats. "That's Lily Bart," I said, "who, down and out, in need of work, could not sew a spangle." Wharton must have seen this illustration, along with the many articles in the very magazines she wrote for concerning working women. Alva Vanderbilt, who gave a costume ball far grander than the Wellington Brys' in the nineties, declared that she knew "of no profession, art, or trade that women are working in today as taxing on mental resources as being a leader of society." Divorced and remarried as Mrs. O. H. P. Belmont, she transformed herself utterly in the early years of the new century, carrying the banner for the Equal Suffrage League of New York City down Fifth Avenue.[19] Grace Dodge, a railroad heiress of Wharton's New York society, devoted her life to working-women's centers.[20] Gerty Farish, therefore, is more than just a virtuous counter to Lily: Gerty is the do-good maiden lady who would have been in the audience when Jane Addams lectured, making a point of the social responsibility which must be assumed by the fortunate. This is the very point that Wharton makes in a letter to the Boston biographer and historian William Roscoe Taylor:

> I must protest, & emphatically, against the suggestion that I have "stripped" New York society. . . . the little corner of its garment that I lifted was meant to show only that little atrophied organ – the group of the idle & dull people. . . . & if, as I believe, it is more harmful in its influence, it is because fewer responsibilities attach to money with us than in any other societies.[21]

The serious theme of social responsibility, as Wharton developed it in *The House of Mirth,* did not adjust easily to her satire. Gerty, Mrs. Haffen, the charwoman, and Rosedale could no longer function as pawns in a narrative game. They are the very outsiders who connect Lily to an urban reality. Wharton gave them dimension. Gerty, unmarriageable, childless, becomes the mother figure for Lily in distress. The scene in which Gerty cradles Lily like a child prefigures the death scene in which Lily feels that Nettie Struther's infant is in her arms, also supposing that she is responsible for this child, whom her single act of charity has begot. Coming of age as a novelist, Mrs. Wharton drew her minor characters to great effect. We must note that as Mrs. Haffen proposes to blackmail Lily, she declares herself to be a good Christian woman.

Mr. Rosedale would not have been a problem for the majority of Wharton's readers of the serialized novel in *Scribner's.* We are troubled reading Judy Trenor's declaration that "he was the same little Jew who had been served up and rejected at the social board a dozen times within her memory" (17). Mrs. Trenor speaks with the unforgivable prejudice of her class. It is more troubling that Wharton in her narrative voice refers to supposed traits of Rosedale's race, but we should not overlook her skill in opposing Rosedale's realistic evaluations of Lily Bart's worth to Lawrence Selden's self-serving, partial assessments. Simon Rosedale is the only man who deals honestly with Lily, the one who, from the first installment to his last chance meeting with her on the street, talks straight to her. He is shown to be no fool and is the closest thing to a sympathetic male in the novel.

We have come to think of Edith Wharton as a self-styled intellectual, an identity hard won. From her letters we know that her reading continued to be deep and wide throughout her life. While she flipped the pages of the popular monthly journals, she was also reading Pater and William James, Proust and Baudelaire. In her unpublished Daybook she copied out passages from Seneca, Donne, Shakespeare, La Bruyère, Goethe, Flaubert's letters, Bernard Shaw, Whitman, and, as she began work on the novel that was to become *The House of Mirth,* she copied lines from Dante, the passage from

The Inferno[22] that concerns the goddess Fortuna, whose "changes have no respite." In one sentence, the depiction of the goddess might seem to be Lily: "This is she who is so reviled by the very men that should give her praise, laying on her wrongful blame and ill repute." In the Daybook of 1903 all of Poe's "To Helen" appears, a poem in which the woman is, to a degree that amazes, an aesthetic object:

> Lo, in your brilliant window-niche,
> How statue-like I see thee stand,
> The agate lamp within thy hand –

Selden, were he not an untalented dilettante, might have written something along those lines about Lily in her classical garb as Mrs. Lloyd.

Wharton took from her reading what could help her to write Lily's story, turning, most particularly, to Dreiser's *Sister Carrie,* which had been published in 1900. She admired the American naturalists,[23] and in her darker work it is evident that she believed, as they did, that natural selection was not benevolent when applied to social and environmental circumstances. Though Lily Bart, transformed to Mrs. Lloyd, displays herself to high, somewhat striving society, her performance recalls the striking scene in which Carrie – upon the stage, in melodrama – transcends her provincial working-class heritage. Untrained, unskilled Carrie Meeber, who has wandered the city looking for work (one job she rejects is the trimming of hats), becomes the desirable Carrie Madenda, an actress. Unlike the tableau vivant, which marks the beginning of Lily's descent, Carrie's performance at the Chicago Elks launches her career. "Hurstwood realized he was seeing something extraordinarily good. It was heightened for him by the applause of the audience as the curtain descended and the fact that it was Carrie. He thought now that she was beautiful. She had done something which was above his sphere. He felt a keen delight in realising that she was his."[24] Hurstwood does not lose sight of Carrie's performance, while Selden, believing that he now sees "the real Lily Bart," buys the illusion of tableau vivant. In their theatrical appearances, both women are removed from their ordinary lives in which they may be possessed by men. Hurstwood and Selden are pathetically wrong. Carrie and Lily's freedom, problematic to be sure, is won by disguise and concealment. Carrie finds herself in being other than she is. Acting is her work, what is destined to be her life/art. Lily's power over her audience cannot be sustained beyond the evening's entertainment; no matter how successful her impersonation of Mrs. Lloyd, it is not a permissible line of work. Edith Wharton's work, we must remember, was still suspect to her New York, as she wrote *The House of Mirth.*

At the end of *Sister Carrie,* Hurstwood's suicide is a determined act. How carefully he tucks his coat and vest along the crack under the rooming-house door! How brief his moment of hesitation before he turns on the gas! In Dreiser's mechanistic system, Hurstwood is weak. But Mrs. Wharton's heroine does not say, "What's the use?" We are told that the action of the drug chloral, a "magic formula" (338) that Lily takes, is "capricious and incalculable" (328). She is far from the calculations that initiated her story. Increasing the dose,

> She knew she took a slight risk . . . – she remembered the chemist's warning. If sleep came at all, it might be sleep without waking. But after all that was but one chance in a hundred; the action of the drug was incalculable, and the addition of a few drops to the regular dose would probably do no more than procure for her the rest she so desperately needed. . . .
>
> She did not, in truth, consider the question very closely – (339–40)

Lily, it would seem, is at last in the hands of Fate. What moves us about her death is that it is not a suicide. She has so fully departed from the world that produced her that she has come to recognize her "deeper empoverishment" (336). As she wanders with the multitudes through an unknown New York, all that has been concealed by the narrowness of her society is now disclosed to her. Lily, homeless, has seen the child and hearth of Nettie Struthers, the poor little "work girl." It is a primal vision of kinship from which the poor little rich girl is no longer closed out. Their chance meeting in Bryant Park is one of the last melodramatic strokes in the novel, to be followed by the final arrival of a letter bearing a check, her inheritance. Money may save the heroine of melodrama (it had saved Nettie), but it cannot save Lily, who is beyond the solution of that genre. She dies of a last, miscalculated dose of chloral, yet another mistake in the long list of bad risks, misunderstandings, and irresolutions that make her story.

Lily Bart is socially unfit, a weak strain, though morally she proves to be a rare subspecies – ultimately an individual, superior to the world that produced her. Fate may dole out the extra dram of chloral, but she has paid her debts, chosen to be good. Lily dies searching for a word she had meant to say to Selden – the man she has idealized, perhaps her fatal mistake; searching for a word, just as he searched for a word to say to her at their last meeting, when Lily spoke clearly without "the conventional outskirts of word-play and evasion" (322). The novelist does not reveal these lost words. After all of Lily's accounts have been settled, literally – the literal is a form of wit in *The House of Mirth* – and all motives, both the bachelor's and the maiden's, revealed, there is a final concealment. As Selden kneels by the dead Lily Bart he is somewhat self-aware, though still self-dramatizing. He is, at last, mute, but he meditates grandly:

> It was this moment of love, this fleeting victory over themselves, which had kept them from atrophy and extinction; which, in her, had reached out to him in every struggle against the influence of her surroundings, and in him, had kept alive the faith that now drew him penitent and reconciled to her side.
>
> He knelt by the bed and bent over her, draining their last moment to its lees; and in the silence there passed between them the word which made all clear.
>
> (347)

It is a scene fit for salon painting or for a tableau vivant: *Lover at the Bier*. It has not kept Lily from atrophy. She is dead. It is Selden's dramatic last moment, not hers. This ending beyond Lily Bart's death scene once again lays open the problems of true feeling against the postured or calculated moment, artifice opposed to authenticity, with which the novel began.

Turning back to the passages leading up to and including Lily's death, we will not find the unuttered word, for it is unknowable, as was the loophole of the unknowable which the American disciples of Spencer grasped and tied into their knot of belief in a transfigured realism. Lily's memory of her rootlessness, her deprivation of a house which stored "visual memories" (337), "the blind motions of her mating-instincts" (337), and her new understanding that "individual existence" may attach to "the mighty sum of human striving" (337) are not Spencer pure and simple. Wharton freed herself from the rigidities of Social Darwinism by throwing her heroine into a world of chance, a chance which implies choice. Lily retains the capacity not only to choose goodness – to connect, however slightly, to social responsibility – but to act against her own interests, which brings Wharton more in line with William James's argument for individual free will. In fact, Wharton rejects not only a passive determinism but the romantic obverse of that notion, which floats through Lily's head: "If only life could end now – end on this tragic yet sweet vision of lost possibilities, which gave her a sense of kinship with all the loving and foregoing world!" (337). If only the arguments which connected an acceptable evolutionary theory to a popular American idealism were not easily refutable: if only Wharton were writing a lesser novel than *The House of Mirth*. In 1898, long before she faced the problems of creating Lily Bart, she copied out a fragment of a letter to J. S. Mill which Spencer published in his *Principles of Ethics,* in which he speaks of "nervous modifications, which by continued transmission & accumulation, have become in us certain faculties of moral intuition – certain emotional responding to right & wrong conduct, *which have no apparent basis in the individual experiences of utility.*"[25] "Nervous modifications" and

"moral intuition" are fudging phrases – vague, unscientific – but the under-
lining is the novelist's and may be read as a note toward the creation of Lily
Bart, who was to be both useless and, in the end, uselessly good.

Edith Wharton, who had just settled into The Mount, the country house
which she built in the Berkshires, came to understand that in writing of her
New York, no matter how amusing or how cutting her attitudes, her novel
would be run-of-the-Scribner's-mill unless she dispossessed herself and took
to the streets with Lily. She added a postscript to her letter to William
Roscoe Taylor, "I wish you felt a little more kindly toward poor Lily!"[26]
Henry James had directed her to the American subject, and she obeyed only
to a degree. "It is vain to write on chosen themes," Thoreau tells us in his
journals. "We must wait until they have kindled a flame in our minds. There
must be the copulating and generating force of love behind every effort
destined to be successful. The cold resolve gives birth to, begets, nothing.
The theme seeks me, not I it. The poet's relation to his theme is the relation
of love."[27] Mrs. Wharton loved the themes of fate and free will, of nature
and artifice, of greedy and generous spirits, large American themes suggested by her discarded New York and further discovered in the city streets,
finding the novel's broad view in a rooming house and a New York tenement. During Lily's accidental dying, the irresolute overdose produces the
flush of loneliness and terror, but her last sensation is that of flesh, the
warmth of the "work girl's" child flowing through her. Lily's body lies
between the baby in her arms, a fantasy, and the bachelor who is unworthy
to claim her in death. Yet Lily's end is surely preferable to Carrie Meeber's,
though Carrie Madenda's name lights up Broadway: "In your rocking chair,
by your window dreaming, shall you long alone. In your rocking chair, by
your window shall you dream such happiness as you may never feel."[28] But
then Wharton, unlike Dreiser, loved her poor heroine from the first exemplary installment to the last, as Jane Austen loved the arrogant Emma and
redeemed her with patience and humor. It was the creation of Lily Bart,
complex and perverse and irresolute, the vision of Lily exiled from the
drawing room and adrift in the other New York of Howells and Dreiser,
which enabled Edith Wharton to rise from her pretty French desk in the
library at Lenox, sluff off the *succes d'estime* of her early work, and march
right into the untidy democratic hall of American letters.

James was right, as he most always was. *The House of Mirth* is two
books, much like Willa Cather's *The Professor's House,* which interrupts a
family story to tell a necessary history, or like Woolf's *Between the Acts,*
which alternates drawing-room comedy with historical panorama. But these

extraordinary novels are not confused in their ingenious assault on structure. Nor is *The House of Mirth* confused, though it is bravely flawed, for in the story of Lily's descent which is not her downfall, Wharton mixed modes in a risky melodramatic rescue – manners with morals, stylish *Scribner's* with serious stuff – depriving her readers of a conditioned sorrow at the death of a beautiful, blameless woman so as to elicit a fresh and complicated response. It is the best book she ever wrote, and in the heroine's elegiac final passages, in which Lily understands that heritage – hers and Mrs. Wharton's – need not be destiny, the novelist delivered her sermon from The Mount.

NOTES

1 Henry James to Edith Wharton, August 17, 1902, *The Letters of Henry James,* ed. Leon Edel (Cambridge, Mass.: Harvard University Press, 1984), 233–6.
2 Ibid., 236.
3 *The House of Mirth,* in *Edith Wharton: Novels,* ed. R. W. B. Lewis (New York: Library of America, 1985), 3. All quotations (hereafter cited in the text) are from this edition.
4 Edith Wharton and Ogden Codman, *The Decoration of Houses* (New York: Scribner, 1897). See R. W. B. Lewis, *Edith Wharton: A Biography* (New York, Harper & Row, 1975), 77–8, for a discussion of Wharton's scoring off her mother's decor.
5 James, quoted in Lewis, *Edith Wharton: A Biography,* 153.
6 Jane Austen, *Emma,* afterword by Graham Hough (New York: Penguin [Signet], 1981), 3.
7 Richard Hofstadter, *Social Darwinism in America* (Philadelphia: University of Pennsylvania, 1944; rpt. Boston: Beacon, 1955). Hofstadter's chapter "The Vogue of Spencer" remains an informative discussion of Spencer's influence on American thought before the Gilded Age and into the first decade of the twentieth century.
8 Edith Wharton, *A Backward Glance,* in *Novellas and Other Writings,* ed. Cynthia Griffin Wolff (New York: Library of America, 1990), 856.
9 Ibid., 94.
10 Edith Wharton, Unpublished Daybook. All material from Edith Wharton's unpublished Daybook by permission of Watkins, Loomis Agency. Copyright © William R. Taylor.
11 Gerald E. Myers, *William James, His Life and Thought* (New Haven: Yale University Press, 1986), 409.
12 Edith Wharton, *Sanctuary* (New York: Scribner, 1903), 66.
13 *Backward Glance,* 939.
14 Judith Fryer has a discussion of the popular modes of tableau vivant as it relates to Lily's presentation of herself, in "Reading Mrs. Lloyd," *Edith Wharton: New Critical Essays* (New York: Garland, 1992), 27–53. See also Candace Wade, *Edith Wharton's Letters from the Underworld* (Chapel Hill: University of

North Carolina Press, 1991). In the chapter "Women and Letters (*The House of Mirth*)," Wade's interest in the Reynolds portrait is in Lily as artist in a self-portrait (27–30).

15 Nicholas Penny, ed., *Reynolds* (London: Weidenfeld & Nicolson, 1976), 275–76.

16 Peter Brooks, *Bodyworks: Objects of Desire in Modern Narrative* (Cambridge, Mass.: Harvard University Press, 1993), 95.

17 Much attention has been directed, in recent criticism, at the representation of women's bodies, with particular insight by Anne Hollander and Linda Nochlin. There is a remarkably perceptive view of the representation of partial bodies, which helps in reading Reynolds' *Mrs. Lloyd,* in Mary Ann Caws, "Representing Bodies from Mannerism to Modernism: Cloaking, Remembering, and the Elliptical Effect," *The Art of Interference: Stressed Readings in Verbal and Visual Texts* (Princeton: Princeton University Press, 1989), 25–50.

18 My discussion of *Mrs. Lloyd* owes much to comments by my daughter, Loretta Howard.

19 William K. Vanderbilt, *Fortune's Children: The Fall of the House of Vanderbilt* (New York: Morrow, 1989), 115–21. The Wellington Brys' evening would also echo the Bradley Martins' ball of 1896. See also Lloyd Morris, *Incredible New York* (New York: Random House, 1951), 152–6.

20 Anne Firor Scott, "Inventing Progressivism: Social Justice," *Natural Allies: Women's Associations in American History* (Urbana, Ill.: University of Illinois Press, 1991), 159–74, is an illuminating discussion of social consciousness and responsibility.

21 *The Letters of Edith Wharton,* ed. R. W. B. Lewis and Nancy Lewis (New York: Scribner, 1988), 96–7.

22 Dante, *Inferno,* bk. 7, lines 73–97, translated by John D. Sinclair (New York: Oxford University Press, 1939, 1982), 103. Wharton copied from the original Italian.

23 *Backward Glance,* 894. See also Lewis, *Edith Wharton: A Biography,* 520.

24 Theodore Dreiser, *Sister Carrie* (New York: Bantam, 1992), 146.

25 Wharton, Daybook.

26 *Letters of Edith Wharton,* 96–7.

27 Henry David Thoreau, *Journal,* ed. Bradford Torrey (New York: AMS, 1968), 3:23.

28 Dreiser, *Sister Carrie,* 400.

8

JAMES W. TUTTLETON

Justine: or, the Perils of Abstract Idealism

Edith Wharton's third novel, *The Fruit of the Tree* (1907), was written toward the end of her residence in New York, while she was yet summering at The Mount in Massachusetts. Her publisher Charles Scribner wanted another best seller just like *The House of Mirth* (1905), that is, a fresh popular exposé of the moral bankruptcy of New York high society. But she was determined not to be typed as a high-society novelist, and she wanted nothing more than to illustrate her capacity for thematic variety. The conflict between capital and labor seemed promising.

Promising – but strange for Mrs. Wharton. Blake Nevius once suggested that Mrs. Wharton "had no community whatsoever" with "Howells and his generation,"[1] but in fact she knew Howells as a friend and must almost certainly have thought about *The Fruit of the Tree* in terms of *Annie Kilburn* (1889) and other popular realist novels dealing with industrial problems in the New England factory town. Howells's generation had produced a long line of popular labor novels, including Elizabeth Stuart Phelps's *The Silent Partner* (1871), Thomas Bailey Aldrich's *The Stillwater Tragedy* (1880), John Hay's *The Breadwinners* (1883), and H. F. Keenan's *The Money-Makers* (1885). In Mrs. Wharton's generation, new writers were bringing into the "Progressive Era" this older mode of writing. Ida M. Tarbell's *The History of the Standard Oil Company* (1904), Lincoln Steffens's *The Shame of Cities* (1904), Samuel Hopkins Adams's *The Great American Fraud* (1906), and scores of nonfiction works like them were exposing corruption in business, industry, and politics that demanded urgent reform. Mary Wilkins in *The Portion of Labor* (1901), David Graham Phillips in *The Deluge* (1905), and Upton Sinclair in *The Jungle* (1906), were – like Mrs. Wharton in *The Fruit of the Tree* – following in this long procession of muckraking prose and popular labor fiction.

For one who had cast a doubtful eye on the impractical theorizing of eighteenth-century reformers in *The Valley of Decision* (1902), Mrs. Wharton's motives in writing this kind of novel seem intriguing. But if she was known as a chronicler of drawing-room society, she had also dealt in a surprisingly extensive way with poverty and its effect on the human spirit. Her first published tale, "Mrs. Manstey's View" (1891), portrayed the grimness of tenement life in New York City. Subsequent tales like "The Confessional" and "A Cup of Cold Water" also touched on the misery of the poor in the city. "Bunner Sisters" – published in *Xingu and Other Stories* in 1916 – was long thought to be one of Mrs. Wharton's later naturalistic portraits of the despair of the poor, but it was in fact drafted as early as 1891 or 1892. The world of Gerty Farish in *The House of Mirth*, and Lily's final months in the cheap boardinghouse – which stand in dingy contrast to the splendor of Bellomont and the Fifth Avenue drawing rooms – were therefore not novelties. All of these early stories suggest how sensitive was Mrs. Wharton, from the beginning of her career, to the problems of the poor.

What could be done in their behalf? Without any very specific notion about the right way to get a "square deal" for the factory worker, Mrs. Wharton turned away from the drawing room to the plight of the textile workers in small-town Massachusetts. "Heaven knows where she got her knowledge of mill-towns,"[2] Q. D. Leavis once wondered, and so may we. She got it by having her chauffeur, Charles Cook, drive her down from her palatial estate at The Mount, near Lenox, to Adams, Massachusetts, where she toured the local textile mills to investigate factory conditions.[3] Unfortunately, the noise of the machines was so great that she could not hear her guide, and so the notes got scrambled. Later, when the story began to appear serially in *Scribner's Magazine,* experts wrote in to call attention to the great lady's technical errors.[4]

These errors seemed minor to Mrs. Wharton in view of her ambitious moral resolve. "It cannot be too often repeated," Mrs. Wharton once observed, "that every serious picture of life contains a thesis."[5] Despite her confusions of fact, Mrs. Wharton's purpose in *The Fruit of the Tree* is perfectly clear: to expose and criticize, in narrative form, an abuse of the industrial system: the irresponsibility of factory managers who fail to look after the physical and spiritual welfare of their employees. The thesis here is expressed through John Amherst, social reformer and assistant manager of the Hanaford Mills. A progressive who undertakes to reform the conditions that make mill work both dangerous and soul-destroying, Amherst seems to be different from the impractical revolutionaries of *The Valley of Decision* whose utopian schemes destroy Pianura.

> John Amherst was no one-sided idealist. He felt keenly the growing complexity of the relation between employer and worker, the seeming hopelessness of

permanently harmonizing their claims, the recurring necessity of fresh compromises and adjustments. He hated rant, demagogy, the rash formulating of emotional theories; and his contempt for bad logic and subjective judgments led him to regard with distrust the panaceas offered for the cure of economic evils.[6]

At the same time, however, Amherst is, like most of us, emotional and inconsistent. He is deeply troubled at the plight of Dillon, a worker whose arm has been mangled in a carding-room accident. If Dillon cannot recover, shouldn't he – Amherst speculates to the nurse Justine Brent – be put out of his misery? And what can be done for Dillon's wife, whose lungs have been ruined by inhaling textile dust, or for the other seven hundred women working in the mills? Feeling both "the menace of industrial conditions" as a whole and the poignancy of the life of the laborers as individuals, Amherst perceives that whatever the philosophic implications of industrialism, "only through sympathy with its personal, human side could a solution be reached" (48). Given the explicitness of Mrs. Wharton's unmistakable theme, then, it is surprising to find Robert Morss Lovett asserting that "the industrial worker" does not "appear in her pages." Quite wrongly, Lovett regarded her as unconcerned with "the relation of class with class," which, he said, eighteen years after her book appeared, was "the vital issue of social morality today."[7]

Yet it must be stressed that *The Fruit of the Tree* does not directly address bread-and-butter economic issues. The question of the fairness of the laborer's wage or the size of the owner's margin of profit is not her point. Amherst makes it very plain that he has "no wish to criticise the business management of the mills – even if there had been any excuse for my doing so." His is a moral argument: that "the condition of the operatives could be very much improved, without permanent harm to the business, by any one who felt a personal sympathy for them; and in the end I believe such sympathy produces better work, and so benefits the employer materially" (100). In this respect Amherst's arguments are in support of the rights of the mill owners as a group, but he is offering them some practical wisdom as to what labor practices best conduce to the profit motive and are consonant with the owners' interests. Yet oddly enough, in some criticism of this novel, Amherst's arguments are seen as expressions of a left-wing labor policy. Mrs. Wharton, however, was a lifelong opponent of socialism, as her correspondence with Upton Sinclair suggests.

One of the greatest wrongs of the new industrial system, according to Mrs. Wharton's protagonist, is that there is no longer any familiar contact between the owner and his employee.[8] "That the breach must be farther widened by the ultimate substitution of the stock-company for the individual employer – a fact obvious to any student of economic tendencies – presented to Amherst's mind one of the most painful problems in the scheme of social readjustment." It is characteristic of Amherst, however, to focus on solving the specific problems that confront him rather than those of the future. He sees his main task as bringing the owner "closer to his workers. Till he entered personally into their hardships and aspirations – till he learned what they wanted and why they wanted it – Amherst believed that no mere law-making, however enlightened, could create a wholesome relation between the two" (48).

Amherst's immediate project is to enlarge the floor space of the mills, so that workers like Dillon will not be endangered by the machines, and to abolish the system of company rentals, so that workers will be able to buy homes from the mills. Green lawns, tennis courts, picnic areas, a reading room, and a gymnasium are seen as low-cost, profit-enhancing ameliorations. But Amherst finds himself handcuffed by the absentee owners. Because they are concerned with profit, they do not take a sufficient interest in the conditions in which the laborers live and work. As she looked about Adams, Mrs. Wharton could not help condemning this absenteeism in very personal – that is to say in aesthetic – terms. What seems to have horrified her most was the visual ugliness of the American factory town, the suburban slum that, in its ugliness, destroyed, she felt, the worker's moral sense:

> With sudden disgust he [Amherst] saw the sordidness of it all – the poor monotonous houses, the trampled grass-banks, the lean dogs prowling in refuse-heaps, the reflection of a crooked gas-lamp in a stagnant loop of the river; and he asked himself how it was possible to put any sense of moral beauty into lives bounded forever by the low horizon of the factory. There is a fortuitous ugliness that has life and hope in it: the ugliness of overcrowded city streets, of the rush and drive of packed activities; but this out-spread meanness of the suburban working colony, uncircumscribed by any pressure of surrounding life, and sunk into blank acceptance of its isolation, its banishment from beauty and variety and surprise, seemed to Amherst the very negation of hope and life. (22–3)

The doubtful plot device by which Mrs. Wharton brings Amherst and the rich owners into closer contact is the marriage of Amherst to Bessy Westmore, a spirited but mindless woman whose family owns the mill. Trying to motivate this frivolous wife to forgo some of her luxuries, so that mill reforms can be accomplished, takes too much out of Amherst. Unable to achieve his goals, he becomes impatient; bored with his mill projects, she drifts away. They become estranged, and his enthusiasm for reform begins to flag. Later, after Bessy's death, Amherst does implement some of his innovations. Rough banks are leveled and sodded, trees are planted, the workers' cottages are freshly painted, the mills are enlarged, and medical facilities are improved. But one's final impression is that these improvements represent only a start: much yet remains to be done to make Hanaford Mills an adequate workplace.

The Fruit of the Tree is not a successful novel, despite its many favorable reviews.[9] What finally subverts it is not Mrs. Wharton's ignorance of mill technology – her errors were corrected, anyway, in the first book edition – but rather her failure to see her subject steadily and see it whole. The novel is, in fact, broken-backed. Midway through the book – probably because she recognized that labor fiction was not her métier – Mrs. Wharton abandoned the theme of labor reform in favor of another: the moral implications of euthanasia. When Amherst's impulsive wife is injured by a fall from a horse, Mrs. Wharton's heroine, the nurse Justine Brent, deliberately puts Bessy out of her misery by giving her an overdose of morphine. Justine's is, ostensibly, a "moral motive" – to put to an end the agonizing pain from which Bessy, it is said, can never recover. Felt compassion, grounded on a rational motive, thus leads her to kill Amherst's wife.

Later, Amherst and Justine are drawn together, fall in love, and marry. They are "soul mates" who have, at the beginning, a perfect married life. As Justine reflects on the marital problems of Bessy and Amherst, it seems to her that

> the tragic crises in wedded life usually turned on the stupidity of one of the two concerned; and of the two victims of such a catastrophe she felt most for the one whose limitations had probably brought it about. After all, there could be no imprisonment as cruel as that of being bounded by a hard small nature. Not to be penetrable at all points to the shifting lights, the wandering music of the world – she could imagine no physical disability as cramping as that. How the little parched soul, in solitary confinement for life, must pine and dwindle in its blind cranny of self-love. (227–8)

Thus the cramping marriage of Amherst and Bessy – and, doubtless, of Edith and Teddy Wharton. But not, apparently, of Amherst and Justine, who enjoy unparalleled marital rapport.

Yet sustained happiness is not characteristic of Edith Wharton's imaginative world. The Fates intrude in this novel in the form of Stephen Wyant, a doctor, who guesses what Justine has done in injecting Bessy with too much morphine, for – of all things – he himself is a narcotics addict. Disintegrating in this addiction, Wyant blackmails Justine. Although she tries to keep her crime a secret, Wyant eventually tells Amherst about the euthanasia. Justine had acted on principles of moral conduct which Amherst had often grandly proclaimed – *"La vraie morale se moque de la morale. . . . We perish because we follow other men's examples. . . . Socrates used to call the opinions of the many by the name of Lamiæ – bugbears to frighten children"* (429). But Amherst is in fact shaken at the revelation of Justine's mercy killing. It is one thing to endorse euthanasia intellectually; it is another to carry it out – particularly on his wife Bessy. Justine reflects that "her fault lay in having dared to rise above conventional restrictions, her mistake in believing that her husband could rise with her." She sees that Amherst "would never be able to free himself from the traditional view of her act" (523–5). Indeed, he cannot.

After Justine's crime is discovered, she and Amherst separate for a year but finally decide that in fact they need each other. Even so, the "secret inner union which had so enriched and beautified their outward lives" (623) has been destroyed by Justine's act and by Amherst's inability to reconcile his rational approval, in principle, of euthanasia with his moral revulsion at the mercy killing of his own wife Bessy. They can only throw themselves into the mill reforms that both are determined to effect. In assisting him, Justine thus pledges herself "to the perpetual expiation of an act for which, in the abstract, she still refused to hold herself to blame" (624).

Calling the novel broken-backed implies that it has just two themes: labor reform and euthanasia. But for Cynthia Griffin Wolff there are many themes embedded in the plot. She has asked:

> What is the "problem" of the novel? Euthanasia, the need for industrial reform, the old problem of idealized expectations coming up against the harsh realities of real-world existence, marriage, the role of women, the devastating results of failures in communication between the sexes, men's unrealistic expectations of women, the insufficiency of women's education and of the roles they are given to enact – the list could go on and on.[10]

All of these may be aspects of Mrs. Wharton's varied story. But most of them, it seems to me, can be subsumed under a rubric we might call "the perils of abstract idealism." A full reading of this theme would of course disclose how abstract idealism permeates several plot elements and is played out in various characters. Despite his seeming practicality, I am convinced that a separate paper could be written with the title "Amherst: or, The Perils of Abstract Idealism." But in the space available here, I should like to concentrate on two important matters: (1) why Justine's idealism is disastrous; and (2) how a misconceived admiration for Justine has produced a false view of Amherst as a misogynist and a false view of the novel as an attack on marriage.

Justine, as I have noted, pledges herself "to the perpetual expiation of an act for which, in the abstract, she still refused to hold herself to blame" (624). Is Justine's feeling of blamelessness justified? The key phrase is of course "in the abstract." But in much current criticism of the novel, this phrase is ignored. Justine is such a strong, independent, freethinking, and self-reliant heroine that – for many readers of the novel – she can do (and indeed *has done*) no wrong. The deliberate fatal injection of morphine, for Cynthia Griffin Wolff, "is unequivocally justified in the mind of the author and narrator." "The text," we are told by Deborah Carlin, "presents un-equivocally Justine's choice to perform euthanasia on Bessy as the morally correct one."[11] It is even rightly pointed out that Mrs. Wharton felt, in the case of an incurable injury to one of her Lenox neighbors, Ethel Cram, that the victim's sufferings might be ended "with a dose of morphine."[12] But such an act, Mrs. Wharton knew, could never be performed "cleanly," that is, without affective consequences to the sensibilities of other people. Hence, the question for criticism is somewhat different: whether the text of the novel endorses euthanasia in actuality, not in the abstract – whether, that is, the novel approves euthanasia in the specific circumstances in which Justine commits it. I do not believe that it does.

Now, to exonerate Justine from the possibility that she has really done something wrong, a number of critics have recently shifted the moral issue away from the euthanasia to Amherst's reaction to it. Elizabeth Ammons suggests that Amherst's estrangement from Justine, after he discovers that she has killed Bessy, arises because she "did not feel bound to seek his approval [for the euthanasia] after the fact." For Ammons, there is appar-ently nothing wrong in Justine's declining "to consider herself morally ac-countable to him," either before the euthanasia or after she married him.[13] The view that a spouse is not ethically accountable to the other, whether held by the husband or the wife, would seem to me to make marriage a moral impossibility. Mrs. Wharton clearly did not mean to suggest this, although some current feminist criticism insinuates as much.

In any case, to salvage Justine as a blameless heroine, this view undertakes to transform Amherst into a typical sexist pig who cannot tolerate moral autonomy in a woman. His dismay at Justine – for actually performing a killing that they have only abstractly and theoretically discussed – automat-ically converts him into a hypocritical villain who is the destroyer of Jus-tine's marriage and her affectional life. Amherst's dismay has the effect of "ruining yet another of his attempts at marriage," Deborah Carlin remarks. That is, if he has killed one woman, he's killed two – by victimizing not only Justine but Bessy before her. The argument that the center of the novel is the destruction of two wives by a misogynistic husband presupposes that Amherst causes Bessy's riding accident. And in fact Carlin transmogrifies the selfish Bessy into the long-suffering, self-sacrificing wife of Victorian sentimental fiction: Bessy "performs the only sacrifice that social and literary traditions have taught her to do; she destroys herself, though even then she still doesn't get it right."[14] Moreover, Amherst is a bogus reformer, since, although he "espouses a kind of socialist democracy in the work place, when it comes to his own spouses, he remains locked in a reading of a natural domination by men and a subordination of women utterly at odds with his reformist ideology."[15]

Instead of labor reform or euthanasia, then, we are now advised to see the tale as really about the victimization of women by men. Elizabeth Ammons goes even further than Carlin, finding in the novel an attack on the institution of marriage itself. When "we last see this brave New Woman," Ammons says of Justine, "she is a prisoner of a paternal, authoritarian husband"; in fact, "the book concludes by arguing that marriage to even the most enlightened man is, in the end, repressive."[16] "Once independent and self-supporting," Susan Goodman complains, "Justine is now 'an angel in the house.'"[17]

That marriage is always repressive certainly was an argument of the free-love advocates of the fin de siècle, but it is surprising to see the notion ascribed to Mrs. Wharton. Does *The Fruit of the Tree* really condemn marriage as such? Does Justine end up as a doormat? Does the book really attack the repression of all impulse in marriage as evil? And supposing that Justine is repressed, what is the agency of her repression? Is it Amherst? Or, when we last see her, has she repressed her own feelings – her contempt for Bessy and disgust at Amherst's idealizing memory of her – in the service of marital harmony? And, if so, is any spouse, man or woman, who compromises in this way – by sidestepping a pointless conflict – a dupe and a fool? These are engaging questions which the reader will want to ponder. But two points must be stressed. First, the novel is a narrative and is not "arguing that marriage to even the most enlightened man is, in the end, repressive." Lesbian sociological polemics and even works of literary criticism may make such arguments, but not novels, which are works of art; and, second, Mrs. Wharton's characterization is much more complex than can be allowed by some ideological critics who wish to see the strong heroine prevail, no matter what act she may have committed, no matter what the ramifications of the act.

Justine Brent is an appealing, well-defined, fully realized woman character, but she is, I submit, far from an ideal heroine.[18] She cannot be, because Mrs. Wharton's whole plot is intended to reveal the train of disasters that follow from Justine's failure to think through the possible consequences of her act and, in particular, to anticipate, once she decides to marry Amherst, what effect a knowledge of the act might have upon him. In reality, as the title suggests, *The Fruit of the Tree* is a modern instance of the fall – Justine and Amherst's fall from purity into sin, from innocence into guilt, from ignorance into a knowledge of the moral life in all its complexity. At the heart of the book is their descent from abstract idealism into a fallen awareness of the contingency of all moral action. Yet the tendency of much criticism of *The Fruit of the Tree* is to see its moral analysis as rigidly inflexible and absolutist. H. Wayne Morgan once said that Mrs. Wharton "committed herself to a system of absolute truth, which required an absolute code of conduct."[19] But this, it seems to me, is a total misreading of the novelist. Edith Wharton had, in fact, immersed herself in the skeptical sciences, especially in evolutionary Darwinism, and she understood both manners and morals to be evolved products of slowly altering social and ethical conventions. It is in fact Justine who is the absolutist: she believes that if, in principle, euthanasia is right, it is always right in practice. And that, the novel shows us, is wrong.

I cannot think of a passage in Mrs. Wharton's work that expresses more vividly than the following her sense of the way in which any abstractly conceived absolute must necessarily – and properly – be constrained and tempered by the weight of the received moral and social tradition. "Life," Mrs. Wharton has Justine at last ruefully perceive, "is not a matter of abstract principles, but a succession of pitiful compromises with fate, of concessions to old tradition, old beliefs, old charities and frailties." That is the lesson that Justine learns:

> that was the word of the gods to the mortal who had laid a hand on their bolts. And she had humbled herself to accept the lesson, seeing human relations at last as a tangled and deep-rooted growth, a dark forest through which the idealist cannot cut his straight path without hearing at each stroke the cry of the severed branch: "*Why woundest thou me?*" (624)

To eat the fruit of the tree is therefore to gain a knowledge of good and evil in their inextricable human entanglement. It is the knowledge of the complexity of the moral life in a world where an idealistic act, abstractly conceived and subjectively justified, may prove destructive because, whether or not it breaks the law, it may ignore a tangle of inconsistencies in the moral sense of another. The opinions of the many create not only the mores but also the morals of society; what society deems immoral, like euthanasia, may be a bugbear to frighten children, or it may not. But the individual who violates a society's ethical judgment on such a matter does so at her own risk. The irony of the novel is that this risk is especially dangerous to the idealist who does not anticipate one recurrent fact of the moral life: that even a person of "emancipated thought," like Amherst, may remain "subject to the old conventions of feeling."

I hope that it will not be perceived as a digression if I observe that in *A Motor-Flight through France,* Mrs. Wharton remarks that the proper way for a modern unbeliever to appreciate the Gothic cathedral is to cultivate, along with one's "enfranchised thought," an "atavism of feeling" – that is, a capacity to feel and appreciate the old religious conviction, the spiritual ardor, and the moral passion that produced the cathedral.[20] Justine and Amherst are "enfranchised" in thought. But Justine does not recognize that an atavism of feeling may prevent Amherst from emotionally assenting to an act like euthanasia, which, historically, has been – and is still – condemned in Western moral thought. A wiser woman than Justine would have known that, in questions of existential value, the emotions of any particular individual may proceed toward enfranchisement at a slower pace than the cognitive faculty.

Justine is surely an admirable woman in many ways, but she is not the morally autonomous and triumphant heroine that some critics want her to be. She is bound to Amherst. They are entangled with each other – not only by marriage but by and through the act that he abstractly endorsed and that she committed. Like Adam and Eve, their paradisal relationship is now denied them. But both are humanized by a new and deeper understanding of the unanticipated irony of fate in human affairs. Justine is, finally, a woman chastened by her experience; she is beautiful in her submission to reality – to that which is, morally, the case; she is, at last, a woman wise in the humility that permits her to learn this hard lesson of life: that if there be virtue in an abstract moral proposition, it can only be fully known in its practical consequences, some of which may be totally unforeseen. Although Justine is one of the earliest of Mrs. Wharton's heroines to discover, as Irving Howe puts it, that "the punitive power of society" is greater than she had supposed and that a moral law "assumed to be lifeless" still retained "a certain wisdom,"[21] she is no doormat or vapid angel at the hearth. And the marital adjustments that she and Amherst finally make, far from enslaving her to him or to the institution of wedlock, define the complexity of living, both in and of itself and certainly in the estate of marriage, where silence may be wisdom rather than servitude. Amherst is not perfect, but he is, as Margaret McDowell has remarked, "one of the few strong, virile, and charitable men in Wharton's fiction," and Justine's decision to stay with him is "a wise compromise."[22] At the same time, Justine's fall into a knowledge of good and evil and the wisdom at which she finally arrives allowed Mrs. Wharton to express – in a way that the simpler Lily Bart did not – her pragmatic view of ethics as a continually shifting question involving one's own immediate relation to life.

NOTES

1. Blake Nevius, *Edith Wharton: A Study of Her Fiction* (Berkeley and Los Angeles: University of California Press, 1953), 24.
2. Q. D. Leavis, "Henry James's Heiress: The Importance of Edith Wharton," in *Edith Wharton: A Collection of Critical Essays,* ed. Irving Howe (Englewood Cliffs, N.J.: Prentice-Hall, 1962), 83.
3. There may be something of a reflexive and ironic self-portrait of Mrs. Wharton in Bessy Westmore, the heiress of the Westmore fortune, descending on the mills at Hanaford to perform an inspection. But whereas Bessy had no interest in the workers and no wish to understand the conditions of their labor, Mrs. Wharton meant serious business.
4. R. W. B. Lewis, *Edith Wharton: A Biography* (New York: Harper & Row, 1975), 181.
5. Edith Wharton, "Fiction and Criticism," 4; unpublished manuscript in the Wharton Archives, Beinecke Library, Yale University.
6. Edith Wharton, *The Fruit of the Tree* (New York: Scribner, 1907), 47–8. Hereafter cited by page number in parentheses, in the text.
7. Robert Morss Lovett, *Edith Wharton* (New York: McBride, 1925), 57–8. One is struck with how often Mrs. Wharton's left-wing critics appear not to have read all – or indeed much – of her fiction.
8. This theme was enlarged upon in 1955 by John P. Marquand in his New England mill novel *Sincerely, Willis Wayde.*
9. For the contemporary reception of *The Fruit of the Tree,* see *Edith Wharton: The Contemporary Reviews,* ed. James W. Tuttleton, Kristin O. Lauer, and Margaret P. Murray (Cambridge: Cambridge University Press, 1992), 145–54.
10. Cynthia Griffin Wolff, *A Feast of Words: The Triumph of Edith Wharton* (New York: Oxford University Press, 1977), 139.
11. Wolff, *Feast of Words,* 137; Deborah Carlin, "To Form a More Perfect Union: Gender, Tradition, and the Text in Wharton's *The Fruit of the Tree,*" in *Edith Wharton: New Critical Essays,* ed. Alfred Bendixen and Annette Zilversmit (New York: Garland, 1992), 69.
12. Lewis, *Edith Wharton: A Biography,* 181.
13. Elizabeth Ammons, *Edith Wharton's Argument with America* (Athens: University of Georgia Press, 1980), 50–1.
14. Carlin, "More Perfect Union," 68.

15 Carlin, "More Perfect Union," 59–60. Amherst, it should be noted, is far from a socialist or social democrat in his economic thought and labor policy.

16 Ammons, *Wharton's Argument,* 48, 25–6.

17 Susan Goodman, *Edith Wharton's Women: Friends and Rivals* (Hanover, N.H.: University Press of New England, 1990), 141.

18 Only Millicent Bell seems to have noticed that in having Justine kill the wealthy Bessy and then marry her husband, thereby securing in one stroke her social and economic future, Mrs. Wharton undercuts Justine's nobility: "few readers, I think, feel complete confidence in Justine's disinterested 'mercy-killing' of Bessy." See *Edith Wharton and Henry James: The Story of Their Friendship* (New York: Braziller, 1965), 256.

19 H. Wayne Morgan, "Edith Wharton: The Novelist of Manners and Morals," *Writers in Transition* (New York: Hill & Wang, 1963), 28.

20 Edith Wharton, *A Motor-Flight through France* (New York: Scribner, 1909), 9–10.

21 Irving Howe, "Introduction: The Achievement of Edith Wharton," in Howe, ed., *Edith Wharton: A Collection of Critical Essays,* 16–17.

22 Margaret McDowell, *Edith Wharton,* rev. ed. (Boston: Twayne, 1991), 32, 35.

WILLIAM L. VANCE

Edith Wharton's Italian Mask:
The Valley of Decision

Edith Wharton's first novel, *The Valley of Decision,* is one of her most important and distinguished novels, yet it has received relatively little (and mostly superficial) attention, in spite of its initial popularity.[1] Set in northern Italy in the late eighteenth century, it concerns the decisions that must be made by Odo Valsecca, a young man of liberal ideas who inherits a dukedom during the years of the French Revolution. Forced to choose between conflicting loyalties – those to the forces of social reform with which he allied himself before he came to power, or those of the feudal tradition to which he belongs by blood – Odo must define himself. Readers familiar with the life of Edith Wharton or the themes of her better-known New York books immediately realize the personal investment Wharton had in her hero's ambivalence and self-definition. Through him she was able to speculate about personal commitments and choices behind the mask of a different time, a different place, and a different gender. Adopting experimental poses, assuming various attitudes, and entertaining contradictory ideas, in fiction she could leave nothing resolved except the fact of the book: it existed, it was hers, it was being widely read. In becoming a writer of novels, she had assumed her rightful identity. Working in the medium of politics rather than literature, her hero was not so lucky.[2]

The genre Wharton chose – historical romance – is conveniently ambiguous. It straddles the worlds of fact and fancy. It assumes the sobriety and impersonality of history while facilitating the expressive imaginative freedom of fiction. We can understand Wharton's choices – of this genre and of period and place – by recalling the particular small circle of readers she inevitably anticipated. They were obsessed with both the history and the romance (in the broad sense) of Italy, going much beyond the superficial acquaintance with that country expected of most people of her class. Wharton herself addressed her prospective readers as "voialtri" – "you others" – those people who had "lived in and *with* Italy" as she had.[3] Among such people were those who would expect Wharton to be a responsible historian of Italy and those who would be more alert to her pretensions as a popular romancer.

Identifying a few of these readers helps us to see precisely the mix of expectations that Wharton would have sensed in the immediate audience she hoped to please – and to equal. They included the two most stimulating writers personally known to Wharton – Paul Bourget and Vernon Lee (Violet Paget). Wharton dedicated *The Valley of Decision* to Bourget and his wife, in remembrance of their travels together in northern Italy. Her next book, *Italian Villas and Their Gardens,* would be dedicated to Lee. Wharton had met Bourget in Newport in 1893, when she was (as she wrote in her memoir of him) "une jeune femme passionnée pour les lettres, mais n'ayant même pas songé à la possibilité de faire elle-même partie de l'illustre fraternité des écrivains!" [a young woman impassioned with literature, but not having even a dream of the possibility of herself joining the illustrious brotherhood of writers!].[4] Bourget was a famous writer, whose novels, psychological essays, and travel book about Italy Wharton had read, and to have him visit her at Land's End seemed to raise her into a special company. It was Bourget who then provided her with a letter of introduction to his friend Vernon Lee, whom Wharton met at Lee's villa outside Florence the following year.[5] This meeting was of even greater importance: "Hitherto all my intellectual friendships had been with men, and Vernon Lee was the first highly cultivated and brilliant woman I had ever known." Lee was a prolific writer about Italy; both her historical studies and her fiction had accompanied Wharton on her Italian travels.[6] These two intellectuals, writers, and cosmopolitan Italophiles became her friends; their respect and example encouraged her to imagine what she might become. In her autobiography, Wharton recalls her pleasure in Vernon Lee's response to her book with exceptional gratitude: "No one welcomed 'The Valley of Decision' more warmly than Vernon Lee, and it was a great encouragement to be praised by a writer whom I so much admired, and who was so unquestioned an authority on the country and the period I had dealt with" (*Backward Glance,* 884).[7]

Wharton would have anticipated with certainty at least three other knowledgeable and critical readers. They included the Harvard art historian Charles Eliot Norton, who supplied her with several of her source books, and his daughter Sara, with whom she was in frequent contact during the two years of its composition (*Backward Glance,* 881–2). And then there was Margaret Terry Chanler, Wharton's Rome-raised friend, now resident in Newport. Chanler was half-sister to Francis Marion Crawford, one of the most popular American novelists of the day, who specialized in Italian romances. Shortly after the publication of *The Valley of Decision,* Wharton received from Crawford the French version of a historical drama he had written for Sarah Bernhardt about the famous Italian lovers Paolo and Francesca. Wharton immediately proposed to William Dean Howells that she write for the *North American Review* an essay on Crawford's drama and two other recent plays on the theme. She told Mrs. Chanler that she was *emballée* about her brother's play, and Wharton's remark that it was "quite different in quality from anything he has ever written" shows her familiarity with his other work. Of her own book, which Chanler had obviously commented on immediately after reading, Wharton adds,

> I shan't pretend to dissemble my pleasure at what you say of my book. I was very nervous of your verdict, I own, for it must seem presumptuous to anyone who knows Italy as you do that I should have attempted to write of it – & not even of the Italy I have seen, but of that vanished civilization which is fading away in the Longhi pictures & in the pages of eighteenth century travellers. It delights me to hear that I produced an illusion to you, but I know you must have detected many mistakes & anachronisms, & some day I hope you will point them out to me.   (*Letters,* 61–3)[8]

Bourget, Lee, and Norton represented published Italophiles of three different nationalities, authorities on the land whose character Wharton wished to evoke. Lee, Bourget, and Crawford were, in addition, novelists, an identity she was attempting to assume. The work of this circle of expected authoritative readers defines the hybrid character of the genre Wharton was engaging. It combined externalizing, objective criteria of accuracy, atmosphere, invention, and "effect" that made a suitable mask for any private anxieties about vocation and competence she might be working out. She had to get her history – both place and period – right; she also had to meet the standards of a popular melodramatic genre, currently set in English by Crawford. One can estimate Wharton's achievement in *The Valley of Decision* by observing how, in writing in this form and for such demanding readers as these, she was able to create a vivid, impersonal mask that is nevertheless revelatory, both in detectable traces of masking and in the fact that the eyes of her hero that peer through the masculine disguise are clearly her own. We may consider these combined issues, for analytic purposes, in this sequence: Italian history; Italian romance; and Wharton as Odo.

Charles Eliot Norton read *The Valley of Decision* immediately when it was sent to him by Wharton. (His daughter had already read it in galleys.) It was as history that in a letter to a friend he hailed this "unique and astonishing performance": "She calls it 'a novel,' but it is rather a study of Italian thought and life during the latter part of the eighteenth century, in the form of a story." Like many readers, Norton thought the characters unsuccessfully realized but that "Mrs. Wharton's imagination has fused her material of reflection, learning, and personal experience into a wonderfully complete and vivid picture of the Italy of the period. . . . Her knowledge of Italy is that of a scholar and a lover of 'that pleasant country,' and her book is to be prized most by those who know Italy best and most love it." Norton was certainly one of those highly qualified judges, having published *Notes of Travel and Study in Italy* (1860), *Historical Studies of Church Building in the Middle Ages: Venice, Siena, Florence* (1880), and a translation of Dante's *The Divine Comedy* (1891–2). His respect for the book's scholarship caused him to believe that it "would not be popular."[9]

It is not quite true, as Wharton believed (*Letters,* 58, 76), that she was the first novelist to set a story in eighteenth-century Italy. James Fenimore Cooper's *The Bravo* (1831) is set in early eighteenth-century Venice. But she was fully aware of the increasing interest in the eighteenth century and contemporary Italy, after a century of American interest focusing first on ancient Rome, then expanding to include the Italian Renaissance and (most recently) the Middle Ages. She was familiar with the works of Howells, and therefore with his extensive treatment of the plays of Carlo Goldoni in *Venetian Life* (1867). And in a letter written in 1905 to William Roscoe Thayer, the Harvard historian, she mentions "how deeply I was indebted to [his book] 'The Dawn of Italian Independence' for such light on that intricate and engrossing period as I needed in writing my Italian novel" (*Letters,* 96). The early part of Thayer's work briefly and incisively defined the eighteenth century in Italy as a period of complete "political and moral decadence," redeemed only by the genius displayed in music, drama, and science. One of the few progressive signs Thayer identified was the framing of a code of laws restricting the Church's privileges by Leopold, Grand Duke of Tuscany. Looking "to economists and philosophers, and not to churchmen, for counsel," he "was the first ruler in Italy to respond to the changing current and to propose laws prophetic of the modern spirit."[10] But Leopold was a foreigner, so the basic hypothesis of Wharton's book concerns a man who had the opportunity to be the first native Italian ruler "to respond to the changing current" but who ultimately refused it. The first person Thayer mentions in the chapter "New Voices and Revolution," which concludes his description of the preliminaries to the Congress of Vienna of 1814, is the poet Vittorio Alfieri, whom Wharton presents as the person who leads Odo into liberal circles.

According to Wharton herself, her interest in eighteenth-century Italy did not begin with anything so exalted as the New Italy, with which indeed she was not even in sympathy. It began with a chair. While sitting for her portrait to Julian Story in his Parisian studio, her eye fell on "the most artlessly simple and graceful arm-chair I had ever seen." Asked its origin, Story replied, "Oh, eighteenth century Venetian. It's a pity no one knows or cares anything about eighteenth century Italian furniture or architecture. In fact everybody behaves – the historians as well as the art critics – as if Italy had ceased to exist at the end of the Renaissance" (*Backward Glance*, 461). This was the "trifling incident" that made Wharton a student of post-Renaissance Italy, giving a specialized focus to her succeeding travels in Italy and the reading that attended them.

But even before her encounter with the chair, Wharton had read Vernon Lee's "enchanting" first book, *Studies of the Eighteenth Century in Italy* (see *Backward Glance*, 461). Vernon Lee was only eight years older than Wharton but, in contrast to Wharton's late beginning, had begun publishing prolifically while in her early twenties. *Studies of the Eighteenth Century in Italy*, written with vigorous scholarly authority and a fine dogmatism, came out in 1880 when she was only twenty-four. It represented research she had begun at the age of fifteen, when her curiosity about the dilapidated Arcadian Academy on the Janiculum Hill in Rome led her into this arcane area of study. In 1884 Lee wrote *The Countess of Albany* for the Famous Women Series of Roberts Publishers in Boston, a biography she considered an extension of her eighteenth-century studies.[11] These are the two books by Lee most directly pertinent to *The Valley of Decision*. The first provided a sense of the nonpolitical dimension of the period, encouraging Wharton to develop the social history that interested her more than the political. The second book gave an interpretation of the most famous Italian of the period – Alfieri, the Countess of Albany's lover – which suggested thematic possibilities for Wharton's hero.

These two historical books are in fact at least as informative and entertaining as Wharton's work of fiction, for two reasons. First, Lee's witty style, which strongly conveys the sense of a lively, engaged, distinctive personality, contrasts with Wharton's cool, impersonal, and grave narrative voice. Lee the historian writes more like Stendhal the novelist, whereas Wharton the novelist writes like Thayer the historian – or rather like Wharton the historian of *The Decoration of Houses* and *Italian Villas and Their Gardens*, the two books that frame *The Valley of Decision*.[12] This suppression of a personal voice in the narrator, with the attendant transfer of value to the third-person central character, is one aspect of Wharton's masking. Second, Lee's historical characters – poets, scholars, pedants, musicians, singers, playwrights, and actors in the book about the eighteenth century and the Young Pretender, the Countess of Albany, and the poet Alfieri in the biography – are far more vivid and vital than Wharton's melancholy inventions. Odo is realized, but realized in his ambivalence and confusion of identity; he cannot have the sharp definition Lee was able to ascribe to persons whose fates were known rather than unfolding in a speculating imaginative process.

According to Lee, the reason why the eighteenth century in Italy had been neglected was that people had not looked in the right place. Nineteenth-century historians interested themselves only in those aspects of the preceding age that had contributed to the great social and philosophical revolutions in their own, and in these respects Italy was merely a pale shadow of France and England. But what was interesting, because original, about Italy in the eighteenth century lay in her drama and comedy and "her own spontaneous national music," which she gave to "the whole of Europe."[13] Although Wharton, knowing this, persisted in making the primary theme of her novel political, Lee's convincing emphasis may have guided Wharton to the area of social history that receives most significant development in *The Valley of Decision*: the theater. *Studies in the Eighteenth Century* contains a chapter on the librettist Pietro Metastasio in which the opera *Achilles in Scyros* is discussed as one of his best works; it is at a performance of this opera that Odo meets Alfieri. Another chapter is "The Comedy of Masks," focusing on Carlo Goldoni and Carlo Gozzi, whose works figure later in *The Valley of Decision*.[14]

Wharton herself was defensive about the large amount of "history" in her novel. To Sara Norton she wrote that there was "undoubtedly . . . too much explanation, too much history &c, for the proper perspective of the novel," but she pled in "extenuation" that the period (in Italy) is "unfamiliar" to most readers, so nothing could be taken for granted, and that

> I meant the book to be a picture of a social phase, not of two people's individual history, & Fulvia and Oddo [sic] are just little bits of looking-glass in which fragments of the great panorama are reflected. But I imagine the real weakness of the book is that I haven't fused my facts sufficiently with the general atmosphere of the story, so that they stick out here & there, & bump into the reader. I knew from the start that this would be the fault – the great fault, I mean – of the book. It is sure to bore people who don't care for Italy.
>
> (*Letters,* 57)

It is difficult (in this post-Michener age) to know what may be considered "too much history" in a historical novel, but clearly what matters is the degree of fusion, a fictionalizing of the texture of the historical material itself so that it does not stand apart from the interests of the characters or impede the development of the plot. In fact, by this criterion Wharton largely succeeds. Her apologetic references to her characters suggest that the work is primarily history, which would raise the question of whether fictional characters are the best reflectors of a "social phase." The comparison with Lee's historical works would seem to suggest not. And it is difficult to believe that Wharton wrote – or that many readers besides Norton read – the novel primarily for its historical content. Yet in writing to her publisher to assist in the publicity for the book, Wharton continued to stress history over fiction as her intention:

> The Valley, then is an attempt to picture Italy at the time of the breaking up of the small principalities at the end of the 18th century, when all the old forms & traditions of court life were still preserved, but the immense intellectual & moral movement of the new regime was at work beneath the surface of things. . . . I have tried to reflect the traditional influences & customs of the day, together with the new ideas, in the mind of a cadet of one of the reigning houses, who is suddenly called to succeed to the Dukedom of Pianura, & tries to apply the theories of the French encyclopaedists to his small principality. Incidentally, I have given sketches of Venetian life, & glimpses of Sir Wm Hamilton's circle at Naples, & of the clerical milieu at Rome, where the suppression of the society of Jesus, & the mysterious death of Ganganelli, had produced a violent reaction toward formalism & superstition. The close of the story pictures the falling to pieces of the whole business at the approach of Napoleon.   (*Letters*, 58)

Wharton gives a very poor summary of her own book. No one would guess from this what kinds of fictional experience would be primary; that, for instance, there would be extensive presentation of the architecture and theater of the time, that the sketch of "Venetian life" includes the escape of a nun from her convent, while the "glimpses" of Sir William Hamilton and of "clerical life in Rome" are precisely that (hardly a page each). So of what does the primary historical content of the book consist?

Wharton's tale is precisely dated as beginning in 1762 and ending in the spring of 1797, in which year the hero has reached the age of forty-four, only slightly beyond Wharton's own age at the time of composition. Book 2 begins in 1774, and Book 3 begins in 1783. Historical fact exists in the book – as in most historical novels – on two planes. On one the narrator occupies herself with the observation of details of social life characteristic of the time and place, these details providing the interest of the exotic by differing substantially from those of contemporary readers. On the other plane are the personages and events of recorded "history" as commonly conceived –

that is, of political and intellectual history. These allude to matters supposedly familiar to educated people, although the narrator must exercise a certain amount of tact in suggesting that the reader is naturally familiar not only with Napoleon and possibly Pope Pius VI, and with Voltaire and Rousseau, but also with Alfieri, Goldoni, and Ganganelli. Much that may actually be quite unfamiliar must be put in the form of a reminder. The reader is flattered into believing that he knows more history than he does. On the other hand, such informed readers as Wharton's first circle of Italophiles would not want to be bored with elementary history lessons.

Wharton's choice of hero, with whose consciousness the book is centrally concerned (although without adopting precisely his point of view), was an excellent one for overcoming the problem of a variously informed readership. By following the developing mind of a neglected boy from a noble family, left for the first nine years of his life in a remote corner of a province and then brought to the capital, Wharton is able to introduce much information as the result of Odo's discoveries about his own world rather than as the superior author's instruction of the ignorant reader. The first action of the novel consists of Odo's removal, after his father's death, from the manor house on the estate of Pontesordo to his mother's palazzo in Pianura, the ducal seat, and from thence to his maternal grandfather's mountaintop feudal castle of Donnaz in the neighboring kingdom of Piedmont. Through architectural descriptions of these three contrasting buildings, Wharton is able to give the reader an efficient exposition of the history of feudalism in the preceding three hundred years, under the guise of Odo's own education. The boy's wide-eyed absorption of the features of the walled town and of the ducal palace itself provides, for instance, a means of evoking eighteenth-century provincial life and architecture in such a way that it seems necessary to the character rather than the reader. Although Wharton does depart briefly from Odo's state of knowledge to mention that one wing and the palace gardens were designed by "the eminent architect Carlo Borromini," the stress is on Odo trembling in amazement at the formal gardens, such as he had never seen before (1:23). Only when Odo returns many years later to live in the palazzo as heir presumptive does Wharton, the learned author who was to write an entire book on Italian gardens the next year, allow a more elaborate statement of architectural history, since Odo himself is now interested in it. Wharton clearly indulged herself in imagining her hero's residence as being "one of the wonders of Italy," celebrated in verse by Aretino, and in assigning to it a long history from the original *rocca* (fortress) through its expansion by a humanist prince (the first duke), who hired Luciano da Laurana to build a proper palace. This duke is present in a "bronze by Verrocchio"; a later duke hired Vignola to remodel and expand the palace and had its interior walls painted by Correggio and Giulio Romano; a still later one hired Borromini; and the present duke has added a chapel "in the florid Jesuit style" (1:240–1). This method of incorporating history into the characterization (or at least making history consistent with the central character's interests, when not directly presented as his thoughts) contrasts admirably with that of George Eliot in *Romola* (1863) (a book Wharton knew), where the weight of historical information about fifteenth-century Florence is far more intrusive and lumpish and is presented almost entirely as a communication from writer to reader.

The chief danger of Wharton's method is that the character will be made to occupy himself excessively with matters that are of particular interest to the narrator, skewing his characterization in the direction of the author's own traits. This indeed happens, and it is one reason why it is possible to see that Odo is Wharton wearing a mask. For instance, the fact that the historical Alfieri had an uncle, Count Benedetto Alfieri, who was a classicizing architect living in Turin in the 1770s, allowed Wharton to have Odo introduced to the count, whereupon he instructs Odo in architectural taste for several pages. "Ignorant as Odo was of all the arts, he felt on the very threshold the new quality of his surroundings" as he entered the architect's lodgings. Not surprisingly, these surroundings are a model of the principles Wharton had propounded in *The Decoration of Houses*. Benedetto Alfieri "represented the old classic tradition, the tradition of the 'grand manner,' which had held its own through all later variations of taste" (1:104–7).

It is clear that Wharton relives her own delight in discovery through Odo's rapid indoctrination. The parallel is furthered by her remark that "Such an initiation was the more precious to him from the indifference of those about him to all forms of liberal culture." Odo's grandfather believes that "there is no need for a gentleman to be a scholar," his stepfather is occupied at court, and his mother "had sunk into a state of rigid pietism." In his mother's world, "art was represented by the latest pastel-portrait of a court beauty," literature by pious homilies or by verses on the death of a pet canary, history by celebrations of Piedmont's defense of the Church (1:108–9). The suffocating nature of the society in which Wharton herself lived and about which she was soon to write directly in *The House of Mirth* is present obliquely in this description, as is Wharton in the characterization of Odo.

After architecture and art, the social element (apart from the political nature of a small court) most developed in the novel is that of theater, which provides both a continuing infusion of popular culture into the setting and a source for recurrent metaphors of masking and role playing. Wharton's inclusiveness amounts to a chronological historical survey, since we are successively introduced to the court entertainments of Metastasio, which Odo attends as a young student at Turin, then to the popular theater of *commedia dell'arte* and Goldoni, which he encounters on his travels, and finally to the heroic political tragedy of his friend Alfieri, which is performed in his own court.

The theater strain sustains the constant motifs of role playing, masking, and ambiguous gender. Near the end of Book 1 (entitled "The Old Order"), Wharton has Odo watching Metastasio's opera *Achilles in Scyros*. She quotes from two widely separated moments in the opera. The first is when Achilles, who is disguised as a woman, sings of his awareness of a repressed heroic masculine identity: "Io sono Achilles." The other comes as Achilles reveals this identity when he cannot resist exclaiming over the beauty of the weapons that the wily Ulysses has mixed in with a gift of jewels (1:98–9).[15] Much later the theatrical motif is developed through the introduction of a "plump abate [*abate,* abbé] in tattered ecclesiastical dress" named Cantapresto, "late primo soprano of the ducal theater of Pianura," now reduced by the loss of his voice to begging. Cantapresto, a castrato, with his ambiguous gender, is one of Wharton's most interesting secondary characters. He accompanies Odo on most of his travels during much of the remainder of the book, both serving him and reporting on his movements to various interested parties. Odo, still a boy when he meets Cantapresto, "had been bred in an abhorrence of the theatre." He is nevertheless intrigued by this strange character, whom he encounters in the midst of a promiscuous crowd while accompanying his aunts on a pilgrimage. It is from Cantapresto that he first hears of "the motley theatrical life of the north Italian cities – the quarrels between Goldoni and the supporters of the expiring *commedia dell'arte,* the rivalries of the *prime donne* and the arrogance of the popular comedians" (1:72). Later Odo twice encounters an itinerant theatrical troupe, and he is enticed into going to a provincial theater to see "a new comedy entitled *Le Gelosie di Milord Zambo.*" The incident, which involves Odo with the Columbine and so has disastrous consequences in the plot, allows Wharton to expatiate for several pages on the nature of this "comedy in the style of Goldoni's earlier pieces, representing the life of the actual day, but interspersed with the antics of the masks (*commedia dell'arte*), to whose improvised drolleries the people still clung" (1:197, 199). An after-theater dinner in the Columbine's room provides a vivid description of the acting company, with their monkeys and parrots and rivalries. An interpolated tale, "Mirandolina's Story," provides another variation on the theme of gender masking: At Pianura, a new strict piety that forbade the appearance of women onstage had required Mirandolina to be announced as her own twin brother, Mirandolino, playing his sister's parts – from which followed a series of farcical mistakes in love familiar to us from Shakespeare's Italian comedies (1:206–16).

Wharton's interests in architecture and theater come together in the second volume, when Odo, traveling to Venice via the Brenta Canal, falls in with a French expatriate nobleman who has enlisted an acting troupe to go to the Procuratore Bra's famous Villa Bellochio for the *villegiatura* (country vacation), during which masked theatrical performances are to be given in the formal garden. Odo is "spell-bound," as obviously is Wharton herself in this fantasy of one possible ideal life: "Never before had beauty so ministered to his every sense" (2:48). All of this has the effect of inviting Odo to a life of passive (not creative) indulgence in pleasure and beauty. The line between actual theater and the metaphor of life-as-theater becomes blurred. The subsequent chapters in Venice bring about the climax of Odo's attraction. The spectacle of Venice, in which "both sexes" wore "white masks" when abroad, encourages a sense of "extraordinary freedom of intercourse. . . . The privilege of going masked at almost all seasons and the enforced uniformity of dress, which in itself provided a kind of incognito, made the place singularly favorable to every kind of intrigue and amusement." Life is imaginable simply as a "huge comic interlude." For many months Odo is able to wear the mask of a gentleman of pure pleasure: "Never had he seen pleasure and grace so happily allied, all the arts of life so combined in the single effort after enjoyment. . . . Nowhere was the mind arrested by a question or an idea. Thought slunk away like an unmasked guest at the ridotto" (2:53–5).

Wharton's description calls to mind her recollection of Newport, "ce milieu ultra-frivole," in her memoir of Bourget:

> La vie de Casino et de sports, de yachting, de bridge, de dîners somptueux, et de sauteries élégantes, qui constituaient la "saison" de Newport. A cette époque . . . cette saison de ville d'eaux avait encore une élégance de bon aloi; mais les aimables personnes qui constituaient cette petite société étaient, à peu d'exceptions près, hermétiquement fermées au mouvement intellectuel et artistique qui, à Paris et à Londres, avait atteint même les milieux les plus frivoles. A Newport il n'était pas encore nécessaire de paraître s'intéresser aux idées.[16]

Wharton shows Odo attracted to this society in which the superficial mask becomes the reality. Only a chance encounter with Andreoni, a bookseller from Pianura, brings him a reminder of the complexities he may face if he comes to rule. Andreoni has been banished because he published a book on tax reform written by Odo's friend, the radical Gamba, who has also fled the duchy. But this momentary reminder of a more troubling reality is canceled by the arrival of the mad carnival season, in which men dress as women, women as men, gentlemen of pleasure as friars, and ladies of the town as nuns. After Easter, Odo is caught up in attendance at dramatic entertainments given by nuns in fashionable convents. The French marquess has fallen in love with a Sister Mary of the Crucifix, and Odo, "cloaked and masked," joins him in a midnight assignation, to which Sister Mary has brought Sister Veronica. This all leads to a *coup de théâtre* in which Sister Veronica, who is dressed as a lady of fashion, is unmasked. She is Fulvia Vivaldi, Odo's estranged love and the feminine embodiment of Liberal Ideas. The effect is to bring Odo a purpose in life, namely to rescue Fulvia from the convent in which she has been imprisoned, which he does. Odo/Wharton, in rescuing an intellectually emancipated woman from the alternative social roles of nun or woman of the world, returns himself/herself to a proper commitment to a free and serious life.

The final theatrical event, occurring in Book 4, develops when Vittorio Alfieri unexpectedly turns up at the dukedom that Odo now rules. Since Odo has last met him, he has become "one of the foremost figures in Italy," having given Italian literature the tragedies that it lacked and the hypothetical Italian nation a voice. "*Liberty* was the cry that rang on the lips of all his heroes." The bookseller Andreoni – who has been reinstalled in Pianura – has even provided Odo with Alfieri's recent (1778) "Odes to Free America." Naturally Odo suggests that a performance of one of Alfieri's tragedies be given, directed by the author himself. The lack of qualified actors in the provincial town is no problem, since "our leading tragedians are monkeys trained to dance to the tune of Goldoni and Metastasio," says Alfieri. Thus Wharton signals that she has now brought in all three of the most celebrated names of eighteenth-century Italian drama. The last – Alfieri – lifts it to the dignity of tragedy. A performance of Alfieri's *Virginia* (1777) is mounted, Wharton's choice of play being motivated by the fact that Fulvia is once more absent and the image of Virginia, a similar woman of stoic republican virtue, will recall Fulvia to Odo's mind. But a full page is devoted to the greater ironies of the occasion. An audience made up of feudal oppressors and a slave-owning bishop displays its "ardent sympathy with the proletariat, their scorn of tyranny and extortion in high places." Only Odo is profoundly affected: "Once more he felt the old ardor of belief that Fulvia's nearness had fanned in him. His convictions had flagged rather than his courage: now they started up as at her summons, and he heard the ring of her voice in every line" (2:192). The

masked comedy of Venice, the life of thoughtless pleasure, is entirely replaced by heroic commitment to action.

The return of Alfieri to the book brings us to the second level of history
characteristic of historical romance: the recorded person and event. In
choosing to invent an entirely fictional dukedom, Wharton had made matters much easier for herself than had, for instance, George Eliot in writing
Romola, who was obliged to restrict herself to the topography, events, and
personages of a very well-known time and place, the final decade of
fifteenth-century Florence. By inventing a typical smaller, less celebrated
dukedom, Wharton is able to exploit the appeal of recognition in her creation of entrance gates, ducal palace, cathedral, marketplace, cobblestone
streets, lamp-lighted shrines, reeking gutters, chilly rooms, and so on – the
generic elements of a northern Italian walled city – without being tied to the
sort of literalism that is so heavy a weight on Eliot's novel. It is also notable
that Wharton keeps Alfieri, a far more colorful character than her hero, in
an extremely subordinate role, whereas in Eliot's novel the brilliant and
fanatic reformer-monk Savonarola eventually greatly overshadows the rela-
tively pallid fictional characters. The historical Alfieri was also an extraordinarily complex figure, and it is clear that Wharton is personally attracted to
him, as Eliot was to Savonarola. Wharton must have seen in Alfieri a
parallel to Odo, or to what stimulated her in the creation of Odo: a contradictory loyalty to both the old order and the new ideas. The poet's incessant
traveling made it wholly plausible that he would show up in her fictional
dukedom, especially as it was near Turin, where Alfieri studied, and near his
native Asti. Alfieri appears five times in the book: first as a student in Turin
when Odo is there, then as a rebellious young man returned from travels
abroad, later in Florence when Odo is visiting that city, at Pianura when his
play is performed there, and near the end, when he passes through Pianura
on his flight from Paris during the French Revolution. In each case he is used
as a way of measuring the spiritual development of the central character,
Odo, even at the expense of departing from historical truth about Alfieri.

In the first place, Wharton exaggerates Alfieri's political liberalism when
he first appears at the age of sixteen. Nothing in his celebrated autobiography (surely Wharton's primary source) suggests that this pleasure-loving
count would have possessed a smuggled copy of Voltaire's *Lettres philoso-
phiques* to give to Odo, as he does at the end of Book 1. Although Alfieri
says that when he read at all he took delight in some of "Voltaire's prose,"
he was far more enamored of popular French novels and would have been
more likely to lend Odo one of these.[17] Wharton has transferred the interests of the later Alfieri to the schoolboy in order to get Odo's revolutionary

thoughts and associations underway. She does, however, successfully convey the dashing young man with a high sense of his own distinction that would have impressed Odo.

Her reason for altering Alfieri's character in the much later encounter in Florence is less apparent. Odo's meeting with him is unsatisfying, because Alfieri is shown to be totally preoccupied with the Countess of Albany. Wharton's account significantly separates Alfieri's vocation to drama from his idealized love for the countess, suggesting that the love inhibited the poetry: "Alfieri's early worship of liberty had not yet found its destined channel of expression, and for the moment his enthusiasms had shrunk to the compass of a romantic adventure" (2:33–4). This is very odd, since by Alfieri's own account – the only source for such a subject – his love for this lady (the first "worthy" one [degno amore] of his life) wholly focused his creative activities: "Within two months it was obvious to me that she was my true woman, since instead of finding again in her (as in all the vulgar women) an obstacle to literary glory, a distraction from useful occupations, and a diminishment [rimpicciolimento] – so to speak – of thought, I found there encouragement [spone] comfort, and example for every good work [bell'opera]." Two years before meeting the countess, Alfieri had dedicated himself to becoming Italy's great tragedian, and, by the time Odo supposedly reencounters him, he had conceived seven tragedies and just completed his Tirannide, a work which was "the unburdening of an overflowing soul that had suffered since infancy from the strokes of an abhorred and universal oppression."[18]

This second alteration in Alfieri's story is more provocative than the first, since it serves no purpose of plot. Its explicit intent seems to be to show that Odo, "to whom the years had brought an increasing detachment," is superior to Alfieri's "self-absorption," which Odo deems "an arrest in growth." But it is the twenty-five-year-old Odo who is wandering pointlessly in exile, with no evident mental growth, no apparent sexual or romantic life at all, and no social function. It seems to have been necessary here for Odo/Wharton to judge that a compelling commitment to another person would be an "arrest," a "self-absorption" that inhibited creative activity. A "romantic adventure" is seen as an obstacle to finding a "destined channel of expression" for one's liberty.

In Alfieri's final appearances, Wharton's adoption of one of the familiar caricatures of Alfieri indicates her awareness (and perhaps fear) that a satirical or polemical idealist frequently traps himself (or herself) in hypocrisy. Such an awareness is consistent with the ambivalence and inconclusiveness of her novel's dénouement. Wharton is sarcastic about the success in court theaters of Alfieri's tyrannicidal tragedies, and finally about his exasperation with the French Revolution, which supposedly was fulfilling the ideals of his own dramas. On all of these occasions Wharton unsympathetically simplifies the issues. But the contradictions Alfieri embodied were those that she herself felt and expressed through Odo. A far more acute account of Alfieri is given by Vernon Lee in *The Countess of Albany,* probably a source for Wharton but one which she seems here consciously to have ignored.[19]

But *The Valley of Decision* is not Italian history, even if read so by Norton. It is an Italian romance. Whether or not Wharton knew Cooper's *The Bravo* or Harriet Beecher Stowe's *Agnes of Sorrento* (1862), she certainly knew (and no doubt sought to improve upon) George Eliot's *Romola.* It is to this tradition that her work belongs. The frequent critical reference to Stendhal's *La Chartreuse de Parme* is prompted by its having been one of Wharton's favorite books and its sharing the same general locale – northern Italy – as her own. Although Wharton noted that her novel differed from Stendhal's in period (the *Chartreuse* beginning where hers ended, at the start of the Napoleonic wars), this is the least of their differences (*Letters,* 58). Stendhal's work is of an entirely different kind.[20] Wharton's book may be better understood in relation to the novels of Francis Marion Crawford, who, from his *To Leeward* and *A Roman Singer* (both 1884) to his *Stradella* (1909, set in seventeenth-century Venice and Rome), established the commercial and critical standard for success in this genre in the 1890s. Written for non-Italian audiences and successful in France (in translation) as well as in England and America, they are characterized by melodramatic characters and plots combined with a wealth of realistic detail of period and place. (Crawford in fact thought of himself as writing contemporary history in the *Saracinesca* series.)[21] Wharton's effort at historical specification provided the equivalent of Crawford's realistic scenography.

In popular romance, what happens is more important than why it happens. Wharton has provided episodes of arbitrarily manipulated melodramatic action that equal those of any romancer. She has made the most of a rigid class system in which the fates of individuals seem determined by accident or by events wholly extraneous to their characters. Unforeseen marriages, births, and deaths quickly alter the course of a life and are great conveniences to a narrator who, after all, has the characters entirely in her power. Odo's father's death; his mother's remarriage to a repellent old count (motivated by her wish to avoid the alternative, a life of total boredom); the birth of a direct heir to the dukedom; his feebleness; the whims of a duke's pious mistress; the intrigues of the luxurious duchess and her *cavaliere servente;* assignations in a malarial hunting lodge; the suave evasions of the art-collecting bishop; the mysterious presence of an agent of the suppressed Jesuits – all add up to an intricate net of connivings and coincidences that have nothing at all to do with Odo's character but affect the course of his life.

Wharton's commitment to the romance genre emerges most dramatically in a few bravura episodes that go beyond anything in Cooper or Crawford. The chapters leading to the end of Book 2 comprise a continuous narrative of suspense, reaching a climax in a bizarre scene that ends in a complete reversal of fortune. Odo has been summoned to live in the ducal palace, since the duke is evidently dying and his young son is none too well. Odo, the duke's cousin, may therefore succeed to power, which means that his own life is in jeopardy. The duke on his deathbed is a grotesque figure, given to pious terrors and haunted by the admonitions of his confessor, Father Ignazio. Also at the court is a certain Count Heiligenstern, a physician administering dubious cures to both the duke and his son. Odo and the reader are consequently treated to a pair of actions, each directed at the cure of the young heir. The first is a pilgrimage to a shrine, advised by Father Ignazio and intended to please the superstitious populace. Its consequence, however, in "spite of the mountain Madonna's much-vaunted powers," is that the duke's illness becomes worse and the condition of the little prince is unaffected. Count Heiligenstern is then allowed to attempt a cure with his mixture of Egyptian necromancy and electric currents.

This grand scene of hocus-pocus brings Volume 1 to a close. The event is made to coincide with Odo's sudden suspicion of his own imminent danger, since he has received an unexpected invitation from the duchess's uncle, ruler of a neighboring duchy, to come to him and then go on a mission to Naples. The duchess has arranged for this exile to protect him from a threat at court owing to his association with liberals. But accepting her protection would bind him to her. His dilemma is resolved, as usual, by circumstance. The ceremony of healing begins with black drapery giving way to a vision of a Temple of Health, at whose center is a crystal ball into which the physician's purified Georgian acolyte gazes while the room fills with per-fumed vapor – and so on. The sickly young prince experiences a heavenly vision that includes a naked Venus, which causes his father to terminate that phase of the cure. Heiligenstern next turns to his electric currents, assisted by an oriental servant, and has gradually encircled the boy in sparks, this phenomenon happily coinciding with a storm of lightning and thunder outside the palace. The observers are stunned by the spectacle, but even more by its sudden termination by the black-hooded Father Ignazio, who arrives with representatives of the Inquisition. Ignazio exposes Heiligenstern as "one of the most notorious apostles" of the atheistic Illuminati, an imposter from Pomerania, a seducer, murderer, family-deserter, and quack. His Georgian "boy" is actually the wife of a Greek juggler from Ravenna. While these wonderful declarations are being made, Odo notices the arrival of the duke's *sbirri* (police), and in the terrified glance of the duchess and the fixed stare of the prime minister he reads the message that he is about to be arrested himself. He makes a quick getaway through the palace-garden wall, gets past the guards with his prepared passport, and hurries down to the dark wharves, and into the waiting boat: "A boatman, distinguishable only as a black bulk in the stern, steadied his descent with outstretched hand; then the bow swung round, and after a laboring stroke or two they caught the current and were swept down through the rushing darkness" (1:434).

Even this summary is hardly sufficient for its purpose, which is to show Wharton's uncompromising inventiveness, or shameless indulgence in the genre. Allusions to *The Valley of Decision* – even critical commentaries on it – seldom even suggest that the book contains such stuff as this. In the second volume, similar set pieces include Odo's elaborately plotted kidnapping of Fulvia from the Venetian convent, followed by a wild Cooperesque night escape over Mount Baldo and a storm-driven crossing of Lake Garda, with not only a representative of the Inquisition but also an agent of the duke's from Pianura in pursuit. A later scene, after the hallucinating duke has died horribly and has been quickly followed to the grave by his son, shows Odo in the bed-chamber from which his religion-mad predecessor had reigned. Odo makes a startling discovery: the image of the Madonna before which the guilt-ridden duke had prostrated himself is merely a cover for a lost painting of Venus by Giorgione, which appears when pressure is put on the kneeling-stool (2:158). This shocker, which throws an entirely different light back on the slobbering prayers of the old duke, goes beyond anything Crawford himself achieved in the way of cheap effects. It should be noted also that Wharton's narrative voice remains persistently sober throughout, with none of the sarcasm by which Crawford sometimes separated himself from the vulgar taste or depravity of what he himself had imagined.

All of these dramatic – even operatic – scenes are narrated with a solid sense of their building tension, and they are undoubtedly the main reason that Wharton's book achieved a popularity approaching Crawford's, in spite of Norton's belief that it was too scholarly to be popular.[22] Ironically, it was Norton who, shortly after reading the novel, provided Wharton with historical evidence that reassured her on one point of her romance-plot: she was pleased to learn that an actual kidnapping of a nun named Camilla Vinati "so quaintly corroborates certain statements in 'The Valley' which some of my Catholic friends have questioned. It will be a great satisfaction to be able to prove, by producing this formidable document, that my Fulvia was not the only nun carried off by an enterprising lover, & that the real convent-doors were as easily unlatched as my fictitious ones" (*Letters, 61*).

Although she may outdo them in sensational incidents, with respect to character Wharton is far more restrained than any of her fellow-workers in the genre of Italian romance. Crawford's characters depended for their degree of plausibility upon certain assumptions (going back beyond Elizabethan drama to Dante himself) about Italian temperament, customs, and behavior, all holding that Italians are more violently emotional than other peoples.[23] In the essay on the Francesca da Rimini dramas, which was written just after *The Valley of Decision*, Wharton praised Crawford's characterization, defending it from the French critics who had taken "exception at the two most characteristic *racial* traits in the drama: the long attachment of the [illicit] lovers, and Malatesta's change from a violent and outspoken man to a stealthy smiling assassin." Wharton claims that precisely these points show Crawford's "insight into Italian character." Crawford's characters are "Italians of the Middle Ages," not "modern altruists" making "lavish use of 'What ho!' and 'Marry come up!' as a satisfying substitute for historic truth and racial psychology."[24] In this spirit Wharton criticized Steven Phillips for the anglicized behavior of Paolo and Francesca in his drama:

> It is still broadly true that *la morale est purement géographique,* and that, in an Italian and an Anglo-Saxon temperament, love and jealousy do not operate in the same way or with the same results. It is safe to say that Giovanni Malatesta . . . would not have made such a to-do about killing his wife and brother. . . . To a lord of the *haute justice* it was as natural, as obligatory, one might say, to kill an unfaithful wife with his own hands, as it would be for a modern Englishman to apply for a divorce.[25]

This sounds like mere repetition of the conventional English idea of Italian mores, but it is confirmed by the views not only of Stendhal – who constantly differentiates Italians from Frenchmen and is equally satirical about the English – but also of an Italian, Vittorio Alfieri himself, who might almost be taken as Wharton's source. In his autobiography, in the midst of recalling an affair he had with a married woman in England, Alfieri expresses the fear that he cannot make the behavior of the participants convincing to his Italian readers:

But here, in describing the extremely strange effects of English jealousy, one sees Italian jealousy forced to laugh, so different are the passions in different characters and climates, and most of all under very different laws. Every Italian reader is now expecting daggers, poisonings, beatings, or at least imprisonment of the wife, and similar well-justified frenzies. Nothing of the sort. The English husband, although in his own way adequately loving his wife, wastes no time in invectives, menaces, or quarrels.[26]

These remarks point up how carefully Wharton has avoided sexual passion and questions of jealousy in her romance, even though there are many opportunities. Indeed, although various passions are often attributed to Odo and Fulvia, they are never directly or convincingly expressed. Only her secondary characters manage to have the vivacity, the stupidity, the madness, the humor of characters of romance. And – most telling of all – there is no villain, major or minor. The forces that oppose Odo and Fulvia are not wicked; they are an array of selfish and amoral interests, entrenched conventions, on the outside; and, in Odo's case, an ambivalence within. This is what makes the central character Wharton's mask.

Within the impersonal evocations of history and the conventions of romance, the core of the narrative concerns what will happen to Odo and what he will *choose* to be and to do. As we have seen, Wharton defensively asserted that the two major characters in *The Valley of Decision* were of secondary importance – mere reflectors of the historical period that is supposed to be the novel's primary interest. Fulvia and Odo "are just little bits of looking-glass in which fragments of the great panorama are reflected" (*Letters*, 58, 57). Such remarks seem intended to divert her friends from thinking about the characters too closely. Many years later, writing in her autobiography, she could admit that during the composition of the book Odo "was more real to me than most of the people I talked and walked with in my daily life." She also recalled how Walter Berry got her going again when she was blocked. "Just write down everything you feel like telling," he had told her, and the words had "sent me rushing ahead . . . and keeping in sight only the novelist's essential sign-post; the inner significance of the 'case' selected." "The *soul* of the novel," she wrote "is . . . the writer's own soul" (*Backward Glance*, 881, 870). Odo is less a reflector of a "social phase" than of a personal one.

In Odo, Wharton created a person who shared her own dilemmas; in Fulvia, she attempted to imagine an intellectual woman engaged in radical politics who might nevertheless be sympathetic. The character of Fulvia is largely a failure, too obviously a contrivance that tries to ally Odo's political liberalism with a romantic interest. At one point both Odo and Fulvia realize that she has become to him a "formula, rather than a woman" (2:222), but in fact she has been that from the beginning. The contradictions of Odo, however, make of him a character both enigmatic and revelatory, the "case selected," the "soul" of this novel. The broad terms of Odo's choices – for he makes more than one – can be put simply: first, to commit himself either to the old order or to the new light, and second, to accept or refuse a position of power. Each of these has, however, several ramifications and ambiguities, both as to what is chosen and the nature of choice. In exploring them, Wharton is able to ponder social hierarchy and social injustice, the function of religion, the philosophy of history, learned women, the new Puritanism, and the limits of power. In the end, none of Odo's alternatives seems quite real to her, and that is where the gender-mask falls. Her own declaration of identity – "Io sono Achilles" – has been achieved by grasping the pen, by writing this novel, but she has given her hero no comparable arena. For him, aesthetic delight has come solely in frivolous social forms; his choices can only be between other types of conventionally masculine action: (liberal) politics or (aristocratic) war. Like Achilles, Odo grasps the sword.

Odo's duchy, Pianura, itself represents merely one manifestation of the old order: its corrupt contemporary state. By having Odo visit his grandfather at Donnaz (which lies within the kingdom of Piedmont), Wharton is able to give a relatively sympathetic view of feudalism in its ancient state as a form of "paternal tyranny" (1:46) preferable to the later system of absentee landlords, which was analogous to depersonalized corporate power. Wharton's depiction of the second element of feudal power – that of the Church – also equivocates. The *Catholic World,* in its review of *The Valley of Decision,* with characteristic hyperbole called it "the subtlest assault ever invented in English literature against the Catholic Church."[27] Yet Wharton is, if anything, excessively cautious in her attempt to treat the Church in a balanced fashion: after all, Catholic friends like Mrs. Chanler and Paul Bourget would be among her dearest readers. In reply to a letter from Alfred Austin, British poet laureate and a Catholic, she wrote: "I tried to hold the balance as evenly as possible in describing the influence of the Church on the various classes of society, & the few Catholics I know who are familiar with the conditions in Italy at that period seem to think, with you, that I have painted them fairly" (*Letters,* 76).[28]

Shortly after Odo's arrival at the court of Pianura, Wharton has him meet the archivist, the *abate* Crescenti, who teaches him that "existing institutions" – both secular and ecclesiastical – must be understood in the light of their evolution from conditions "five hundred or a thousand years ago," not measured by "the standard of some imaginary Platonic republic." This conservative position weighs against Odo's hunchbacked friend's radicalism; from now on, this view of history "tempered his judgments with charity and dignified his very failures by a tragic sense of their inevitableness" (1:260). Such a view considerably inhibits a wholehearted adoption of the New Light, those modern ideas undermining both cunning priests and rapacious princes, ideas that rejected the medieval past and accepted only some elements of ancient political thought. Odo's youthful devotion to these new ideas is also compromised by the fact that his attraction to them owes much to Fulvia's being their advocate; whenever she disappears, his liberalism wanes. Fulvia is introduced as the daughter of the philosopher Vivaldi, who is at the center of the secret liberal club in Turin to which Alfieri takes Odo. At first Fulvia seems directly parallel to Eliot's Romola, the dutiful motherless daughter of a scholarly father. But, unlike Romola, when her father dies she does not become the passive instrument of her husband and then of a religious movement. Instead, after Vivaldi's death Fulvia emerges as a powerful intellectual and orator, and, when she becomes Odo's mistress, the true ruler of the duchy of Pianura.

Wharton does not know quite what to make of her leading female character. Fulvia is introduced in the most extravagant terms, as the ideal young woman of romance: "Nature . . . had indeed compounded her of all fine meanings, making each grace the complement of another and every outward charm expressive of some inward quality. Here was as little of the convent-bred miss as of the flippant and vaporish fine lady; and any suggestion of a less fair alternative vanished before such candid graces" (1:138). Odo, from the first, cannot distinguish his love for Fulvia from his love for the new learning, which does not in his mind yet extend to the idea of a liberated woman. Alfieri assures him that although Fulvia is "one of your prodigies of female learning, such as our topsy-turvy land produces," she has not yet aspired to "academic honors" like the famous Laura Bassi or Gaetana Agnesi. She is above all "a good daughter." Odo imagines her as "a vestal cherishing the flame of Liberty" – not exactly sexy (1:148–9). But her comparative attractiveness is reinforced by a page of remarkable satire against academic women who "order about their servant-girls in Tuscan, and scold their babies in Ciceronian Latin," none of whom "wore her learning lightly. They were forever tripping in the folds of their doctors' gowns, and delivering their most trivial views ex cathedrâ; and too often the poor philosophers, their lords and fathers, cowered under their harangues like frightened boys under the tongue of a schoolmaster" (1:151). This page ought to prepare the reader for the fact that on the same day that Fulvia receives her doctorate and delivers her oration, Wharton has her shot.

But Fulvia must first serve the purpose of returning the wandering Odo to liberalism without compromising herself sexually. In their romantic escape over the mountains, Fulvia and Odo feel the strangeness and intimacy of their situation. Wharton chooses to introduce here a somewhat irrelevant historical survey in favor of middle-class chastity, protesting the comic tradition of the poor "cheated husband," "the plausible adulteress and the adroit seducer," even though neither of her characters is married. Oddly, the New Light of Liberty approves of monogamy and fidelity:

> Faithfulness to the family sanctities, reverence for the marriage tie, courage to sacrifice the loftiest passion to the most plodding duty. . . . [L]ove as a moral emotion might be called [the discovery] of the eighteenth-century philosophers, who, for all their celebration of free unions and fatal passions, were really on the side of the angels, were fighting the battle of the spiritual against the sensual, of conscience against appetite. (2:121)

For Odo and Fulvia, the "new idealism" triumphed over "youth and propinquity." "The girl stood for the embodiment of the purifying emotions that were to renew the world" (2:122).

Wharton's anachronistic celebration of Victorian morality (no doubt motivated by both personal need and a sense of her readership) creates a difficulty in the plot. When it appears that Odo's accession to power will mean the loss of Fulvia, Odo at first renounces power. "My choice is made," he tells her. But she refuses to join him in a flight to France, reminding him that "the duty to which a man is born comes before any of his own choosing." In her view, he is "called to serve liberty on a throne." They will be united only in their common purpose – payment of the age-old debt to the people, which Odo as heir cannot escape. Like the heroine of an Alfieri tragedy, Fulvia renounces him with stoic virtue. To which he says: "You are right . . . I have no choice." But there is an alternative to lonely rule. She can come to Pianura with him as his mistress. "According to the code of the day there was no dishonor in the offer." Wharton nevertheless will not allow it – yet. Fulvia must first be the renouncing heroine: "To love you I must give you up" (2:133–40). This scene concludes Book 3, which is called "The Choice." Obviously that title is ironic, but this virtuous drama is in any case entirely undercut by the fact that later on Wharton contrives circumstances by which Fulvia does in fact become Odo's mistress and the power behind the throne, after he has married the previous duke's widow. Now that the relationship must be adulterous, neither Fulvia nor her creator seems concerned about the "sanctities" of the new religion. They seem only to regret that the union of Fulvia and Odo "came too late" for its most passionate realization; but the novelist is in this way freed from showing that passion.

Ironic also is the title of the final book: "The Reward." Odo enters into his power committed to the gospel of service to the people, hoping to find compensation in it for his private loss. But to break "the chains of feudalism" in an Italian state proves to be a nearly impossible task (2:180). The difficulty is not, however, merely with entrenched interests and ingrained habits of thought. The problem is also with Odo. He is not drawn to political power. From the beginning Wharton imagined him as a person given to speculation and revery, gazing at the fresco of Saint Francis instead of that of Saint George. She attributes to him "a kind of imaginative sympathy, a wondering joy in the mere spectacle of life, that tinged his most personal impressions with a streak of philosophic temper." This trait is, moreover, "the best gift of the past from which he sprang," not a gift of the "new light" (1:91). But even beyond this, Odo is exceptional among those of his race, given to a "sensitiveness" to nature, a consciousness of its most "delicate changes," a "tenderness for every sylvan function of renewal and decay." Odo is laughed at for this effeminacy; only in the pages of Rousseau does he find a confirmation of his feelings (1:115–17).

Young Odo is also ambivalent about the ideal of social life. He admires the "grave men" he meets at the Honey-Bees club for their "frugal" life "in dignified contrast to the wasteful and aimless existence of the nobility." Yet "None was more open than he to the seducements of luxurious living, the polish of manners, the tacit exclusion of all that is ugly or distressing; but it seemed to him that fine living should be but the flower of fine feeling, and that such external graces, when they adorned a dull and vapid society, were as incongruous as the royal purple on a clown" (1:150).

In all this we see that Wharton has made Odo a character so much in her own image that he can never be wholly devoted to reform, whatever action Fulvia supposedly inspires him to. Like James's Hyacinth Robinson in *The Princess Casamassima* (1886), he loves too much the things his theory tells him he must destroy. When his wife (a distant relative of Marie Antoinette) asks him plainly whether what they have is "ours or theirs," he replies that the rulers hold everything in trust "for our people." Then he makes a survey of the room, with Wharton's own informed eye:

He looked at the delicate adornment of the walls, the curtains of Lyons damask, the crystal girandoles, the toys in porcelain of Saxony and Sevres, in bronze and ivory and Chinese lacquer, crowding the tables and cabinets of inlaid wood. Overhead floated a rosy allegory by Luca Giordano; underfoot lay a carpet of the royal manufactory of France; and through the open windows he heard the plash of the garden fountains and saw the alignment of the long green alleys set with the statues of Roman patriots.   (2:177)

The words with which Odo warns his wife that the people may take everything from them some day "sounded strangely in his own ears" (2:179). Odo himself has had sense enough to move the Giorgione Venus from the bedroom shrine to his study.

Odo's equivocating character is developed in contrast to Fulvia's monomaniacal rigidity. "With Fulvia, ideas were either rejected or at once converted into principles; with himself, they remained stored in the mind, serving rather as commentaries on life than as incentives to action. This perpetual accessibility to new impressions was a quality she could not understand, or could conceive of only as a weakness. . . . He perceived that to a spirit like Fulvia's it might become possible to shed blood in the cause of tolerance" (2:222–3). It would appear that Odo wants to be a novelist like Henry James, given to "perpetual accessibility to new impressions" and converting ideas into "commentaries on life." Wharton attributes to Odo a "duality that so often paralyzed his action" (2:238), but as the book reaches its dénouement, the real Odo, conservative and feminine, clearly shows that one half of the duality was a mask. Like Alfieri (which is what makes her satire of him odd), Wharton in the end does not believe in social reform; her concern for the injustices to "the people" is small. What does concern her, like Alfieri, is personal freedom. She even cites Alfieri's attack on the "false liberty" of the French (2:301). Although Fulvia exults in the news from France, Odo is appalled by it. In the authority of narrator, Wharton herself says: "Religion, monarchy, law, were sucked down into the whirlpool of liberated passions. Across that sanguinary scene passed, like a mocking ghost, the philosopher's vision of the perfectibility of man. Man was free at last – freer than his would-be liberators ever dreamed of making him – and he used his freedom like a beast" (2:303).

But one irony of Wharton's plot is that its own "sanguinary scene" shows the embodiment of liberalism – Fulvia herself – being shot by the "beast." After the riot that culminates in her death, Odo suspends the constitution he has just proclaimed, primarily at her urging (his doubts about it persisted). After a spell in a Benedictine monastery, sympathetically listening to long rationalizations justifying the Church's power from his Jesuit friend, he returns to court but leaves actual power in the hands of his conservative prime minister, for "His mind was lost in a maze of metaphysical speculations; and even these served him merely as some cunningly-contrived toy with which to trick his leisure" (2:298). Wharton herself is speculating freely in these last pages, working her way out of a maze of her own creation. She turns the political irony two twists further, as though to justify complete detachment.

Two years pass; the French Revolution is reaching its crisis. Odo exists in a state of conscious impotence. Andreoni and Gamba – his liberal friends – have risen to power *without* the constitution and are now ready to give the duchy over to French domination. Austria and the Holy See, Odo's natural protectors in his now reactionary stance, cannot defend him. None of the small Italian states has chosen to unite behind conservative Piedmont's king to resist France. "The ideas he had striven for had triumphed at last, and his surest hold on authority was to share openly in their triumph." But "a profound horror dragged him back. . . . The goddess of the new worship was but a bloody Mænad who had borrowed the attributes of freedom. He could not bow the knee in such a charnel-house. Tranquilly, resolutely, he took up the policy of repression" (2:305).

Finally, emboldened by the French Revolution, the people of Pianura seize Odo's citadel. "The revolution took place quietly, without violence or bloodshed." Andreoni and Gamba, whom Wharton has portrayed sympathetically, demand that he proclaim a constitutional monarchy and declare allegiance to the French. Why (apart from the fact that history offered no parallel instance) should it not all end in radical triumph – the new light conquering the old order? Because Wharton does not like the actuality of popular democracy, however sentimentally she can agree with the justice of liberal theories. So Odo must follow suit. He absolutely refuses to participate in its next stage, even though he is promised "more power than you ever dreamed of possessing" (2:308). Odo realizes that a liberal leader is a leader who is led. He sees the "waves of destiny" closing over him. But the "circumstances of his past" suddenly bring a revelation, and his "indifference fell from him."

> The old passion of action awoke and he felt a new warmth in his breast. After all, the struggle was not yet over: though Piedmont had called in vain on the Italian states, an Italian sword might still be drawn in her service. If his people would not follow him against France he could still march against her alone. Old memories hummed in him at the thought. He recalled how his Piedmontese ancestors had gone forth against the same foe, and the stout Donnaz blood began to bubble in his veins. (2:307)

How arbitrarily manipulative Wharton has become is evident enough in the dry externality of the description of the radical changes of heart. The confusion continues to the end, for as Odo flies from Pianura toward Piedmont, where he will join the deeply conservative Savoyard resistance against the liberal forces of France, represented (at that moment) by Napoleon, he stops at the chapel in Pontesordo where the story had begun. In the old chapel he kneels and feels "a prayer, yet not a prayer – a reaching out, obscure and inarticulate, toward all that had survived of early hopes and faiths, a loosening of old founts of pity, a longing to be somehow, somewhere reunited to his old belief in life" (2:311–12). Just before he leaves, "the face of Saint Francis shone out on him," the face that on the first page of the novel had been said to express "the mute pain of all poor downtrodden folk on earth" (2:112; 1:3).

Wharton ought to have selected Saint George instead, for in the end Odo is choosing to be a person of action in defense of constituted authority and social tradition. But Odo – and Wharton – remain partially masked to the very end. The image of Saint Francis cannot efface the most extended statement of Odo's final position, offered as mature truth. The riots that had brought about the death of Fulvia and the end of the constitution had seemed to represent a direct opposition of the Church party's Virgin to Fulvia as Liberty. But in fact the apparent "blind outburst of religious fanaticism" had been merely a front for the "concerted efforts of the liberal and court parties." The countermovement was not religious but "at bottom purely political, and represented the resistance of the privileged classes to any attack on their inherited rights." And in fact Odo "could no longer regard it as completely unreasonable.

> He was beginning to feel the social and political significance of those old restrictions and barriers against which his early zeal had tilted. Certainly in the ideal state the rights and obligations of the different classes would be more evenly adjusted. But the ideal state was a figment of the brain. The real one, as Crescenti had long ago pointed out, was the gradual and heterogeneous product of remote social conditions, wherein every seeming inconsistency had its roots in some bygone need, and the character of each class, with its special passions, ignorances and prejudices, was the sum total of influences so ingrown and inveterate that they had become a law of thought. (2:292)

On such a basis Wharton could turn to a criticism of New York life that focuses exclusively upon limitations of personal freedom, and not at all upon the existence of social injustices of a larger sort. Odo's last view might allow for "adjustments" in class relationships, but the classes themselves are permanent. Yet individuals, given – or taking – their freedom, could choose. Obviously, beyond the sustained act of the scholarly imagination that had allowed her to create an Italian duchy of the eighteenth century, beyond the inventiveness that had permitted her to write a romance with thrilling scenes, Wharton had in *The Valley of Decision* managed to argue with herself over many ideas of history and society, and the individual's place in both – vicariously imagining what "decision," what "choices" she would make if she were Odo – and what would be her "reward." She projects upon Odo her own speculative, curious, independent, novelistic attitude toward life, which wholly inhibits him as a politician but makes possible precisely her own self-realization as a novelist: the genre in which curiosity issues in its own kind of action.[29]

Edith Wharton distinguished herself from those fashionable women whom she satirized years later in "Roman Fever" by turning the pleasure of Italy into a fact of knowledge and enlightened creative labor. For those still unwilling to interest themselves in Wharton's Italian mask, it might be added that in her view the knowledge required for its construction provided her with the perspective by which to paint her own time and place. One of the things for which she praised Paul Bourget, with obvious sincerity, was his cosmopolitan perspective, a quality that is commonly missing from American critiques of American authors and of American society. Citing Kipling's "How can they know England, that only England know?", she concludes: "En effet, c'est seulement en ayant vu d'autres pays, étudié leurs mœurs, lu leurs livres, fréquenté leurs habitants, que l'on peut situer son propre pays dans l'histoire de la civilisation."[30]

NOTES

1 Grace Kellogg, in *The Two Lives of Edith Wharton* (New York: Appleton-Century, 1975), 87, dismisses the novel as "tedious" and misplaces the period of its action by three hundred years. R. W. B. Lewis, in *Edith Wharton: A Biography* (New York: Harper & Row, 1975), justly rates the book as "unmatched in its generation for its presentation of the conflict between the stiffening old and the radically new" and also sees that there is "a profoundly personal element" in the struggle she depicts (104), but his summary of its concluding chapters is erroneous on several counts (103), most particularly in stating that it is the Church party that brings the hero down. Similarly, Cynthia Griffin Wolff sees the book as bearing "a direct relation to Wharton's life" and quotes Blake Nevius's observation concerning the parallel between the historical period she chose and the one she lived in. Yet Wolff oddly reads the hero as an "Everyman," whereas Wharton was at pains to point out his essentially distinctive qualities (reflecting her own). Wolff's confusion of the French Revolutionary period with the "Napoleonic Era" (which is only just beginning at the end of Wharton's book and takes on a quite different character) further muddles her generalizations. See *A Feast of Words: The Triumph of Edith Wharton* (New York: Oxford Univer-

sity Press, 1977), 91–7. Cf. Blake Nevius, *Edith Wharton: A Study of Her Fiction* (Berkeley and Los Angeles: University of California Press, 1953), 48–50.

2 Wharton's identification with her hero has been frequently noted, as, for example, by Marilyn Jones Lyde, *Edith Wharton: Convention and Morality in the Work of a Novelist* (Norman: University of Oklahoma Press, 1959), 82–3: "Like most first novels, it is intellectually the most autobiographical work Edith Wharton ever wrote and the clearest statement of many of her beliefs." My concern is to show the means by which Wharton created an autobiographical mask and to suggest that the mask's value as a fiction was to allow the evasion of a "statement" of any of her "beliefs."

3 *The Letters of Edith Wharton,* ed. R. W. B. Lewis and Nancy Lewis (New York: Scribner, 1988), 76. Cited hereafter in the text as *Letters.*

4 Edith Wharton, "Souvenirs du Bourget d'outre-mer," *Revue hebdomadaire* 6 (June 1936), 268.

5 Wharton, "Souvenirs," 280.

6 Edith Wharton, *A Backward Glance,* in *Edith Wharton: Novellas and Other Writings,* ed. Cynthia Griffin Wolff (New York: Library of America, 1990), 884, 882. Hereafter cited in text as *Backward Glance.*

7 Lee wrote an introduction to the proposed Italian translation of the novel, but the translation apparently never appeared in volume form. The introduction was in Wharton's possession (*Backward Glance,* 884), but is not among her papers at the Beinecke Library at Yale. The review reprinted in Chapter 10 of the present volume perhaps indicates its character.

8 Apparently Chanler mentioned some errors when they met shortly afterward in Newport; there is a record only of Chanler having told Wharton that she had mistakenly placed the Feast of the Purification in November. See *Letters,* 69.

9 *The Letters of Charles Eliot Norton,* ed. Sara Norton and M. A. DeWolfe Howe, 2 vols. (Boston: Houghton Mifflin, 1913), 2:319.

10 William Roscoe Thayer, *The Dawn of Italian Independence: Italy from the Congress of Vienna, 1814, to the Fall of Venice, 1849,* 2 vols. (Boston: Houghton Mifflin, 1892), 1:82, 90, 91–2. The first hundred pages of Thayer's book review Italian history before 1814; Wharton undoubtedly drew upon the last two sections, "Science and Folly," and "New Voices and Revolution."

11 Vernon Lee, *The Countess of Albany* (Boston: Roberts Brothers, 1884), vii.

12 In both of the nonfiction books a formal, anonymous authorial tone is rigorously maintained. In the first, *The Decoration of Houses* (written with the architect Ogden Codman), authorial identity is fully obscured by the dual authorship. Furthermore, according to Wharton, the two authors discovered that they could not write, so a third person – Walter Berry, unacknowledged in the book – had to reshape the whole. See *Backward Glance,* 865. The biases and preoccupations of this book do, of course, reveal something about the authors relevant to the biases and preoccupations of *The Valley of Decision.* But there are two important additional things to note about *The Decoration of Houses.* First, it is based upon much historical research, authoritatively marshaled to support an aesthetic thesis (interior and exterior should be treated as one, with simplicity as a guide). The conservative value of history and tradition is asserted, and so is a value less obvious to Americans: that of the compatibility

of beauty and comfort. Second, it traces practically every good principle of architectural taste back to Italy.

13 Vernon Lee, *Studies of the Eighteenth Century in Italy* (London: Satchell, 1880), 3.

14 While writing *The Valley of Decision,* Wharton was also engaged in writing a play. See *Letters,* 44.

15 See *Tutte le opere di Pietro Metastasio,* ed. Bruno Brunelli (Milan: Mondadore, 1953), 1:759, 782.

16 Wharton, "Souvenirs," 269–70: "The life of gambling, sports, yachting, bridge, sumptuous dinners, and elegant parties, that constituted the Newport season. At that time . . . the season of the watering place still had an authentic elegance; but the amiable people who made up that little society were, with few exceptions, hermetically closed to intellectual and artistic movements that in Paris or London had reached even the most frivolous milieux. At Newport it was not yet necessary to appear to be interested in ideas."

17 *Vita di Vittorio Alfieri da Asti scritta da esso,* ed. Giampaolo Dossena, 2nd ed. (Turin: Einaudi, 1974), 57 (my translation, here and throughout). A good modern translation is *The Life of Vittorio Alfieri Written by Himself,* trans. Henry McAnally (Lawrence: University of Kansas Press, 1973). The James R. Osgood (Boston: 1877) edition (anonymously translated) for which William Dean Howells wrote the introductory essay has had "objectionable matter" removed, which means that some episodes in Alfieri's early life have been rendered incomprehensible.

18 Alfieri, *Vita,* 178, 175.

19 See Lee, *Countess of Albany,* 117–18, 128.

20 Major differences include the focus of the narrative, which in Stendhal is on the energetic monologues of the characters, whether interior or (as is their wont) delivered at length to a sympathetic party, and the facts that the *Chartreuse* is a comic novel and a contemporary one, which allows Stendhal to make frequent present-tense comments on the differences between Italy and France. The witticism, dogmatism, irony, and brio of Stendhal's highly personal narrative style make reading him a very different experience from reading Wharton, whose style is self-effacing. A difference from Wharton's narrator that Stendhal's shares with Cooper's in *The Bravo* is a strong sense of foreign nationality. The most extended (and to my mind distorting) comparison and contrast between Wharton and Stendhal is in Wolff, a *Feast,* 92–5.

21 See Francis Marion Crawford, *Sant'Ilario* (New York: Macmillan, 1889), 434. For a full discussion of the historical value of Crawford's Roman romances, see Alessandra Contenti, *Esercizi di nostalgia: La Roma sparita di F. Marion Crawford* (Rome: Izzi, 1992).

22 The book had sold 25,000 copies in the first five months, at which point it was reprinted in a one-volume edition. See Stephen Garrison, *Edith Wharton: A Descriptive Bibliography* (Pittsburgh: University of Pittsburgh Press: 1990), 37.

23 For a discussion of traditional Anglo-American characterizations of Italians and Crawford's Roman romances, see "The Reality of Roman Romance," in my *America's Rome,* vol. 2: *Catholic and Contemporary Rome* (New Haven: Yale University Press, 1989), 228–61.

24 Wharton, "The Three Francescas," *North American Review* 175 (July 1902), 29–30.

25 "Three Francescas," 19–20.

26 Alfieri, *Vita,* 113. This is among the passages deleted from Howell's edition.

27 *Catholic World* 75 (June 1902), 422–3; quoted in Kristin O. Lauer and Margaret Murray, *Edith Wharton: An Annotated Secondary Bibliography* (New York: Garland, 1990), 177.

28 Wharton's worries are particularly evident in the equivocal treatment she gives the Jesuits, often letting a Jesuit friend of Odo's speak in their defense. For vacillating views, see *The Valley of Decision,* 2 vols. (New York: Scribner, 1902), 1:110, 286–7, 2:24–7, 59–60 ("the greatest organized opposition to moral and intellectual freedom that the world has ever known"), 129–30. The Benedictines, as was the custom, get favorable treatment as monks of *exceptional* virtue and usefulness and comparative modesty (2:27–9).

29 See Ross Posnock, *The Trial of Curiosity: Henry James, William James, and the Challenge of Modernity* (New York: Oxford University Press, 1991).

30 Wharton, "Souvenirs," 276. It is not accidental that the best recent reading of *The Valley of Decision* is the first chapter of Janet Goodwyn's *Edith Wharton: Traveller in the Land of Letters* (New York: St. Martin's, 1990), in which the stress is upon Wharton's cosmopolitan perspective on American life and letters.

Edith Wharton's *Valley of Decision:*
A Rediscovered Contemporary Critique

I do not know whether Mrs. Wharton's novel will be appreciated in Italy. The feelings a country can arouse in the imagination of foreigners is one of the greatest gifts that country can give to the world (and every country, like every epoch, climate, or personality can lend to the great symphony of the universe, one note, one timbre, sometimes a wondrous stretch of melody, completely individual). Yet mostly this gift exists only in the perception of whoever receives it and cannot be conveyed to the inhabitants of the country that has bestowed it. Later, when cosmopolitan scholarship has explained foreign literature and created a taste for it, that country's readers may learn to enjoy those same impressions that their landscapes, their cities, their very physical and spiritual attributes had produced in the minds of others. Thus Taine succeeded in conveying to Italian readers the full impact of the terrible or exquisite images that Italy had induced in the bizarre minds of Elizabethan dramatists. Thus my treasured and greatly esteemed friend Enrico Nencioni superbly managed to extract from Shelley's poetry (and, above all, from Browning's) that marvelous essence which those two supreme poets had distilled from Italy.

But this is a critical essay and, like all really fertile criticism, a second flowering sprouted from the original seed. And, in my opinion, it is quite possible that Mrs. Wharton's fine book will, for the present, remain as little appreciated by today's Italian readers as Goethe's *Italian Journey*. It would have been appreciated by Italians living in 1780, those same Italians whom the American novelist has described.

This is because her book is concerned with a strangely neglected aspect of the Italian eighteenth century. It is the intimate biography of a typical and fictional character: a minor Lombardian nobleman. We follow the spiritual and secular progress of this small provincial aristocrat, related to an illustrious Renaissance family, from his neglected childhood, through his travels, his loves, his friendships, his reading, right up to the day when his humanitarian and liberal dreams are horribly shattered by clerical plotting, by

Jacobin fanaticism, by stupid peasant brutality, all conspiring against him to ruin the work so generously started, to thrust the state he had envisaged as happy, free, and enlightened, under the dishonored Bonapartian rapacity, the enervating and cruel tyranny of Austria and the Vatican. Oddone Valsecca, duke of Pianura, disciple of the Encyclopedists, friend of Filangieri and Pimentel, who studied in the same academy as Vittorio Alfieri, sacrificed his personal independence, his free development as an individual, was even ready to sacrifice the only great love of his life in order to reign over a small state and reform it. His reforms are rejected, his people incited by the clerical rabble, provoked by pseudophilosophers, and set against him; in the rioting, his own beloved, the adored Egeria who had inspired him, is killed. The book ends with him deposed, exiled, disillusioned, heartbroken, going off with the Sardinian army to fight that same revolution in which he and his woman had so fervently believed.

Is this probable? Is it historically accurate? My research of long ago on that same eighteenth-century Italy gives me (among other pleasant and perhaps less deserved things) the great pleasure of answering, yes: Mrs. Wharton's novel is indeed a wonderful account of historical truth, both in the actual facts and in their human environment – a truth which, however, is not merely objective. This Italy of the second half of the eighteenth century is something more than a topographical map, displaying with admirable accuracy and clarity the absolute contours, distances, and real proportions, together with all the incidents, of the historical terrain. Mrs. Wharton gives us something more: a picture, a series of pictures, viewed through an artist's personality and translated into artistic symbols: the subjective truth of the soul of an age and of a country, revealed through the eyes of a real writer.

And here I return to my first subject: I shall explicitly say that – in my opinion – the historical novel (long dead, or rather living sporadically only through Scott, Manzoni, George Sand, or that admirable Menhold of the *Bernstein Hexe*) can come back to life only if it is made more subjective, becoming a narrative (as the pseudo-Cavalca said of the life of the Magdalen) not of facts that have actually happened but of facts that the writer has wished to happen. A new school of historical novel seems to be slowly emerging in England today. Leaving aside the splendid adventure stories of the greatest of our present-day storytellers and novelists, Robert Louis Stevenson, I would draw special attention to a type of novel that started some twenty years ago with Shorthouse's *John Inglesant* and that includes a recent masterpiece, Hewlett's *Richard Yea-and-Nay*. These novels are notable for having originated not simply from the study of a specific age but particularly from the fascination that a specific age has exercised over the mind of an individual.

Modern man travels not merely through space but also in time, and the past, glimpsed as a landscape through the window of a train, can awake in him that nostalgic desire, that Faustian "Stay, you are so fair," which is the true intimate motive of all works of art. A fresco, a deserted room in some Gonzaga or Farnese palace; the view from the ruined parapet of a Roman villa; a shepherd's path through an oak wood where an abandoned chapel or a black cross stands as witness to some forgotten tragedy turn and drive our imagination into the hidden distance. All of these things, along with a word or two in a letter or biography, a face looking at us from some portrait by a "pittore ignoto," above all, some bars of a melody, recall to our soul a past that is real because we have lived it. Such was the genesis of Short-house's *John Inglesant*, an unforgettable novel to which Mrs. Wharton's book is closely related. But whereas Shorthouse's book deals with the fascinating, terrible, and mysterious Italy, as it was perceived by the English of 1600, Mrs. Wharton's shows us eighteenth-century Italy, as it appears to a modern lover of art and justice whose desire for a better future is in contrast to her nostalgia for those times – and they may never have existed! – when tradition and privilege, sophistication and dignity, reigned before being lost forever.

And here, before ending this comment on a book that will find few capable of appreciating it (though those few will appreciate it as only the few can do), I would venture to ask the author a question that I have been unable to answer myself: What feelings moved her to write this book? Was this novel prompted by discouragement? Is it a work of pure art and fantasy, conceived by someone who no longer believes in life and truth? This Oddone Valsecca, who has given all and lost all, who is kneeling in the chapel where he prayed as a child before going on a useless journey, to fight a senseless war, how will he end? Should we imagine him as an embittered man whose ideas have become narrow, like the Alfieri of *Il Misogallo*? Or will he, like De Maistre, become converted to all those forms he has staunchly opposed? Or may we hope that this man, already mature in 1796, will live on, like Botta and a few more generous souls, to fire the enthusiasm and the endeavors of 1830 and 1848?

Faith in truth, goodness, and progress, an ardent aspiration toward fraternity, were the feelings that, together with their noble and timeless love, united the duke of Pianura and his woman. Should all this be considered a little like those old palaces, those deserted gardens, those half-forgotten melodies, as fodder for the fastidious and pointless dilettantism of our present time?

I do not believe so. I, at least, have felt that by dwelling in my mind with the characters of this book I have emerged with a greater, not a lesser, faith in the future. We too are, to a large extent, disillusioned people. We should draw courage from the example of those who, a hundred years ago, suffered from the same appalling disillusionment in their time. Events march backward sometimes because they have rushed forward too quickly, but the going forward continues, even when it is violently interrupted.

Let us not be seduced by our epicurean melancholies, let us not offer our sword to the ancien régime as Oddone Valsecca offered his to the king of Sardinia; let us not even kneel too long in the chapel where we prayed as children. To Mrs. Wharton's hero, Italy and Europe must have appeared as hopelessly lost, and yet, at that very moment, they were rising again.

BIBLIOGRAPHY

Many of Edith Wharton's books are individually available in various reprint editions, but no uniform, edited collection of all of her works is in print. The best partial collection is provided by the Library of America's two Wharton volumes, *Novels,* edited by R. W. B. Lewis (New York, 1985), and *Novellas and Other Writings,* edited by Cynthia Griffin Wolff (New York, 1990). References to Wharton's writings in the *Cambridge Companion to Edith Wharton* are, wherever possible, made to these volumes.

SELECTED CRITICAL AND BIOGRAPHICAL STUDIES

Ammons, Elizabeth. *Edith Wharton's Argument with America.* Athens, Ga.: University of Georgia Press, 1980.

Auchincloss, Louis. *Edith Wharton.* Minneapolis: University of Minnesota Press, 1961.

Bell, Millicent. *Edith Wharton and Henry James: The Story of Their Friendship.* New York: Braziller, 1965.

Brown, E. K. *Edith Wharton: Études Critiques.* Paris: Droz, 1935.

Erlich, Gloria C. *The Sexual Education of Edith Wharton.* Berkeley and Los Angeles: University of California Press, 1992.

Fryer, Judith. *Felicitous Space: The Imaginative Structures of Edith Wharton and Willa Cather.* Chapel Hill: University of North Carolina Press, 1986.

Gimbel, Wendy. *Edith Wharton: Orphancy and Survival.* New York: Praeger, 1984.

Joslin, Katherine. *Women Writers: Edith Wharton.* London: Macmillan, 1991.

Lewis, R. W. B. *Edith Wharton: A Biography.* New York: Harper & Row, 1975.

Lindberg, Gary. *Edith Wharton and the Novel of Manners.* Charlottesville: University Press of Virginia, 1975.

Lubbock, Percy. *Portrait of Edith Wharton.* New York: Appleton-Century-Crofts, 1947.

McDowell, Margaret B. *Edith Wharton.* Boston, Hall, 1976.

Nevius, Blake. *Edith Wharton: A Study of Her Fiction.* Berkeley and Los Angeles: University of California Press, 1953.

Waid, Candace. *Edith Wharton's Letters from the Underworld*. Chapel Hill: University of North Carolina Press, 1991.

Walton, Geoffrey. *Edith Wharton: A Critical Interpretation*. Rutherford, N.J.: Fairleigh Dickinson University Press, 1970.

Wershoven, Carol. *The Female Intruder in the Novels of Edith Wharton*. Rutherford, N.J.: Fairleigh Dickinson University Press, 1982.

Wolff, Cynthia Griffin. *A Feast of Words: The Triumph of Edith Wharton*. New York: Oxford University Press, 1977.

INDEX

Cambridge Companions to Literature